THE BALLAD OF
CARSON McCULLERS

The Ballad of Carson McCullers

A BIOGRAPHY

Oliver Evans

COWARD-McCANN, Inc.
NEW YORK

B
M133

FOR ARDIS, AGAIN

ACKNOWLEDGMENTS

For their help in the preparation of this book, the author wishes to thank Dr. Mary Mercer, Edwin Peacock, John Zeigler, Major Simeon Smith, Paul Bowles, Floria Lasky, Dorena Knepper, Anaïs Nin and Gypsy Rose Lee. Thanks are also due to the University of California at Los Angeles, and to the San Fernando Valley State College Foundation and Faculty Research Committee, who awarded the author a fellowship that enabled him to complete the book.

The publishers would like to thank the following for their kindness in granting permission to use extracts: Houghton Mifflin Company for permission to quote extensively from *The Heart Is a Lonely Hunter, Reflections in a Golden Eye, Member of the Wedding, The Ballad of the Sad Café* and *Clock Without Hands,* Copyright © 1940, 1941, 1946, 1955 and 1961, respectively, by Carson McCullers; Random House, Inc. for permission to quote from W. H. Auden's "September 1, 1939," Copyright 1940 by W. H. Auden, reprinted from *The Collected Poetry of W. H. Auden,* and from William Faulkner's "A Rose for Emily," Copyright 1930 and renewed 1957 by William Faulkner, reprinted from *Collected Stories of William Faulkner.* The publishers would also like to thank the *New Statesman,* London, and *The Times Literary Supplement* for permission to quote from reviews.

CONTENTS

Illustrations will be found
following page 126.

CHAPTER ONE

THE TOWN WAS DREARY

In 1917 the little town of Columbus, Georgia, had fewer than thirty thousand inhabitants. It was a typical small town of the Deep South; its principal industry was, of course, cotton, and it was here that Lula Carson Smith was born on February 19th. (She retained the 'Lula' only for as long as it took her to dislike it, which was not very long.) Her father, Lamar Smith, was a watchmaker and jeweller of French Huguenot stock who had come to Georgia some years previously from Society Hill, Alabama; her mother, Marguerite Waters, a native of the little town of Dublin, Georgia, was of Irish ancestry.

The family lived on Thirteenth Street, in a house owned by Carson's maternal grandmother. It was a neighbourhood that already, by the time Carson was born, had begun to decline considerably, though it was still 'respectable'. It was close enough to the cotton mill for the child, at a very early age, to become aware of the poverty of the workers, whom she could see passing by on their way to and from their jobs; the experience made an ineradicable impression on her and may partly account for the strong proletarian sympathy that characterizes her early work, such as her first novel, *The Heart Is a Lonely Hunter*:

> These cotton mills were big and flourishing and most of the workers were very poor. Often in the faces along the streets there was the desperate look of hunger and loneliness.

She has always been haunted by this memory. In 1943 she wrote in her novella, *The Ballad of the Sad Café*:

> There were always plenty of people clustered around a mill— but it was seldom that every family had enough meal, garments and fat-back to go the rounds. Life could become one long dim scramble just to get the things needed to keep alive.

It is almost certainly true too that Mr Smith's occupation was the source of Mrs McCullers's obsessions with the theme of time: watchmakers appear in three of her books, and *Clock Without Hands* is the title of her latest novel.

When Carson was seven, the family moved to Macon Road, which at that time was almost in the country. It was a wonderful place for children, with a magnificent pine tree in the yard, and they lived there for five years, whereupon, Mr Smith's jewellery shop having flourished, they decided to move to a more affluent neighbourhood—the suburb of Wynnton. It was here, in the white, two-storey bungalow with a big, shady yard at 1519 Starke Avenue, that Carson spent her adolescence: this is the house which she described in *The Member of the Wedding*, which of all Mrs McCullers's books is the most frankly autobiographical. Like most Southern families of the middle class, the Smiths had a series of Negro housemaids, and when she was lonely Carson would while away the long, hot afternoons in interminable conversations with them. The profound understanding of Negroes which many critics (such as Richard Wright) have admired in her work derives directly from this early association, and two of her most memorable characters—Portia, in *The Heart Is a Lonely Hunter*, and Berenice, in *The Member of the Wedding*—are composite portraits of several such servants.

Carson McCullers's childhood was similar to that of many other writers of the Deep South (William Faulkner, Eudora Welty, Tennessee Williams, Truman Capote, Flannery O'Connor), which is to say that it was almost singularly lacking in the excitement of external events, and in her imagination she compensated, as did these other writers, for this lack. She invented elaborate fantasies involving imaginary playmates ('They were all of them', she says, 'from far-away, improbable places'), and as soon as she was able to read she devoured not only the books in the family library—some of those which she particularly enjoyed were *Little Women, Little Men, Hans Brinker and the Silver Skates,* and *Twenty Thousand Leagues Under the Sea*—but most of the children's fiction in the Carnegie-endowed Columbus Public Library as well. By the time her adolescence was over she had read every work of fiction in the local collection.

In 'The Discovery of Christmas' (*Mademoiselle*, December, 1953), Mrs McCullers has written charmingly about this early period in her life, and of how, at the age of five, she made the shattering discovery that Santa Claus was a mere fiction. Christmas was an important occasion in the Smith household—so important that Carson began dreaming about it in midsummer, when it was pleasant to think about the North Pole and the snow that she had never seen. But this snow, or rather the lack of it, used to cause her a great deal of worry, for it was a matter of common knowledge that Santa Claus made his visits in a sleigh drawn by reindeer, and if there were no snow how could he manage? Then one day at a Christmas party where there was a Santa Claus she recognized in him the voice and mannerisms of a neighbour, Mr Lewis, and received her first great shock of disillusionment. The discovery that, as she puts it, 'Santa Claus is parents', solved a problem that even then had for her a moral dimension:

> With a great leap of logic I understood why Santa Claus gave rich people big presents and poor people little or none, things like apples and oranges, or, worse than all, 'useful clothes'. Although it did not explain the rich and the poor, it explained why a bad, rich child like Sport Richards kicked me when I was waiting in a line at school and had a grand Santa Claus while another poor child I know had *shoes* from her Santa Claus.

Shortly after this, Carson discovered the hiding place where her parents concealed the family presents, and the whole mystery was made sadly clear. Nevertheless, she could still enjoy the privilege of sitting up late on Christmas Eve waiting for her father to come home (Mr Smith, for whom it was the busiest time of the year, worked in his shop until midnight); the fish roe and grits that were always served for breakfast on Christmas morning; the elaborate fruit cake which her mother had baked weeks ahead and soaked in brandy; the glass of wine that she was permitted to drink on Christmas Day with her dinner of turkey, cornbread-and-oyster dressing, cranberry sauce, candied yams and sillabub; the glittering tree and the presents which, though divested of the glamour of their origin, never failed to be exactly what she had wished for.

If we are to accept Mrs McCullers's testimony, she was already, at this early age, preoccupied with the riddle of time:

> Here I was on this August afternoon in the tree-house, in the burnt, faded yard, sick and tired of all our summer ways . . . How could it be that I was I and now was now when in four months it would be Christmas, wintertime, cold weather, twilight and the glory of the Christmas tree? I puzzled about the *now* and *later* and rubbed the inside of my elbow until there was a little roll of dirt between my forefinger and thumb. Would the *now* I of the tree-house and the August afternoon be the same *I* of winter, firelight and the Christmas tree?

By her own admission, her parents spoiled her. A brother, Lamar Junior, arrived in 1920, when Carson was three, and a sister, Margarita, when she was six, but Carson remained the favourite. Mrs Smith, in particular, maintained that nothing was too good for 'Sister'—which, after Rita's birth, is what her family has always affectionately called Carson—and was determined that she should have a brilliant future: she was, as the late Ford Madox Ford once remarked of his own childhood, 'trained to be a genius'. Her mother always had this feeling about her—that she was a very special person, intended for no ordinary career—and indeed, in the light of what has actually happened, Mrs Smith's prescience can only be marvelled at. It failed her, however, in one respect: she had expected a boy, and had decided to name him Enrico Caruso. Music, as it happened, was Carson's first love, and it was prophesied in the neighbourhood that she would one day become a great concert pianist.

Though she was only five, Mrs McCullers remembers vividly the day her father bought her a piano, and how she threw her arms about his neck in a delirium of joy. Within a few days she had begun to make up pieces of her own. She received her first music lessons from a Mrs Alice Kierce, meantime entering the Wynnton elementary school, where she neglected her class work for the piano, spending as many as four hours a day at the keyboard.

Carson had always been a rather delicate child, and when she was still quite small suffered a severe attack of rheumatic fever which was misdiagnosed by the small-town family doctor as 'growing pains' and which left her, though no one suspected it at the time, with a seriously damaged heart: the series of strokes that was destined to cripple her in later life (the first one occurred when she was only twenty-three) had this early illness for its origin. She has also, since childhood, suffered from almost yearly onslaughts of pneumonia.

These illnesses, however, did not prevent her from being more active even than most children of her age. She would climb trees and run races with boys, so that by the time she was twelve she had acquired a local reputation for being a tomboy, rather like Mick Kelly in *The Heart Is a Lonely Hunter*, who 'would rather be a boy any day', climbs sharp-pointed roofs in her tennis shoes, and of whom Biff Brannon observes that 'she was at the age when she looked as much like an overgrown boy as a girl' and wonders

if he should have sold her the pack of cigarettes and if it were really harmful for kids to smoke. He thought of the way Mick narrowed her eyes and pushed back the bangs of her hair with the palm of her hand. He thought of her hoarse, boyish voice and of her habit of hitching up her khaki shorts and swaggering like a cowboy in a picture show.

Frankie Addams, in *The Member of the Wedding*, is also a tomboy, with hair that 'had been cut like a boy's, but it had not been cut for a long time and was not now even parted'. She steals her father's pistol and shoots up the cartridges in vacant lots; practises knife-throwing in the kitchen, to the terror of Berenice; stomps her feet and whistles at the movies; and when a soldier makes a pass at her she calmly breaks a pitcher of iced water over his head. Perhaps it should also be pointed out here that the names Mick and Frankie, like Carson's own, are, though sexually ambiguous, more generally applicable to boys than to girls.

Carson was taller, too, than most girls her age: she was not slow in attaining her present height of five feet, eight and a half inches. Children would ask maliciously, 'Is it cold up there?' while adults would advise her humorously to keep a brick on top of her head. The hypersensitive girl resented the attention that her height never failed to create, and this physical peculiarity was responsible for some of the more agonizing experiences of her childhood. She recalls that when she was old enough to go to her first dance none of the boys wanted her for a partner. 'They would look at me,' she says ruefully, 'or rather, look *up* at me, and go away.' Readers familiar with *The Heart Is a Lonely Hunter* will remember that Mick suffers for the same reason:

> She knew what he was thinking. It used to worry her all the time. Five feet six inches tall and a hundred and three pounds, and she was only thirteen. Every kid at the party was a runt beside her, except Harry, who was only a couple of inches shorter. No boy wanted to prom with a girl so much taller than him. But maybe cigarettes would help stunt the rest of her growth.

In *The Member of the Wedding*, Frankie has the same problem:

> Frankie was too tall this summer to walk beneath the arbor as she had always done before. Other twelve-year-old people could still walk around inside, give shows, and have a good time. Even small grown ladies could walk underneath the arbor. And already Frankie was too big; this year she had to hang around and pick from the edges like the grown people.

And again:

> She stood before the mirror and she was afraid. It was the
> summer of fear, for Frankie, and there was one fear that could
> be figured in arithmetic with paper and a pencil at the table.
> This August she was twelve and five-sixths years old. She was
> five feet and three-quarter inches tall, and she wore a number
> seven shoe. In the past year she had grown four inches, or at
> least that was what she judged . . . If she reached her height
> on her eighteenth birthday, she had five and one-sixth growing
> years ahead of her. Therefore, according to mathematics and
> unless she could somehow stop herself, she would grow to be
> over nine feet tall. And what would be a lady who is over nine
> feet high? She would be a Freak.

By the time Carson was twelve she had learned all that Mrs Kierce
was capable of teaching her in the way of music. Now it happened
that at nearby Fort Benning there lived an Army officer, Colonel
Albert Sidney Johnston Tucker, whose wife, Mary, was an unusually
talented musician who occasionally gave piano lessons to a few
pupils of exceptional talent. The Smiths and Mrs Kierce hoped they
could persuade her to include Carson among them, and Mrs Tucker
consented to an audition. For this occasion, Carson chose to play
Liszt's Second Hungarian Rhapsody: it was her showpiece, of
which she was particularly proud, and she played it in trip-hammer
fashion, with the amazing energy that, according to people like
Edwin Peacock, who remember hearing her play in her youth, before she became crippled, characterized her musical style. 'It was,'
she recalls, 'the fastest, loudest Hungarian Rhapsody that had ever
been heard in this world.' In spite of her nervousness, the audition
was a success: Mrs Tucker agreed to take her on, and thus began
the first of a series of several relationships that Mrs McCullers, who
has always had the faculty of endearing herself to a small group of
intensely devoted friends, considers to have been of the greatest importance in the shaping of her life and thought; she and Mrs Tucker
still continue to correspond.

Her new teacher began with Bach, who remains one of Mrs
McCullers's favourite composers, and under her direction the girl
made rapid progress as a virtuoso. Mrs Smith would drive her to
and from Fort Benning in the family car, and it was not long before
the Tucker residence became a kind of second home to her. These
visits (which continued until she was seventeen) were important to
Carson in a way that she did not, of course, realize at the time. The
Tuckers participated actively in the social life of the garrison, and

there was not much that escaped the watchful, inquisitive eyes and the precocious intelligence of this awkward, overgrown adolescent: it was in this way that she became familiar with the side of Army life that she later described so vividly in *Reflections in a Golden Eye*.

Mrs Tucker had a daughter, Virginia, who was about Carson's own age, and the two girls became fast friends: at weekends, before Virginia went away to boarding school, they would play games that satisfied the longing both of them had for far-away places, unfamiliar experiences, and glamorous acquaintances. Switzerland, which they thought of as always shining with snow, was about as different from Georgia as any place could possibly be, and one of their favourite games was 'Whom shall we invite to our Swiss chalet?' Carson, who had been reading Isadora Duncan's scandalous autobiography (which had a great vogue in the Twenties and Thirties) and studying Bach, wanted to invite these celebrities, but Virginia objected, saying, 'That's not fair—they're dead.' 'But it's all make-believe anyway,' Carson protested. Virginia, however, would not give in, and Mrs Tucker was obliged to intervene. 'Girls,' she said firmly, 'you must make up your minds one way or the other. Personally I see no reason why the dead should have to be invited; it will be quite grand enough as it is.' So the matter was settled, and Carson then decided on Marlene Dietrich, Myra Hess, and Rachmaninov.

It is interesting to note that snow scenes figure importantly in the adolescent fantasies of both Mick and Frankie. Just as Carson, in mid-August, dreamed of Christmas, so Mick, under the blazing summer sun, dreams of snow and ice:

A lot of times the plans about the things that were going to happen to her were mixed up with ice and snow. Sometimes it was like she was out in Switzerland and all the mountains were covered with snow and she was skating on cold, greenish-coloured ice.

She tells Singer, the deaf-mute protagonist of *The Heart Is a Lonely Hunter*, 'I mean to travel in a foreign country where there's snow,' and later, when she develops a 'crush' on him, she dreams of

just the two of them in a foreign house where in the winter it would snow. Maybe in a little Switzerland town with the high glaciers and the mountains all around . . . Or in the foreign country of Norway by the gray winter ocean.

At another point she asks Singer, 'Have you ever lived in a place where it snowed in the winter-time?' and when, reading her lips, he writes on his pad that he has once visited Canada, she falls to dreaming of the 'deep forests and white ice igloos' that she imagines to be there, 'the arctic region with the beautiful northern lights'. Frankie, in *The Member of the Wedding*, is similarly obsessed. When her brother, Jarvis, is sent to Alaska, she imagines

> the snow and frozen sea and ice glaciers. Eskimo igloos and polar bears and the beautiful northern lights. When Jarvis had first gone to Alaska, she had sent him a box of homemade fudge, packing it carefully and wrapping each piece separately in waxed paper. It had thrilled her to think that her fudge would be eaten in Alaska, and she had a vision of her brother passing it around to furry Eskimos.

When Jarvis picks his bride from a town named Winter Hill, the associations of the name do not escape her:

> 'I think it's a curious coincidence that Jarvis would get to go to Alaska and that the very bride he picked to marry would come from a place called Winter Hill. Winter Hill,' she repeated slowly, her eyes closed, and the name blended with dreams of Alaska and cold snow.

Seated across from the soldier in a booth at the Blue Moon Café, she has another vision:

> She suddenly saw the three of them—herself, her brother, and the bride—walking beneath a cold Alaska sky, along the sea where green ice waves lay frozen and folded on the shore; they climbed a sunny glacier shot through with pale gold colors and a rope tied the three of them together . . .

One of her favourite treasures is a glass ball with snow inside that could be shaken up into a snowstorm:

> She could hold the snow globe to her narrowed eyes and watch the whirling white flakes fall until they blinded her. She dreamed of Alaska. She walked up a cold white hill and looked on a snowy wasteland far below. She watched the sun making colors on the ice, and heard dream voices, saw dream things. And everywhere there was the cold white gentle snow.

Frankie is even envious of Berenice, the cook, because years ago she and her ex-husband, now dead, lived in Cincinnati, where snow fell every winter.[1]

In much of Mrs McCullers's fiction the heat and glare of summer are associated with boredom, monotony, and sorrow. 'Yes, the town is dreary,' she writes in *The Ballad of the Sad Café*, the most melancholy of all her works, and one of the saddest stories in English. 'On August afternoons the road is empty, white with dust, and the sky above is bright as glass . . . There is absolutely nothing to do in the town . . . The soul rots with boredom.' Here is Malone, in *Clock Without Hands*:

> As he walked he felt the blazing sky, the sun, weigh down his shoulders. An ordinary, practical man who seldom daydreamed, he was daydreaming now that in the autumn he was going to a northern country, to Vermont or Maine where again he would see snow . . . He saw in his mind's eye the polar enchantment of snow and felt the cool of it. As he thought of snow he felt a freedom . . .

And it may be no accident that in the short story, 'Madame Zilensky and the King of Finland', the protagonist (a musician who derives much of her mysterious energy from fantasies) regards as the high point of her existence the 'fact' that she has once seen the King of Finland passing by on a sled when she was in a pastry shop in Helsingfors: when it is cruelly pointed out to her that Finland is a democracy, she is crushed. Here once more snow is associated with the world of dreams, the world of glamorous but impossible happenings.

Another, less persistent symbol of excitement and romance in Mrs McCullers's work is the sea. Mick, who, like Carson, had never seen it, says wistfully to Harry: 'I wish we was at the ocean. On the beach and watching the ships far out on the water. You went to the beach one summer—exactly what was it like?' And next to her glass ball Frankie's most cherished possession is a lavender seashell: 'When she held the seashell to her ear, she could hear the warm

1 Truman Capote, another Southern writer, makes an almost identical use of snow symbolism in *Other Voices, Other Rooms* (New York, Random House), pp. 57-59. *The Heart Is a Lonely Hunter* and *The Member of the Wedding* appeared in 1940 and 1946 respectively; Mr Capote's novel, in 1948. Numerous critics, *e.g.* Mark Schorer (in *The Creative Present*, ed. by Nona Balakian and Charles Simmons, New York, Doubleday & Company, 1963, p. 96) have commented on specific instances in which Mr Capote's work resembles Mrs McCullers's. Perhaps the most striking of these occurs in *The Grass Harp*, where Verena's crossed eyes 'peering inward upon a stony vista' recall Miss Amelia's, similarly crossed, in *The Ballad of the Sad Café*, and 'exchanging with each other one long and secret gaze of grief.'

wash of the Gulf of Mexico, and think of a green palm island far away.'

On one occasion the monotony of the long, lonely days was broken when Carson's family received an unexpected visit from an elegant old lady dressed in black. It was her father's second cousin, once removed, and she had not been long in the house when she calmly made the announcement that, as she had always been fond of it and of them, she had decided it would be unwise for her to leave, and that she planned to spend the remainder of her days there. (Her children finally succeeded in luring her away with an ice-cream cone.) It was the child's first contact with the bizarre, and it appears to have made a profound impression upon her.

Carson's childhood and adolescence were, on the whole, happy. Her parents let her do very much as she wished; they appear to have been what, in the jargon of modern child psychologists, is known as 'permissive', even to an extreme degree. Their liberalism extended to religion also: Mr Smith was an Episcopalian, his wife a Baptist, and as a small child Carson attended the services of either denomination according to their mood. After she was ten, however, she ceased to accompany them, and eventually the whole family came to prefer spending their Sundays in the woods.

From the point of view of the literary historian, this early period in Mrs McCullers's life is interesting for two reasons: it illuminates those portions of *The Heart Is a Lonely Hunter* and *The Member of the Wedding* which are of an autobiographical character, and it accounts for the small-town setting of four of her major works—*The Heart Is a Lonely Hunter, The Member of the Wedding, The Ballad of the Sad Café,* and *Clock Without Hands.* Certainly the resemblances between Lula Carson Smith and Mick Kelly are too obvious to be ignored: both are tall for their age, both are tomboys, and the fathers of both of them are small-town jewellers. The resemblances between Lula Carson Smith and Frankie Addams are stronger still. And there is little doubt that it was her home town of Columbus, Georgia, that furnished Mrs McCullers with the generic image of the Southern small town that, with various modifications, is the scene of the above-mentioned works. It is a depressing image, on the whole: of a cotton mill, of poor whites and poorer Negroes, of a few middle and upper middle class white families with coloured servants. There is a main street lined with business establishments and having two or three cafés on it, there is a court-house set in the centre of a little park, there is a post office and a few movie theatres. In the residential area there are a few peach trees, a few oaks, a few magnolias, and a few bushes of crêpe myrtle. In the poorer section there are tumble-down shacks that need painting and dusty streets that need paving and lights; in the more prosperous area there are big white cottages built for coolness—they have screened porches and shady lawns, and convey an impression of somnolent self-satisfaction. In this town the season is always summer, the time of day always afternoon. The heat is suffocating, the glare all but unbearable. And there is absolutely nothing to do.

* * *

CHAPTER TWO

WUNDERKIND

In an early story, 'Wunderkind' (*Story*, December, 1936), Mrs McCullers describes an afternoon in the life of a fifteen-year-old girl who has been a child prodigy—a *Wunderkind*. It is no ordinary afternoon, for during the course of it she experiences the first great disappointment of her life. Mister Bilderbach, the piano teacher who three years previously, when she first came to him, had applied to her the glamorous-sounding foreign word, and for whom she has conceived an admiration bordering on idolatry, listens to her playing of Beethoven's Variation Sonata, Opus 26, with a disapproval that he is too honest to conceal. But when he sees how seriously she takes his criticism, he tactfully suggests that she play 'The Harmonious Blacksmith'—one of the first pieces they worked on together, and which in the past she has always rendered impeccably. However, the girl, who is in a state of emotional tension caused by an overpowering awareness of his physical presence and her own feeling of self disappointment, is unable to do justice to this either, and flees tearfully from his studio.

In a sense this story anticipates what occurs as a minor theme in *The Heart Is a Lonely Hunter* and as a major one in *The Member of the Wedding*. For, like Frankie Addams, this girl (whose name, incidentally, is Frances), straddles the uncomfortable fence that separates childhood from adulthood: she is not yet sufficiently mature to play Beethoven with the proper feeling, nor can she retreat to the earlier, less troubled period when she was capable of turning out a flawless performance of 'The Harmonious Blacksmith'. But there is another reason why this story is interesting. When we read that the first piece Frances chooses to play for Mr Bilderbach is Liszt's Second Hungarian Rhapsody, and that after listening to her he starts her on Bach, we are reminded immediately of Carson's own audition, which took place at the same age (twelve). Frances's experience is described as follows:

The first day she came to the studio. After she played the whole
Second Hungarian Rhapsody from memory. The room graying
with twilight. His face as he leaned over the piano. 'Now we
begin all over,' he said that first day. 'It—playing music—is
more than cleverness. If a twelve-year-old girl's fingers cover
so many keys to the second—that means nothing.'
He tapped his broad chest and his forehead with his stubby
hand. 'Here and here. You are old enough to understand that.'
He lighted a cigarette and gently blew the first exhalation over
her head. 'And work—work—work—. We will start now with
these Bach Inventions and these little Schumann pieces.' His
hands moved again—this time to jerk the cord of the lamp behind her and point to the music. 'I will show you how I wish
this practiced.' She had been at the piano for almost three hours
and was very tired. His deep voice sounded as though it had
been straying inside her for a long time. She wanted to reach
out and touch his muscle-flexed finger that pointed out the
phrases, wanted to feel the gleaming gold band ring and the
strong hairy back of his hand.

It would of course be absurd to maintain that this incident is
entirely autobiographical: Mrs Tucker never had any reason to be
seriously disappointed in Carson's playing; on the contrary, she encouraged her ambition to become a concert pianist and predicted
great successes for her. But it is easy to see that an important part
of Carson's own real-life experience went into the making of this
fictional situation (she too must have had afternoons that were less
successful than others), and the worship that Frances feels for Mr
Bilderbach, though it is confused and complicated with sexual overtones, is perhaps no less intense than that which Carson once felt for
her own teacher.

Mrs McCullers's early musical training has been valuable to her
as a writer in several ways, and she has several times observed that
the best possible preparation for a writer is by way of music. (The
case of Paul Bowles, the distinguished composer and music critic
who has also earned for himself an enviable reputation as a novelist,
comes immediately to mind.) First of all, this training has provided
her with a good ear—or rather, it has developed in her the feeling
for rhythm that enables her to choose the most effective of several
alternative ways of combining words into sentences, and sentences
into paragraphs: it has made her peculiarly conscious of the caden-
ces of prose composition. Secondly, it has taught her the strategy
by which literary themes, like themes in music, can be suggested, developed, and finally resolved. (Among twentieth-century novelists
Proust and Mann have been unusually successful with this technique,

which is essentially musical; Huxley attempted it, with less success, in *Point Counterpoint,* and Faulkner practised it with considerable skill in his longer and more ambitious novels.) Finally, her know-ledge of music and her experience as a musician have supplied her with a large area of important experience, thereby increasing and enriching the sources of her material and furnishing her with a frame of reference that is unavailable to writers lacking this experience [1]. 'Wunderkind' is not the only one of Mrs McCullers's works that is concerned with music; musical references abound in both the short stories and the novels, and when Mick Kelly listens for the first time to Beethoven's Third Symphony played on a neighbour's radio, the experience comes as the emotional climax of her entire adolescence :

> She could not listen good enough to hear it all. The music boiled inside her. Which? To hang on to certain wonderful parts and think them over so that later she would not forget— or should she let go and listen to each part that came without thinking or trying to remember? Golly! The whole world was this music and she could not listen hard enough. Then at last the opening music came again, with all the different instruments bunched together for each note like a hard, tight fist that socked at her heart. And the first part was over.
> This music did not take a long time or a short time. It did not have anything to do with time going by at all. She sat with her arms held tight around her legs, biting her salty knee very hard. It might have been five minutes she listened or half the night . . . But maybe the last part of the symphony was the music she loved the best—glad and like the greatest people in the world running and springing up in a hard, free way. Wonderful music like this was the worst hurt there could be. The whole world was this symphony, and there was not enough of her to listen.

Passion and discipline are the two qualities Mrs McCullers believes are essential to any artist. The former is innate, though of course it is subject to cultivation and development, while the latter can only be acquired by hard work—and Mrs Tucker saw to it that her pupil worked very hard indeed. Carson was now a student at Columbus High School, and continued, with the indulgence of her parents, to work four hours a day at the piano and as little as possible at the preparation of her other lessons, which naturally

---

[1] One of Mrs McCullers's French critics, Pierre Brodin, has observed: 'Notons, au passage, que la musique, non moins que l'enfance et l'atmosphère sudiste, a marqué fortement la romancière : sa sensibilité, son art seront plus proches de ceux du musicien que ceux du peintre.' (*Présences Contemporaines, Ecrivains Américains d'Aujourd'hui,* Nouvelles Editions Debresse. Paris, 1964, p.99.)

suffered. Nevertheless, she managed to pass all her subjects with fairly good grades—testimony, perhaps, at once of her own adaptability and intelligence and of a certain laxity of standards in the small-town high school. Mrs McCullers has never valued formal education, with its complicated system of 'credits' and 'units' very highly, and she has really had only two overwhelming intellectual interests in her life: music and writing.

She made her first experiments in writing when she was fifteen. Eugene O'Neill was her favourite author at the time, and her first literary compositions took the form of drama. She wrote three plays in rapid succession, the first of which, she says, was 'thick with incest, lunacy, and murder'. (The first scene was laid in a graveyard and the last required a catafalque.)

Her startled but ever-obliging father, impressed by this latest manifestation of his daughter's talent, bought her a typewriter—just as, ten years before, he had bought her a piano—and Carson considered that her literary career was launched in earnest. She wrote a story called 'The Fire of Life' containing only two characters who compensated in distinction for what they lacked in number (they were Nietzsche and Jesus), and she began a novel, *A Reed of Pan*, which concerned a musician in New York who 'sold his soul' by writing jazz, and hopefully sent it off to an agent. Carson was familiar with the setting of her story only, of course, through what she had read and heard about the great city: she knew that there were subways, and she presumed that passengers bought tickets to ride on them. In the letter with which the puzzled agent returned the manuscript, he inquired, 'How old were you when the subways sold tickets?' As he could not recall such a time within his own memory, he apparently thought his would-be client was an elderly woman instead of a fifteen-year-old girl! She then wrote a second novel, *Brown River*, about which she remembers little except that it was inspired by, and imitative of, D. H. Lawrence's *Sons and Lovers*, which she had recently discovered. She even tried her hand at verse, producing some 'rather queer poems that nobody could make out, including their author'. Mainly traditional in form, there were odd and unexpected lapses into *vers libre*: when she found regular metrical patterns too confining, or when she had trouble with rhymes, she simply abandoned them.

The first story she thought good enough to show to her parents was called 'Sucker'. This story has an interesting history: written when she was barely seventeen, it had never been published until, rummaging in some old papers recently, a relative (Major Simeon Smith of West Point) discovered it and turned it over to her literary agent, Robert Lantz, who promptly sold it to *The Saturday Evening Post* for fifteen hundred dollars. Though slight, and of only minor interest in its own right, it is nevertheless an extraordinary achievement for a girl in her middle teens, and to students of Mrs McCullers's mature work it is of particular interest because it proves that already, at this early age, its author was concerned with what was to become one of her major themes: frustrated love and loneliness. Told in the first person by Pete, a sixteen-year-old boy, it explores his relationship with two other persons—Maybelle, a girl of about his own age with whom he is infatuated, and a twelve-year-old boy, a first cousin, who is infatuated with *him*. The cousin's nickname is Sucker (he is called this because he believes whatever is told him), and the older boy treats him sometimes kindly and sometimes cruelly, depending on how Maybelle treats *him*. When she rejects him finally for a football player, Pete suddenly turns upon Sucker and says terrible things to him—things that he later regrets and cannot even understand how he could have brought himself to utter. But it is too late; his cousin's love for him has been permanently destroyed, and shortly after this Sucker undergoes a metamorphosis. He becomes hard and tough, and loses his childish quality: the moment of betrayal is the moment that separates the boy from the child. Thereafter Pete and the other boys call him by his proper name, Richard.

The frustration pattern that is here handled so simply receives much more elaborate treatment in *The Heart Is a Lonely Hunter*, but it is essentially the same pattern. Singer, the protagonist of that novel, worships Antonapoulos, a half-wit who is incapable of reciprocating his devotion; Mick Kelly adores Singer, who would be amazed if he knew she follows him on his lonely evening strolls; Biff Brannon, the café owner, loves Mick, who thinks he despises her; Lucile, Biff's sister-in-law, loves Leroy, who has deserted her; Mick's playmate, Harry Minowitz, has a crush on Jake Blount, the political agitator, though Jake does not know it; and Dr Copeland, the Negro physician, loves his people, who are afraid of him. The same pattern is repeated in *Reflections in a Golden Eye*, where Private Williams longs for Leonora, the wife of his superior officer; and Captain Penderton, Leonora's husband, loves Private Williams, though he will not admit it to himself; there is also frustration in the wistful love that Anacleto, the Filipino houseboy, has for Alison Langdon, and she for him. In *Clock Without Hands* Ellen, the protagonist's daughter, loves Jester, who is scarcely aware of her existence; Jester nurtures a secret love for Sherman, a blue-eyed Negro who constantly mistreats him; and Sherman worships Zippo, a man of his own race who mistreats *him*. But it is in *The Ballad of the Sad Café* that the pattern of 'Sucker' is duplicated most precisely. Marvin Macy has been in love with Miss Amelia (though later his love, because she rejects it, turns to hate); Miss Amelia loves Cousin Lymon, the hunchback; and Cousin Lymon is enamoured of Marvin. Miss Amelia's rejection of Marvin's love corresponds to Maybelle's rejection of Pete's, and Cousin Lymon's betrayal of Miss Amelia's love corresponds to Pete's betrayal of Sucker's. Pete observes toward the beginning: 'There is one thing I have learned . . . If a person admires you a lot you despise him and don't care—and it is the person who doesn't notice you that you are apt to admire.'

Nearly ten years later Mrs McCullers was to write, in what has become one of the most frequently quoted passages from *The Ballad of the Sad Café*:

> The curt truth is that, in a deep secret way, the state of being beloved is intolerable to many. The beloved fears and hates the lover, and with the best of reasons. For the lover is forever trying to strip bare his beloved. The lover craves any possible relation with the beloved, even if this experience can cause him only pain.

Readers familiar with *Clock Without Hands* will recall that when Jester attempts to kiss Sherman the caress is returned with a blow, and when Malone's wife makes advances to him he is repelled and rushes out of the house.

Mrs McCullers is not, of course, the first writer to express this idea (it occurs, for instance, in Stendhal's *Le Rouge et le Noir*), but it is doubtful if any other author—at least any other author writing in English—has articulated it quite so simply and so succinctly, or has posited it so firmly as an axiom of the human psyche.

Apart from these general similarities to her later work, and from the fact that Sucker is the first in Mrs McCullers's gallery of memorable adolescents, this story recalls an analogous incident (of which it may well have been the genesis) in *The Heart Is a Lonely Hunter* —where, to be sure, it plays only a small part. Mick's seven-year-old brother, whose nick-name is Bubber, runs away from home when, as a punishment for his misbehaviour, she tells him a made-up yarn to the effect that the police are looking for him and that, when they find him, they intend to put him in the penitentiary. And though she begs his forgiveness when the family at last succeeds in finding him, he is never quite the same after this experience.

But after that night there was not much of a chance for her to tease him any more—her or anybody else . . . He always kept his mouth shut and he didn't fool around with anybody else . . . Most of the time he just sat in the back yard or in the coal house by himself . . . He hid his marbles and jack-knife and wouldn't let anybody touch his story books.

After that night nobody called him Bubber anymore . . . But he didn't speak much to any person and nothing seemed to bother him. The family called him by his real name—George. At first Mick couldn't stop calling him Bubber and she didn't want to stop. But it was funny how after about a week she just naturally called him George like everybody else did. But he was a different kid—George—going around by himself always like a person much older and with nobody, not even her, knowing what was really in his mind.

Here, too, betrayal engenders suspicion and produces in the small boy, as a defence reaction, a precocious toughness.

People who remember Carson McCullers as a girl of fifteen and sixteen all agree on one thing: her amazing creative energy, which overflowed in all directions. Isadora Duncan's autobiography, as has been mentioned, made a strong impression on her, and she decided to start her own school of the dance. Gathering a few recruits from among the neighbourhood children, she insisted that they wear sheets and go barefooted in the Greek manner. The dances were done in what they imagined was the Duncan style—they were loosely interpretive, sometimes wildly fanciful, and always highly dramatic. There were two kinds of performances: yard dances and living-room dances. The yard dances were of a semi-public type, performed by various members of the 'school' before an audience consisting of their parents, other children, and anyone at all who was willing to watch. Living-room dances were private—for members of the family only. Rita participated in these ventures a bit reluctantly, but only once was Carson able to persuade her little brother to help: on this occasion, wrapped in a sheet, he condescended to do a solo performance in the living room.

Sometimes Carson composed the music for these dances herself. For some years now she had been making simple experiments in musical composition, and they gave her a feeling of deep satisfaction. Again, we are reminded of Mick Kelly: 'And she made up new music too. That was better than just copying tunes. When her hands hunted out these beautiful new sounds it was the best feeling she had ever known.'

She was also an indefatigable reader, and when she was engrossed

in a good book was almost entirely oblivious of her surroundings—
a fact that on one occasion nearly proved disastrous. Curled up in
bed with a Dostoevsky novel one afternoon—it was when she was
sixteen—she heard a loud noise upstairs. Thinking it was Lamar
Junior, she called out to him to be quiet. Presently the room began
to fill up with smoke, and she realized, just in time, that the house
was on fire, that she was alone in it, and that the noise had been
caused by the roof's collapsing! Mrs Smith, who had gone out on
an errand, saw the fire engine racing down the street and, unaware
that its destination was her own house, remarked to a neighbour, 'If
they're not careful they'll run over somebody.' The blaze was finally
put out, but a substantial part of the house had to be rebuilt.

Carson was always startling her parents with sudden, unexpected
announcements—as when, under the spell of the Duncan book, she
one day calmly informed her father that when she was grown up
she did not want a husband, but only lovers; this is one of the very
few occasions when she can recall seeing a look of genuine shock
on her father's face. On another occasion, she came into the house
with a decisive air and said they would all have to go abroad
immediately. 'Whatever for?' Mr Smith asked, and his daughter
answered him: 'Why, to dance, of course.' Abroad, abroad: the
word was constantly in her mind and evoked associations of such
magnificence that when, thirteen years later, she was able to visit
some of the scenes she had dreamed of for so long, the experience
was almost anticlimactic—the fact was not nearly so wonderful as
the image.

In 1933, when she was still in high school, Carson met, through
Mrs Tucker, a man who for many years exerted an important influence on her intellectual development: Edwin Peacock, a twenty-
three-year-old worker in the Civilian Conservation Corps, an organization of young men who, under Franklin D. Roosevelt's New Deal
administration during the Great Depression, were given federal em-
ployment preserving valuable forest areas and improving natural resources generally. Peacock was a sensitive, well-read man with a
genuine interest in the arts; he had a particular fondness for music,
and, in spite of the difference in their ages, shared many of Carson's
enthusiasms.

Like many government workers during the Roosevelt administration—and like many American intellectuals in the Thirties—Peacock had strong liberal leanings. Political liberalism, of course,
formed an important part of the literary climate of the time (it was
the period of the early Sandburg, the early Steinbeck, and the early
Dos Passos), and Mrs McCullers would have been certain, sooner

or later, to be affected by it. It is difficult to exaggerate the importance of this influence: Mrs McCullers is not essentially a political writer, and the theme of social justice enters importantly into only two of her novels (the first and the latest), but no one who reads *The Heart Is a Lonely Hunter* can overlook in it the struggle between organized religion and dialectical materialism—between the view of life held by characters such as Portia, who see it as planned for better or for worse by a divine intelligence, and that held by characters such as Jake Blount and Doctor Copeland, who would like to reshape it by humanitarian means.

Mr Peacock's camp was at Fort Benning, but he had an apartment in Columbus. He and Carson became close friends, and she valued this relationship almost as much as the one which she enjoyed with Mrs Tucker. The latter, however, was interrupted the following year, when Carson was seventeen, by an unexpected development: Colonel Tucker was ordered to a new post in California. For Carson it meant the end not only of the good times the three of them had together socially, but also of her music lessons, for there was no teacher comparable to Mrs Tucker anywhere near, and Carson had now begun to think quite seriously of following a professional career in music. Though Mrs Tucker was of course in no way to blame for this change of plans, and regretted it almost as much as her protégée, Carson brooded over it ceaselessly and came to regard it finally, in her unconscious mind, as a kind of desertion or betrayal. This was the first appearance of a pattern which was to repeat itself in Mrs McCullers' life, when she has made emotional investments in individuals which, often through no fault of these persons, failed to prosper as she might have wished.

After graduating from Columbus High School, and with the Tuckers in California, Carson was at a loose end; the only friend in whom she could confide now was Edwin, and he was available only when he could leave his camp. She took a job as a reporter on the small-town paper, the Columbus *Enquirer*—a provincial, folksy sheet—but did not keep it very long. Unlike Hemingway and Sherwood Anderson, she was not destined to learn her craft in a newspaper office, and frankly admits that she made a poor reporter. 'I would always,' she recalls, 'write "the murderer in the city jail" instead of "the alleged murderer in the city jail".' Then she tried to found a literary magazine, but this came to nothing because of lack of funds.

Now, more than anything else, she longed to get away. Mrs Tucker had spoken to her often of the Juilliard School of Music in New York, and had even offered to pay her tuition there, but Mr

Smith, who had a strong sense of pride, would not allow his daughter to take advantage of this opportunity. But Carson could not quite put the idea out of her mind, and dreamed about New York and the triumphs that might be awaiting her there. As a second possibility there was always her writing, and if the Juilliard, which was expensive by Depression standards, proved out of reach, she could always take a course in creative writing at Columbia University. From a friend she learned that there was another Columbus girl, with whom Carson was unacquainted, who was then in New York studying at Columbia, and Carson wrote asking her for details. The girl wrote back answering all her questions and offering, if she should decide to come, to let her share her room.

Carson made up her mind, and her parents, as they had always done before at such times, supported her. In the Smith household there was then only one way of raising enough money to finance such an enterprise, which was by far the costliest that their daughter had yet conceived, and that was by selling a diamond-and-emerald ring that had belonged to Carson's maternal grandmother. Her parents did not hesitate : the ring was sold for a good price, and the money was hers. With careful managing, it might even be enough for the Juilliard.

The house was in a turmoil, and with all the hubbub there was a certain sadness. They were all pleased for Sister's sake, since this was what she had been wishing for, but they found it hard to imagine what the place would be like without her; besides, Mr and Mrs Smith worried about her going off all alone. Carson herself was in a fever of anticipation. A passenger steamship service existed at that time between Savannah and New York, and, as Carson had never seen the ocean, she decided on this means of making the trip— the more so as it was relatively inexpensive. At last the great day came : good-byes were said all around—Lamar Junior and Rita were inconsolable—and the seventeen-year-old girl, her eyes wide with excitement but also a little frightened, left the house on Starke Avenue whose memory has never since then ceased to haunt her imagination.

* * *

CHAPTER THREE

MISHAP ON THE SUBWAY

It was a cold winter day early in 1935 when Carson's steamer entered New York harbour, and her first glimpse of the towering skyscrapers made her catch her breath. She was met by her new 'pen pal' whose room she was going to share; it turned out to be a rather dingy, sparsely furnished bed-sitting room over a linen store on the upper West Side, and here she installed herself and the few belongings she had brought with her.

It is doubtful whether she had formed, at this stage, any very definite plans about her immediate future, and her real reason for coming to New York was not so much to attend Columbia, nor even the Juilliard, as it was to experience the adventure of living in a great city where—for those who could afford them—concerts, operas, plays, and lectures were available every single night of the week. And even without money, or with very little, it was still possible to enjoy many things that were not available elsewhere—the great museums and libraries, the elevated railways and the subways, the big double-deck buses on Fifth Avenue, the windows of the huge department stores, Chinatown, Central Park, the Staten Island ferry —and of course snow, of which there was a great deal that year. Best and cheapest of all were the dreams with which she was filled.

The Great Depression was at its height, or rather at its depth, and there was plenty of suffering in evidence, but she was used to that : what was unfamiliar to her was the luxury that existed alongside it. Contrasts of wealth, common at all times in large cities, were particularly striking in New York during the Thirties, and Carson used to marvel at the long, shiny limousines driven along Park Avenue by chauffeurs in livery; the elegantly dressed crowds pouring out of Carnegie Hall and the Metropolitan Opera House just before midnight; and the dazzling displays of jewellery in the windows of Cartier's and Tiffany's that almost made her regret having sold her grandmother's ring. She was torn between an admiration of these glamorous spectacles (and a wistful longing to identify herself with them in some way) and the promptings of her recently awakened social conscience that told her they were but the symptoms of disease in a society which persisted in living by a code of ethics that was barbaric and outmoded.

For the first few days she was terrified, afraid to leave her room. The only other places which offered comparative security and privacy were telephone booths: she had no one to telephone, but sometimes she would sit in them and read by the hour. There were so many booths at Macy's Department Store that she never felt she was inconveniencing anyone by her habit, and Macy's became her favourite rendezvous, a home away from home.

She was fascinated by the subways, but always getting lost in them. Instead of depositing her money in a bank, or buying travellers' cheques with it, she carried it around with her in her purse, and one day, shortly after her arrival, her room-mate suggested she turn it over to her for safe-keeping, saying, 'You might lose it on the subway or something.' Carson consented, and the following evening her room-mate, apparently in a state of great agitation, told her a piece of dreadful news: *she* (or so at least she said) had lost the money on the subway! It was every cent that Carson had in the world, and she was obliged to write home for more. Gone forever were her dreams of the Juilliard, and she decided to take a job during the day and attend classes at Columbia in the evening. She also decided, not surprisingly, to get another room—at the Parnassus Club, a woman's residence hall on the West Side which accommodated a good many Columbia students. After a month here she settled at the Three Arts Club, another residence hall for women located at 240 West Eighty-fifth Street, where she found company that no longer made it necessary for her to sit in telephone booths. The second semester was just getting under way, and she registered for a course in philosophy, one in psychology, and one in the short story taught by Helen Rose Hull, a well-known novelist, anthologist, and author of several books on the craft of fiction.

It is thus owing to an accident on the subway (if it was an accident —Carson has never been able to decide) that Mrs McCullers finally exchanged a musical for a literary career: it did not cost quite so much to be a writer. And though up until the time of her third stroke—which paralyzed the left side of her body—piano playing continued to be her favourite recreation, she has never seriously regretted making this decision. Carson's room-mate, however dubious her motives, may therefore have rendered her a more valuable service than if she had persuaded her to open a bank account—only one of several ironies in this writer's life.

Her daytime jobs gave her no end of trouble, and she drifted helplessly from one to another. 'I was always fired,' she says. 'My record is perfect on that. I never quit a job in my life.' In quick succession she worked as a typist, a waitress, and a clerk in a real estate office; she played the piano for a dancing class in a settlement house and worked for a comic sheet named *More Fun*, which contained jokes and cartoons. Ironically again, *More Fun* offered her the presidency of the firm—because it was going bankrupt!

It was when she was working in the real estate office that she discovered Proust: she would put *Swann's Way* on her lap, concealing it beneath the big ledger on her desk, and read from it surreptitiously. When her employer, Louise B. Field, discovered her at this trick she was so enraged that she fired her on the spot. 'You will never amount to a thing in this world!' she shouted, and emphasized her prophecy by hitting her over the head with the ledger. Solacing herself with a hot chocolate at Schrafft's, Carson wired Mr Smith for more money.

She managed to stick out another semester at Columbia, and during the day, in between jobs, she wandered about the city soaking up impressions and storing them—sometimes consciously, sometimes not—in her mind. In the summer she went back to Columbus, where she renewed her friendship with Edwin. The months in New York had done wonders for her, and her family and friends marvelled at the change: the overgrown, gawky-looking girl was now a poised young woman with a quick, charming smile, and a figure that, though slim, was well-proportioned. The good ladies of Columbus agreed that Carson Smith had 'got her growth' at last.

As autumn approached, a plan that had been in the back of her mind began to take definite shape. A number of people had told her about Sylvia Chatfield Bates, whose class in creative writing at Columbia was immensely popular. Once more Carson made her choice, and September found her back at the Three Arts Club. Miss Bates's class proved to be everything that she had hoped for, and it was under her supervision that Carson McCullers began to achieve maturity as a writer. 'I do not know how anybody teaches writing,' she has said, 'but I found in Miss Bates's class a sympathy and criticism and the discipline of constant work that were invaluable.'

She supported herself, as she had the previous year, by means of various part-time jobs, and would get up as early as four and five in the morning to accomplish the daily quota of writing that she had set for herself. In this way she wrote story after story, destroying everything with which she was dissatisfied—a practice, incidentally, to which she still adheres. And she continued to read, and to reread, her favourite authors: Tolstoy, Dostoevsky (she preferred, and still prefers, the former), Proust, Flaubert, and Faulkner. She also found the time to write to her mother and Edwin almost daily. It was a period of the most intense activity, and her health was beginning to show the strain: at the end of every day she would sink into bed exhausted. But she was supremely happy.

She went back to Columbus in June. Edwin had written her about a young army corporal at Fort Benning with whom he had become intimate and whom he wanted her to meet; he had a feeling, he said, that they would like each other. The corporal's name was James Reeves McCullers, and Edwin's intuition had not been mistaken: almost from the moment he introduced them they fell in love.

Reeves McCullers was also from a small town in Georgia—Jesup, near the Florida line. He was twenty-three, of Irish ancestry, and handsome in a virile kind of way—blond, with grey-blue eyes, unusually regular features, and a hard, well-knit body which he kept in perfect condition. His height—fairly short for a man—was approximately Carson's own. He had not gone to college—this was to be a source of dissatisfaction to him later—but he was intelligent, well-read and well-spoken. There was even something a little disconcerting about his charm—not that it was 'professional' in any sense (on the contrary, it was supremely natural) nor that he 'traded' on it, at least not consciously, but nearly everyone who knew this man, whose career was destined to be such a tragic one, agrees that there was something almost uncanny about the way he attracted people to him—all kinds of people, and animals as well. This was one of the ways in which he and Carson were different: she did not make friends easily (though she was fiercely loyal to them when she did), while Reeves would not have found it easy, even if he had tried, to make an enemy.

Reeves helped to fill the place in Carson's affections that Mary Tucker had left vacant by her departure, and she found the new relationship all the more exciting because it combined sexual passion with the emotional dependency that had now become a firmly fixed part of her character: for the first time she discovered the joy of loving completely, with all of her nature, and of being loved in return. The days sped by. She and Reeves were together as often as he could arrange it, and Edwin joined them when he was able. Carson was planning to return to Columbia in July, to attend Whit

Burnett's class in the short story. The decision was harder to make this time, because of Reeves, but already she had come to understand that where her writing was concerned she could not afford to compromise. And Reeves, though it was not easy for him, agreed with her. He was enthusiastic about her plans to write; his own secret ambition, he confided to her, was to be a writer, and this made her feel even closer to him. Now she thought less and less about making a career of music: her head was humming with ideas for stories and novels.

Whit Burnett, her new teacher, was the influential editor of *Story*. It is scarcely possible to overestimate the importance of this magazine in the Thirties and Forties, which published the first stories of William Saroyan, J. D. Salinger, Tennessee Williams, Jesse Stuart, Frederick Prokosch, Truman Capote, Nelson Algren, and Norman Mailer, and which numbered among its regular contributors William Faulkner, Sherwood Anderson, and Erskine Caldwell. At one time or another Gertrude Stein, William March, Kay Boyle, James T. Farrell, and Richard Wright had all appeared in it, as well as a good many writers from across the Atlantic: Frank O'Connor, Graham Greene, Seán O'Faoláin, and, in translation, Ignazio Silone and two distinguished Nobel Prizewinners, Luigi Pirandello and Ivan Bunin.

Two of the stories Carson wrote that summer in New York so impressed Mr Burnett that he bought them for his magazine: 'Like That' and 'Wunderkind'. The first, for some reason, never saw print, but the second, as has been previously mentioned, appeared in December, 1936, and is thus Mrs McCullers's first published story. To Miss Bates and Mr Burnett, then, must properly go the credit for having 'discovered' Carson McCullers.

Reeves wrote to her daily; he was beginning to grow restive. Self-indulgent by nature, he found it hard in Carson's absence to practise the literal fidelity that he seemed to feel he owed her, but he succeeded. Edwin Peacock recalls trying to persuade him to accompany him to a Columbus bordello: he finally consented, but on arriving there refused to join his friend in enjoying the hospitality of the establishment; he was keeping himself 'pure' for Carson. Occasionally he would overdrink, but this was the only outlet for his frustration that he permitted himself. In the autumn he inherited from his aunt a small sum with which he bought himself out of the Army.

Carson, meantime, had worn herself out with her self-imposed work schedule and was obliged to return to Georgia. She had lost weight and become extremely nervous; and her new habit of chain-smoking as she worked at the typewriter—she had begun a long, rambling novel that was still only half-plotted in her mind—excited some comment among the neighbours, who also observed that, though she was friendly enough when spoken to, she had begun to hold herself somewhat aloof. Her opinions, they suspected, were 'radical', and her way of expressing herself was not sufficiently conventional for their taste. There was some justification for this feeling: in her attitudes and in her manner Carson corresponded rather closely to the stereotype of the bohemian intellectual of the middle and late Thirties—passionately liberal in her views on politics and sexual morality (the influence, respectively, of Marx and Freud), 'advanced' in her aesthetic tastes, and somewhat indifferent where her personal appearance and the ordinary routines of daily life were concerned. It was a type that was more appropriate to the precincts of Greenwich Village than to a small town in Georgia.

Carson's illness, which put her to bed during the winter of 1936-37 and which was vaguely thought to be 'tuberculosis', is now believed to have been rheumatic fever. Had this diagnosis been made at the time, and had she been enjoined by her physician to lead a more restful life, she might well have been spared her subsequent strokes. Now that Reeves was free, Carson encouraged him to go to New York to try his luck in the literary world: as soon as she was better, she said, she would join him there. He was naturally reluctant to leave her, and only agreed to do so on condition that she write to him every day. It was not until the spring, however, that she was able to meet him at Golden's Grove, the little town outside New York where he established his studio. Shortly after her arrival she fell ill once more, whereupon Reeves accompanied her South by steamer. Temporarily abandoning his plans for a literary career, he found a job as a credit manager in Charlotte, North Carolina. The following autumn he and Carson were married by a Baptist minister in a simple ceremony in the house on Starke Avenue. Though there was no 'best man', Edwin of course was present, and he was given an assignment—to play one of their favourite records (Bach's Concerto for Two Violins in D Minor) on the phonograph while the couple entered the living-room arm-in-arm. He was supposed to play the *largo* movement, but in his excitement he put on the other side of the record, which was *vivace*, and caught himself just in the nick of time. Mrs Smith cried when her daughter's handsome husband took her off with him to their new home in Charlotte but consoled herself by repeating the old rhyme: 'A son is a son 'til he gets a wife; a daughter's a daughter the rest of her life.'

CHAPTER FOUR

THE TONGUE AND THE HEART

The Case of the Silent Singer

1

The novel on which Mrs McCullers had started to work during the year she was 'resting' in Columbus did not begin to take definite shape until after her marriage, and even then it did so very gradually. She knew that it was to be a book whose central theme was loneliness and love, and she had roughly decided on its pattern: the protagonist was to be a Jew about whom the other characters knew very little but to whom, for some reason, they all turned in their distress and confided their innermost hopes and fears. Somewhere in an art gallery she had seen a portrait of a Jew whose expression —wise, kindly, and compassionate—supplied her with the physical image of her character, whom she named Harry Minowitz. It is also possible that, unconsciously, she was endowing Harry Minowitz with some of the characteristics of her own father, and that this character represents to that extent a projection of the father image: Minowitz, like Mr Smith, is a jeweller, and his relationship with the other characters is of a distinctly paternal type. It had not yet occurred to her to make her protagonist a deaf-mute, and Mick, at this stage, was not a girl at all but a boy named Jester.[1]

It was during the first year of her marriage, when she and Reeves were living in Charlotte, that she had what she sometimes refers to as an 'illumination':

> For a whole year I worked on this book and I didn't understand it at all. All the characters were there and they were all talking to this man—but I didn't know why they were talking to him. Then one day, after working very hard on this novel I

[1] Readers familiar with *Clock Without Hands* will recall that this is also the name of a character in that novel: there is no other resemblance, however, between the two characters.

did not understand, I was walking up and down the floor when suddenly it came to me that Harry Minowitz (his name) is a deaf-mute and immediately the name was changed to John Singer.[2] The whole focus of the novel was fixed and I was, for the first time, committed morally, ethically, and with my whole soul to *The Heart Is a Lonely Hunter*.

This statement suggests that Mrs McCullers is, like many romantics, a writer of the compulsive type, and it is her conviction that the writer discovers his purpose in the act of composition by a kind of 'dawning' process. It may be remarked that this is not, perhaps, the way in which allegories are commonly thought of as being written—and *The Heart is a Lonely Hunter*, like most of Mrs McCullers's work, is largely allegorical. But all allegorical writers do not work in precisely the same way, and in any case no real inconsistency is involved, for allegory, if it is to be other than merely mechanical, presupposes an intuitive faculty that invents incidents and relationships as well as a rational faculty that orders and arranges them according to a conscious plan. In allegory, which by its nature involves the use of symbols, the selection and integration of them is naturally more rigorous than in non-allegorical writing, but the source and growth of any work of art remain, as Mrs McCullers has said, 'as mysterious as the formation of life in the womb.'

At any rate the idea of making her protagonist a deaf-mute was a happy one, not merely for the obvious reason that he constitutes an excellent symbol of isolation but also because the nature of his handicap contributes greatly to the irony that is at the centre of the novel. For the reason Singer is so highly esteemed by the other characters is that, being mute, he cannot make himself fully known to them. Not that there is anything dubious about his character—he is simply lacking in the godlike qualities that they imagine they see in him, as is made clear from the letters he writes—and never mails —to his friend Antonapoulos. He himself wonders why it is that the others are always seeking him out. He writes to Antonapoulos: 'They come up to my room and talk to me until I do not understand how a person can open and shut his or her mouth so much without being weary.' Of Jake Blount he says: 'The one with the mustache I think is crazy . . . He thinks he and I have a secret together but I do not know what it is.' And of Mick: 'She knows I am deaf but she thinks I know about music.' About the whole situation he confesses:

---

[2] The name Harry Minowitz in the final version designates another character—the playmate with whom Mick has her first experience of sex.

'I do not understand, so I write to you because I think you will understand.'

It is tempting to speculate that the reason Singer is able to get along so well with these so different characters (who often quarrel among themselves) is that his understanding of them does not greatly exceed theirs of him. Certainly it is because they know so little about him that they are free to imagine him as they wish him to be, so that the image of him which they fashion is really a projection of their own desires. The rumours that exist about him are therefore many and varied:

> The Jews said that he was a Jew. The merchants along the main street claimed he had received a large legacy and was a very rich man. It was whispered in one browbeaten textile union that the mute was an organizer for the C.I.O. A lone Turk who had roamed into the town years ago and who languished with his family behind the little store where they sold linens claimed passionately to his wife that the mute was Turkish. He said that when he spoke his language the mute understood. And as he claimed this his voice grew warm and he forgot to squabble with his children and he was full of plans and activity. One old man from the country said that the mute had come from some place near his home and that the mute's father had the finest tobacco crop in all the county. All these things were said about him.

There is surface irony in the choice of the name Singer as applied to a deaf-mute, but there is also a sense in which the name, as I shall presently show, is peculiarly appropriate.

'I never knew a deaf-mute,' Mrs McCullers once admitted in an interview. To write about one so knowingly, and at such length, posed a problem that was not to be solved overnight, but her imagination proved equal to the task and in none of her other novels, with the possible exception of Clock Without Hands, has she been quite so successful in the handling of realistic detail. When the book was nearly finished, her husband told her about a convention of deaf-mutes which was being held in a nearby town and suggested they go to observe it, but Carson refused: 'I already had made my conception of deaf-mutes and didn't want it to be disturbed.'

The two years during which she worked on The Mute (whose title was later changed by the publisher to The Heart is a Lonely Hunter[3]) were amongst the happiest of Mrs McCullers's life. She

---

3 Probably after a poem, 'The Lonely Hunter', by William Sharp ('Fiona MacLeod') in which occurs the line, 'My heart is a lonely hunter that hunts on a lonely hill.' See Poems and Dramas, by 'Fiona MacLeod' (William Sharp), New York, Duffield & Company, 1914. p. 27.

and Reeves were poor but they were in love, and as yet no cloud had appeared which threatened to trouble their peace of mind. During the day she would write, play the piano, and go for long walks in the country; in the evening, when Reeves came home, she would read aloud what she had written during the day and discuss with him the plan of the book. Occasionally he would make a suggestion, but what he mainly had to offer was not criticism so much as encouragement and enthusiasm. He had not altogether forgotten his own literary ambitions, and Carson made a point of reminding him of them from time to time. Between them they made a pact: she would write for a year while he worked to support them, and the following year the parts would be reversed—he would work at his writing while she acted as breadwinner. By this means they hoped in time to arrive at the point where it would be possible for both of them to devote all their time to fiction.

When Carson was in New York she had met, through Miss Bates, the novelist William March, author of *Company K,* which was perhaps the best American novel to come out of the First World War. Miss Bates, with whom she continued to keep in touch and who knew that she was working on a novel, now suggested that she apply for a Houghton Mifflin Fiction Fellowship and advised Carson to send several chapters of *The Mute* to March for his opinion and criticism. He was enthusiastic: not only, he declared, was the book worth subsidizing, but it contained some of the most sensitive writing that he had ever read; it was hard for him to believe it was a first novel. Encouraged by his and Miss Bates's support, Carson submitted the outline which appears in the Appendix of this book to the Houghton Mifflin Company, which awarded her a Fiction Fellowship of $1500.

2

The essential loneliness of individuals in a world full of other individuals as lonely as themselves is the paradox about which *The Heart Is a Lonely Hunter* is constructed. It would, I think, be an impertinence to suggest specific biographical reasons why Mrs McCullers chose this particular theme—or rather (since, as I have said, she is a compulsive writer) why it chose her. Beyond noting that she had always been conscious of the sense of difference that separates creative from ordinary people (and conscious also that ordinary people were conscious of it) and that during her first months in New York she came to know what it was to be lonely in the midst of crowds, there seems to be no particular point in speculation of this type: what is important is that the theme is a valid—indeed, a traditional—one, and that she recognized in it an opportunity to communicate her experience of life.

The structure of the book is strictly symmetrical. At its apparent centre is Singer, about whom the other main characters are grouped in satellite fashion, or to whom they stand in the same relation as the spokes to the hub of a wheel: Mick Kelly, the adolescent tomboy who struggles fiercely but hopelessly against the fate that denies her the money for piano lessons and that forces her finally to exchange her dream of becoming a concert pianist for a job at Woolworth's; Doctor Copeland, the agnostic Negro physician whose mission in life is the advancement of his race and who is willing to sacrifice everything, including his own health, toward this end—yet who is feared and mistrusted by even the members of his own family; Jake Blount, the Marxist proselytizer whose excess of zeal and refusal to compromise render him so ineffectual that he takes refuge in alcohol; and Biff Brannon, the proprietor of the New York Café, who watches everything from behind his counter with an attitude that is half ironic, half compassionate, and who, when his wife (for whom he feels no special fondness) dies, expresses the feminine side of his nature, hitherto held in abeyance, by using perfume and bleaching his hair.

Though Singer is the protagonist and the apparent centre of the book, its real centre is Spiros Antonapoulos, a grotesque character who is not merely a deaf-mute but a half-wit as well. For, while all the above-mentioned characters are attracted to Singer, Singer himself—unknown to the others—is attracted to Antonapoulos, so that Singer stands in the same relation to Antonapoulos as the other characters do to Singer. Singer's suicide removes the apparent centre of the structure, which thereupon collapses, but Singer commits suicide because Antonapoulos, the real centre, has died in a mental hospital. Alternatively, the structure of the novel, as Frank Durham has observed in an interesting essay ('God and No God in *The Heart Is a Lonely Hunter*', *South Atlantic Quarterly*, Fall, 1957), may be considered to be pyramidal, with Antonapoulos at the apex, Singer just below him, and the other four major characters forming the base.[4]

When Singer, to whom everyone looks up, commits suicide (the situation reminds one irresistibly of that in Edwin Arlington Robinson's well-known poem, 'Richard Cory'), the shock is indeed great

[4] Other structural patterns in the novel have been pointed out by Klaus Lubbers, 'The Necessary Order: A Study of Theme and Structure in Carson McCullers' Fiction', *Jahrbuch für Amerikastudien*, No. 8 (1963), p. 188 ff.

for the four characters who, as we have seen, have imputed to him an omniscience that he really lacks, but the shock is no less severe for Singer when he learns of the death of his friend, to whom *he* has ascribed a similar power: indeed, judging from his reaction, it is far more severe, since it leads him to end his life while the other characters, though temporarily stunned and confused, continue their frustrated search for love.

Granted that the novel is an allegory, what is the symbolic function of Antonapoulos, and what is the moral truth that the author wishes to dramatize by causing the least attractive character in the book to be the object of Singer's love? These are difficult questions, but they must be answered if we are to understand *The Heart Is a Lonely Hunter*. We have seen that Mrs McCullers did not, as many reviewers thought, make Singer a deaf-mute because she has a fondness for the unusual as such but because of his symbolic value. Antonapoulos' defect, which is mental as well as physical, is likewise essential to the moral of the story. The fact that Singer's four friends do not see him as he really is but as they imagine him, and that Singer does not see Antonapoulos as *he* really is but as he imagines *him*, suggests that what men see in other men whom they admire or love is not what is 'really' there but what they wish to find: this is one of the truths with which Mrs McCullers is concerned in her novel, and it ought to be obvious that the more grotesque and repulsive a character is who is yet capable of inspiring love in another, the more forcefully he illustrates this thesis.

That there is religious symbolism in *The Heart Is a Lonely Hunter* cannot, I think, be denied, but it is religious only in the general sense that Singer may be said to be 'deified' by the others, and Antonapoulos by him. I think it is safe to infer, especially in view of the evidence in her outline, that Mrs McCullers means that men invent the kind of gods that best serve their own purposes, but I do not think it is possible to find specific religious meanings in the novel in spite of a number of false clues which the author—I think unfortunately—scatters throughout. Of these the most obvious are the attempts (noted by Durham and others) to make of Singer a Christ figure.[5] For if Singer represents Christ, whom then does Antonapoulos represent? Mr Durham's speculation (that he symbolizes the gods of classical antiquity, and that the outcome of the novel illustrates 'how, with the destruction of the pagan past, the Christian

5 Chester E. Eisinger (*Fiction of the Forties*, University of Chicago Press, 1963, p. 247) argues, not very plausibly, that Singer, because he is bisexual, combines the double function of the Virgin Mary and her Son—that, however, because he lacks omniscience, he is 'the false Virgin and the false son'.

myth derived from it collapses') is certainly ingenious, but it is inconsistent with some of the circumstances in the story, such as Antonapoulos' prayers to the Virgin Mary.

Of Antonapoulos (who, incidentally, was modelled—with a few radical alterations—after a Greek produce dealer in Columbus) Mrs McCullers has deliberately made an enigmatic figure. Singer has the following dream about him, which has a Dostoevskyan quality:

> Out of the blackness of sleep a dream formed. There were dull yellow lanterns lighting up a dark flight of stone steps. Antonapoulos kneeled at the top of these steps. He was naked and he fumbled with something that he held above his head and gazed at as though in prayer. He himself knelt halfway down the steps. He was naked and cold and he could not take his eyes from Antonapoulos and the thing he held above him. Behind him on the ground he felt the one with the mustache and the girl and the black man and the last one. They knelt naked and he felt their eyes on him. And behind them were uncounted crowds of kneeling people in the darkness. His own hands were huge windmills and he stared fascinated at the unknown thing that Antonapoulos held.

It is tempting, but not very rewarding, to speculate concerning the unknown thing which Antonapoulos is holding above his head 'as though in prayer', for it may supply the key to the meaning, or one of the meanings, of the novel. The context establishes that it is an object of worship, which would make of Antonapoulos not so much a god as a high priest or religious champion (*In hoc signo vinces*). The possibility that it is a cross,[6] however, is less likely—since it is Singer rather than Antonapoulos who has been endowed with Christlike qualities—than that it is a pagan idol of some kind, perhaps a phallus (the author has previously suggested that Antonapoulos has both onanistic and exhibitionistic tendencies), so that the ironic source of Singer's 'selfless' love may be sexual after all, and the meaning of the dream may be that the spirit must ultimately kneel before the altar of the flesh—a meaning which does not fit easily into the ideological pattern of the novel. I rather wish that Mrs McCullers had made the import of this dream more apparent or omitted it altogether, for I cannot resist the feeling that she has invested Antonapoulos with a mystery and an importance that are incommensurate with what we actually know of him.

6 Lubbers errs when he claims (op. cit., pp. 189-90): 'The "thing" that the Greek holds in his hands is later identified as his little brass cross'. The passage to which he refers is ambiguous.

There is in Singer more than a slight resemblance to Prince Myshkin in *The Idiot* of Dostoevsky: about both characters there is an aura of holiness which is associated with their simplicity, and both inspire confidences from the most unlikely persons. In neither novel is the attempt to make a Christ figure of the protagonist entirely successful, and both books suffer from a certain fuzziness in their symbolism. And when we read of Singer that he has in his face 'something gentle and Jewish, the knowledge of one who belongs to a race that is oppressed . . . a brooding peace that is seen most often in the faces of the very sorrowful or the very wise,' we are reminded of the Dostoevskyan doctrine that it is suffering which ennobles and redeems mankind.

Mrs McCullers once described *The Heart Is a Lonely Hunter* as 'an ironic parable of fascism . . . presenting the spiritual rather than the political side of the phenomenon,' a statement which has puzzled many critics and which, as Ihab Hassan has commented, 'seems to have encrusted itself like a barnacle in the standard reference works on contemporary authors.'[7] But while this description of the novel is indeed misleading in the sense that it limits the real subject too narrowly, it is possible if we think of Singer and Antonapoulos as leaders, blindly invested by others with attributes in which they are only too conspicuously (for those whom they fail to hypnotize) lacking, for us to see the terrifying meaning of the parable: in this absurdly grim game of follow-the-leader, the ultimate leader, the power beyond the power, is a lunatic. Chester E. Eisinger is therefore mistaken when he says concerning Mrs McCullers's description of the book as an 'ironic parable of fascism': 'The comment makes sense only if we assume that the economics of capitalism and the racial practices of the South suggest to her the barbarism of fascism.'[8]

At is broadest level of meaning, however, the allegory of *The Heart Is a Lonely Hunter* is neither religious nor political but concerns the struggle of individuals to free themselves from the cells of their beings—to achieve communication with other individuals similarly imprisoned and to identify themselves in some way with something bigger than themselves and outside themselves. Now of all the practical means of communication the most obvious is speech, and it is another irony of this intricate narrative that its two most articulate characters (Doctor Copeland and Jake Blount) are also the most miserable, while the only one who achieves a sort of happiness, however provisional and short-lived, is Singer, the deaf-mute. Speech

7 In *Modern Fiction Studies*, Winter, 1959-60, p. 317.
8 Op. cit., p. 251.

indeed, only leads in this novel to further confusion, frustration, and loneliness, as witness the bitter quarrel between Jake and the Doctor—two men with very similar interests—in the latter's bedroom. And it is because the Doctor must always say what he thinks, with a monumental tactlessness that is really a form of egotism, that he alienates his own children; and the one lesson that this would-be teacher has not learned himself is that the language of the mind is less eloquent than that of the heart, as his daughter, Portia, reminds him.

> None of us ever cares to talk like you. Us talk like our own Mama and her peoples and their peoples before them. You think out everthing in your brain. While us rather talk from something in our own hearts that has been there for a long time.

Portia, uneducated though she is—perhaps even *because* of her lack of education—is more adept than her father at the language of the heart, the language of ideal communication. Another would-be teacher, scarcely less effective than Copeland and Jake, is Alfred Simms, the mad evangelist who tries to substitute for the language of the heart the language of Scripture, to which he gives his own private meanings: he lives in a world of utter fantasy.

Any practical attempt at communication between individuals must end in failure, Mrs McCullers is saying. The only way in which man can escape from his cell is through ideal communication, or love, and it is interesting in this connection to contrast Jake and the Doctor with Singer, for what the former are filled with is ideological enthusiasm rather than love. Of all the lovers and would-be lovers in the book the most passionate—and the most successful—is Singer. It is in this sense that, although a mute, he is the most eloquent of all the characters: the language of the heart does not require a tongue and may even be the more eloquent for lacking one—just as, in the case where one of the physical senses is impaired, another will occasionally compensate for it. The deaf-mute is indeed a *singer*, and his song—like that of the shepherd on the Grecian urn—is all the sweeter for its silence.

It is one of the characteristics of ideal romantic love, derived from Platonism, that it need not be reciprocal; the beloved, indeed, may even be unaware of the lover's existence, and while this is not precisely the case with Singer and Antonapoulos, it is, in view of the latter's limitations, an approximation of it. Singer's love does not require reciprocation but it does require an object, and when Antonapoulos dies his own reason for living is removed: suicide is a not

uncommon outcome of romantic love. Grotesque though it may
seem, Singer is in fact the archetype of the romantic lover, and the
fact that the object of his love is unworthy of it makes him not the
less typical but the more so, since idealization is the essence of
romantic love.

What we have in The Heart Is a Lonely Hunter is a group of
characters seeking release in love from the bondage of self, but,
since it is 'natural' for most men to think and act selfishly, their
capacity for love is limited. The book presents us with a hierarchy
of lovers, and of these Singer is the most eminent because he is the
most selfless. The other characters seek out Singer chiefly because
of what they think he has to offer them, not because they wish to
offer him anything of their own. This point has been elaborated by
John B. Vickery (in 'Carson McCullers: a Map of Love', Wisconsin
Studies in Contemporary Literature, Vol. I, No. 1, 1960) and by
Horace Taylor (in 'The Heart Is a Lonely Hunter: a Southern
Waste Land', Studies in American Literature, Louisiana State University Studies, Humanities Series No. 8, 1960). Mr Taylor points
out that the selfishness of the other lovers is demonstrated in the
scene when all of them meet by chance in Singer's room—an extremely awkward occasion, for while each of them was able to talk
freely when he was alone with the mute, none of them is able to do
so with the others present:

> They cannot say anything. Each of them regards the others as
> intruders and considers his own need of Singer as paramount.
> When they are finally able to talk it is about the most super-
> ficial subject of all, the weather . . . What is revealed in the
> incident is the unconscious but utter selfishness of these people.
> Each of them is solely concerned with the pouring out of his
> own inner compulsions to Singer.[9]

But the gift of love which Singer makes to Antonapoulos is very
nearly unqualified: it is true that his sessions with the Greek are
consoling to him, but he is prepared to offer sympathy and understanding whether he receives any or not. (Actually, of course, he is
the gainer, since the gift that Antonapoulos makes to him—of an
object to love—is greater than that which he makes to Antonapoulos, who is incapable of the selflessness demanded of a true lover:
Singer, however, never consciously entertains this motive.) It is this
selflessness which is the source of the spiritual superiority that the

9 p. 157.

other characters recognize in him, so that their feeling about him is, at least to that extent, justified.

The Platonic and Neo-Platonic aspects of Mrs McCullers's theory of the nature of love have been tentatively explored by Frank Baldanza ('Plato in Dixie', *The Georgia Review*, Summer, 1958). Their presence in *The Heart Is a Lonely Hunter* is undeniable, but I am not at all sure that they are consistent with the central irony of the parable. One is forced, I think, to choose between the popular view of love that it is blind—on which depends the irony of Mrs McCullers's story—and the view that it is clairvoyant, endowing the lover with special vision which enables him to see qualities in the beloved to which others, because they do not love, are blind. It is repeatedly suggested throughout the novel that this clairvoyance is but a projection of what the lover wishes to find, and this is a psychological rather than a metaphysical theory of love.

But whatever its source, love, the author is saying, offers man his only hope of escape from the fate of spiritual isolation. The hope, however, is a slight one, and most attempts to love end in frustration : even Singer cannot endure the thought of life without Antonapoulos. The next most selfless seeker after love and happiness is Mick, who longs to express herself and to communicate with others through music, and her failure is pathetic because it is not the result of a flaw in herself but of economic necessity. One of the most moving passages in the book is that in which she still persists in clinging to her impossible ambition with a desperation which is the measure of her suspicion that it is all in vain :

> But maybe it would be true about the piano and turn out O.K. Maybe she would get a chance soon. Else what the hell good had it all been—the way she felt about music and the plans she had made in the inside room? It had to be good if anything made sense. And it was too and it was too and it was too and it was too. It was some good.
> All right!
> O.K.!
> Some good.

More than a piano, of course, is involved here : Mick is trying to persuade herself, in the face of all evidence to the contrary, that life has some meaning, that it 'makes sense'. Young as she is, she realizes that life without love is scarcely worth the living and that life therefore contains for most people more pain than happiness. Hitherto she has been able to escape this realization by retreating into an

'inner room', a private world where she can be alone with her
dreams:

> With her it was like there was two places—the inside room and
> the outside room. School and the family and things that
> happened every day were in the outside room . . . Foreign
> countries and plans and music were in the inside room. The
> songs she thought about were there . . .The inside room was a
> very private place. She could be in the middle of a house full of
> people and still feel she was locked up by herself.

The conflict between the world of dreams and the world of reality
is very strong in Mick. In an early scene, when her effort to convert
a ukelele into a violin ends in failure, she bursts into tears:

> It seemed to her as she thought back over the last month that
> she had never really believed in her mind that the violin would
> work. But in her heart she kept making herself believe. And
> even now it was hard not to believe a little.

That illusions are necessary for human happiness is also the theme
of another early story, 'Madame Zilensky and the King of Finland'
—as it is of Henry James's 'The Tree of Knowledge', Ibsen's *The
Wild Duck,* and Tennessee Williams's *A Streetcar Named Desire,*
to name only three works by twentieth-century authors in which this
theme is found. When Mick takes the job at Woolworth's, the inner
room becomes increasingly difficult of access, and the dream dis-
solves into a sordid reality.

Doctor Copeland and Jake Blount are, as we have seen, doomed
to isolation because of defects in their own character. Biff Brannon's
situation is less desperate than that of the other main characters
because he has achieved a sort of adjustment: the mechanical
relationship which, in his role of restaurant proprietor, he enjoys
with them alleviates somewhat his sense of loneliness. Even though
the place loses money, he continues to maintain it: 'The business
was losing money. There were many slack hours. Still at meal-time
the place was full and he saw many hundreds of acquaintances as he
stood guard behind the café counter.'

Biff is the least ardent of all the lovers. He is conscious of Singer's
charm, but he does not depend upon him as do the others, and because he has less need of him he is the only one who does not
fashion the mute according to his own wishes and who can see him
with anything approaching objectivity: it occurs to him to wonder
how much Singer really understands of all that is said to him. He is

attracted to Mick in a wistful way that is half paternal, half maternal, but as she grows older she loses interest for him and he is able to play with greater efficiency his role of detached observer. He is important to the symmetry of the book: he is one of the first characters we meet, and the final chapter, a kind of coda, is written from his point of view.[10]

No fewer than six cases of frustration occur in *The Heart Is a Lonely Hunter*. Five of them involve the love of one individual for another which is either unreturned (Singer-Antonapoulos), unrecognized (Harry-Jake, Mick-Singer), spurned (Lucile-Leroy), or mistaken for its opposite (Biff-Mick). Three of them involve the love of an individual for an ideal: Copeland longs for racial equality, Jake for social justice, and Mick for her music. (The case of Simms must, I think, be overlooked: it is hard to think of him as a lover in any sense.)

But the fact that love, whether it be for a person or an ideal, is seldom completely or permanently successful does not mean that it is not valuable while it lasts. Its value, however, is chiefly *to the lover* (something that must be constantly kept in mind as one reads Mrs McCullers) in that it affords him release, however partial and temporary, from his cell, so that for the time that he loves he is happy, as was Singer. The wish to love, also, is so universal that it tends to join men together, often without their realizing it: in the very attempt to love—however awkward that attempt and however unworthy its object by standards inadmissible to the lover—man finds a measure of relief from his loneliness. Finally, love invests its possessor with a certain dignity: without her dream, which she clings to so stubbornly (as if realizing that without it she is nothing), Mick would lack the interest that she has for us, and certainly the same is true of Doctor Copeland.

The emphasis on social reform, without which almost no writer in the Thirties would have dared to offer a first novel—especially one with a Southern setting—to a reputable publisher, occurs most overtly in the speeches which Copeland and Jake are forever making. At his annual Christmas party, the Doctor tells the assembled guests:

10   René Micha ('Carson McCullers ou la Cabane de l'Enfance', in *Critique*, Paris, Août-Septembre, 1962) says that when he told Mrs McCullers that Biff reminded him of Charles Bovary, she was greatly pleased. But the resemblance is very weak: Charles is stupid; Biff is not. Charles worships his wife; Biff does not. When Emma dies, Charles no longer wishes to live; when Alice dies, Biff for the first time begins to live according to his own nature. It is difficult, indeed, to see what they have in common, except perhaps a certain sluggishness of temperament.

One hundred and twenty years ago another man was born in the country that is known as Germany—a country far across the Atlantic Ocean. This man understood as did Jesus. But his thoughts were not concerned with Heaven or the future of the dead. His mission was for the living. For the great masses of human beings who work and suffer and work until they die. For people who take in washing and work as cooks, who pick cotton and work at the hot dye vats of factories. His mission was for us, and the name of this man is Karl Marx.

In one of his curious sessions with Singer, Jake lashes out against organized religion as follows:

The things they have done to us! The ideals they have fouled and made vile. Take Jesus. He was one of us. He knew. When he said that it is harder for a camel to pass through the eye of a needle than for a rich man to enter the kingdom of God—he damn well meant just what he said. But look what the Church has done to Jesus during the last two thousand years. What they have made of him. How they have turned every word he spoke for their own vile ends. Jesus would be framed and in jail if he was living today. Jesus would be one who really knows. Me and Jesus would sit across the table and I would look at him and he would look at me and we would both know that the other knew. Me and Jesus and Karl Marx could all sit at a table and—

The humanitarianism in *The Heart Is a Lonely Hunter* reveals itself in two ways: in a sympathetic concern for the wage slaves in the town's textile mills, and in a passionate protest against the situation of the Southern Negro. On neither subject is Mrs McCullers sentimental, and—unlike a good many of her contemporaries—she never idealizes the social victim. When Jake tries to tell the workers how they are being taken advantage of, he is met with indifference and even derision:

'What I'm trying to tell you is plain and simple. The bastards who own these mills are millionaires. While the doffers and carders and all the people behind the machines who spin and weave the cloth can't hardly make enough to keep their guts quiet . . .
'Don't it make you mad? Don't it?'
Jake's eyes were flushed and dark and his lips trembled.
The three men looked at him warily. Then the man in the straw hat began to laugh.
'Go on and snigger. Sit there and bust your sides open.' The men laughed in the slow and easy way that three men laugh at

one. Jake brushed the dirt from the soles of his feet and put on
his shoes. His fists were closed tight and his mouth was con-
torted with an angry sneer.
'Laugh—that's all you're good for. I hope you sit there and
snicker 'til you rot.' As he walked stiffly down the street the
sound of their laughter and catcalls still followed him.

These workers, to whom Mrs McCullers has given a collective
identity ('The men laughed in the slow and easy way that three
men laugh at one'), remind us of that other group, equally unattractive, in *The Ballad of the Sad Café*, who comes to Miss
Amelia's house to investigate Cousin Lymon's 'murder': there they
serve as a symbol of suspicion; here, of the kind of caution that proceeds from ignorance and self-interest.[11]

Doctor Copeland has the same problem with his own people. 'The
Negro race,' he tells Portia bitterly, 'of its own accord climbs up on
the cross on every Friday.' A little later, in the same scene, it occurs
to him that 'the whole Negro race was sick'. A firm believer in birth
control, he distributes contraceptives that he pays for himself:

> All his life he had told and explained and exhorted. You cannot
> do this, he would say. There are all reasons why this sixth or
> ninth child cannot be, he would tell them. It is not more children
> that we need but more chances for the ones already on earth.
> He would tell them in simple words, always the same way, and
> with the years it came to be a sort of angry poem which he had
> always known by heart. He studied and knew the development
> of any new theory. And from his own pocket he would distri-
> bute the devices to his patients himself. He was by far the first
> doctor in the town to even think of such. And he would give
> and explain and give and tell them. And then deliver maybe two
> score times a week.

So the frustration pattern in *The Heart Is a Lonely Hunter* involves not merely individuals but large masses of people; it persists
on a social level as well. How private fear stands in the way of public
reform is illustrated most dramatically in the incident involving
Willie, the Doctor's son, who, because he 'sassed back' one of the
white guards at the penitentiary where he was sent for wounding
another Negro with a knife, was punished—together with two other
convicts—by having his feet tied for three days to a rope suspended
from the ceiling of a 'cold room': gangrene developed, and his feet
had to be amputated. When Willie returns, Jake has the idea of

---

11 Lubbers (op. cit., p. 193) sees a parallel between this scene and that in
Matthew (X, 11-14) in which Jesus sends forth his apostles.

publicizing his mistreatment by exhibiting him in a wheelbarrow, and urges Willie to give him the names of the other two convicts. But Willie refuses to co-operate: he has been warned at the penitentiary that he must keep quiet about what has happened or suffer further imprisonment. Besides, he has quarrelled with the two convicts ('Us all has had a big falling out') and has no desire to help them. As Portia explains: 'You see, during them two days when they hurt so bad they commenced to quarrel. Willie don't ever want to see any of them again.' Mrs McCullers's moral here is very plain: individuals are prevented from uniting for a useful purpose by fear and by petty differences which divide them and weaken their force, driving them deeper than ever into the isolation which is the result of their failure to achieve harmonious social union. Long-range ideals are thus defeated by purely personal fears and obstinacies, and I can agree only partially with Mr Eisinger when he says, 'The failure of love is the failure of communion, not of labor unions or Negro-white relations.'[12]

Of the various symbols for loneliness and incompletion in *The Heart Is a Lonely Hunter*, physical deformity and freakishness are the most obvious, and this explains not only the presence of many freakish characters in the book but also the constant references to freakishness. There is something a little odd about most of the main characters: Mick is overgrown and a tomboy, and here is Jake as seen by Biff:

> There were many things about the fellow that seemed contrary. His head was very large and well-shaped, but his neck was soft and slender as a boy's. The mustache looked false, as if it had been stuck on for a costume party and would fall off if he talked too fast. It made him seem almost middle aged, although his face with its high, smooth forehead and wide-open eyes was young.

Biff (like Miss Amelia in *The Ballad of the Sad Café*) has an affinity for freaks that is, of course, symbolic:

> What he had said to Alice was true—he did like freaks. He had a special friendly feeling for sick people and cripples. Whenever somebody with a harelip or т.в. came into the place he would set him up to beer. Or if one of the customers were a hunchback or a bad cripple, then it would be whiskey on the house. There was one fellow who had had his peter and his left

12 Op. cit., p. 251.

leg blown off in a boiler explosion, and whenever he came to town there was a free pint waiting for him.

Mick's divergence from the norm is the source of the attraction that she has for him:

> Mick had grown so much in the past year that soon she would be taller than he was . . . She was at the age when she looked as much like an overgrown boy as a girl, and on that subject why was it that the smartest people mostly missed that point? By nature all people are of both sexes. So that marriage and the bed is not all by any means. The proof? Real youth and old age. Because often old men's voices grow high and reedy and they take on a mincing walk. And old women sometimes grow fat and their voices get rough and deep and they grow dark little mustaches. And he even proved it to himself—the part of him that sometimes wished he was a mother and that Mick and Bubber were his kids.

There is one passage concerning Mick—as a student in Vocational High School—that is particularly interesting because it suggests a theme that Mrs McCullers was later to explore much more thoroughly:

> Here was the thing that soon began to bother her. In the halls the people would walk up and down together and everybody seemed to belong to some special bunch. Within a week or two she knew people in the halls and in classes to speak to them—but that was all. She wasn't a member of any bunch.

In the desire to belong to some 'bunch', to be a 'member' of something outside herself and greater than herself, Mick anticipates Frankie Addams in *The Member of the Wedding*.

3

A study of Mrs McCullers' preliminary outline reveals that the departures which she made from it in the final version are, for the most part, of a minor and mechanical kind. She altered a few of the circumstances in the lives of certain minor characters, dropping one of them altogether—'Lily Mae' Jenkins, the homosexual Negro, who turns up several years later in *The Member of the Wedding*, where he never actually appears but is merely mentioned by Berenice—and made several changes in the sequence of events. The most radical differences between the novel-as-projected and the novel-as-written are in the character of Alfred Simms and in the scene involving Jake and the Doctor in the latter's bedroom. Simms, as originally planned, was 'a pitiable, fragile old fellow whose senses are muddled' and who appears on the street 'in clean, ragged clothes and holding an old woman's pocket-book'. His function was to dramatize the contrast between Biff's kindness and the indifference of his wife, Alice—a contrast which reverses the conventional role of the sexes, in which the husband is generally (as in Robert Frost's poem, 'The Death of the Hired Man') thought of as being more unfeeling than his wife. This contrast is necessary, for it underscores Biff's sexual ambivalence, and Mrs McCullers wisely did not omit it: she merely makes Jake rather than Simms the target of Alice's unkindness. Another function Simms originally served was to cause Biff to experience pangs of conscience after he ejected him from the café at Alice's insistence. In the final version, Biff is spared this necessity, for Singer offers to take Jake home with him. The Alfred Simms whom Mrs McCullers originally had in mind has almost nothing in common with the religious fanatic whom we meet in *The Heart Is a Lonely Hunter* and for whom it is not easy to see a *raison d'être* unless it be that he contributes a certain local colour (almost every Southern town of any size contains such a madman) and lends a bizarre, Dostoevskyan quality to the scenes in which he appears.

The other departure from the original plot, that involving the scene between Jake and Doctor Copeland, is far more important. Mrs McCullers first planned for this meeting between the two men (who have been prevented by a misunderstanding from knowing each other more fully but whose purpose in life is very similar and in whom the zeal for social reform is equally passionate) to end in a harmonious reconciliation: 'In the course of a few hours these two men, after a lifetime of isolation, come as close to each other as it is possible for two human beings to be.' But in the final version exactly the opposite occurs: after an all-night argument in which Jake calls the Doctor a 'short-sighted bigot' and the Doctor retaliates with the epithet 'white fiends', Jake rushes violently from the house and Copeland (who is tubercular)[13] quite literally foams at the mouth and is ill for a long time thereafter.

The advantages of the revised over the original version of the incident are that it fits more easily into the general pattern of frus-

---

[13] Copeland's disease and Jake's alcoholism are the external signs of the sickness which is destroying the souls of both men.

tration and that it adds to the irony which, as we have noted, is all-pervading. This scene occurs immediately after Jake's unsuccessful attempt to extract from Willie the names of the two ex-convicts and to persuade him to allow himself to be exhibited, and the two failures of communication are played off against each other. It may be worth noting that the relationship between Jake and the Doctor is based on a mis-understanding from the very beginning. When they first meet, Jake is drunk and the Doctor (who has more than his share of the persecution complex that is apt to characterize minority groups, especially minority groups that *are* persecuted) gives him 'a look of quivering hatred'. The second time they meet they collide physically on the stairs leading to Singer's room and Jake tells Singer, 'I never had anybody look at me so dirty.' Copeland thinks Jake despises him, while actually Jake is curious to know more about the Doctor: the situation here is very similar to that in Sherwood Anderson's story, 'Queer', where Elmer, a paranoid character, convinces himself that George, the small-town news editor, hates him while in truth George has been hoping for a chance to make a friend of him. The isolation that results from mutual miscomprehension is also the theme of that story.

In the case of Portia, Mrs McCullers also made an interesting alteration. Originally she had planned for this character's husband, Highboy, to be unfaithful to her, and in the outline Portia experiences strong feelings of jealousy where her rival, a 'light-colored, good-looking girl', is concerned. But in the novel Highboy continues to be faithful, so that of all the relationships depicted theirs is the only one that remains untroubled. At first thought this may seem inappropriate to the general pattern, but if one reflects on Portia's value as a foil to such characters as Jake and her father, and on her mastery of the language of the heart, one may see a certain rightness in the exception which the author has made in her favour. The speech in which Portia originally referred to this rival now refers, with a few changes, to the girl over whom Willie has the fight that sends him to the penitentiary:

> What I can't understand is how come he would be messing around with that Love. She at least ten shades blacker than I is and she the ugliest nigger I ever seen. She walk like she had a egg between her legs and don't want to break it. She ain't even clean. And here Willie done cut the buck like this over her.

Were Portia one of the major characters she would be doomed by the logic of the allegory to an unsuccessful love life, like the others.

Because she is not, she is permitted to remain as the single exception to the pattern.

There is some reason for believing that Mrs McCullers originally intended the novel to end on a more 'positive' note than it actually does. 'A few of the people in this book,' she writes in her outline, 'come very near to being heroes and they are not the only human beings of their kind. Because of the essence of these people there is the feeling that, no matter how many times their efforts are wasted and their personal ideals are shown to be false, they will someday be united and they will come into their own.' In view of the actual outcome, however, it is easy to escape this feeling: Singer dies by his own hand; Mick's dream becomes a conscious illusion; Jake leaves town only, presumably, to repeat his blunders elsewhere; Doctor Copeland is forced to accept the charity of relatives to whom he has always felt himself superior. Only Biff remains undefeated—but this is because he has been too cautious to make investments in the ideal. And at the end even he is frightened. The last chapter, seen from his point of view, contains a passage which is a coda to the entire work:

> . . . in a single radiance of illumination he saw a glimpse of human struggle and of valor. Of the endless fluid passage of humanity through endless time. And of those who labor and of those who—one word—love. His soul expanded. But for a moment only. For in him he felt a warning, a shaft of terror. Between the two worlds he was suspended. He saw that he was looking at his own face in the counter glass before him. Sweat glistened on his temples and his face was contorted. One eye was opened wider than the other. The left eye delved narrowly into the past while the right gazed wide and affrighted into a future of blackness, error, and ruin. And he was suspended between radiance and darkness. Between bitter irony and faith. Sharply he turned away.
> 'Louis!' he called. 'Louis! Louis!'
> And again there was no answer.

His moment of vision over, he finds it is his own face that confronts him in the mirror: was the vision valid, or was it but a projection of his own desires? Suddenly, as the latter possibility dawns on him, he becomes terrified, and, feeling himself alone, calls for help. But there is no answer.

4

The Heart Is a Lonely Hunter was published in the spring of 1940.

On Sunday, June 16th, the day it was reviewed by *The New York
Times,* its publisher ran a large advertisement describing it as 'a
book that brought down the house before it appeared on the stage',
and quoting opinions by T. S. Stribling ('the literary find of the year')
and Katherine Gauss ('a perfectly magnificent piece of work, one of
the best first novels I think I have ever read . . . one thinks about it
for days'). Rose Feld's review, in the same issue, was scarcely less
enthusiastic. 'Mrs McCullers's imagination is rich and fearless; she
has an astonishing perception of humanity,' she wrote, and added:

> No matter what the age of its author, *The Heart Is a Lonely
> Hunter* would be a remarkable book. When one reads that Carson
> McCullers is a girl of twenty-two it becomes more than that.
> Maturity does not cover the quality of her work. It is something
> beyond that, something more akin to the vocation of pain to
> which a great poet is born.

The two other most influential popular reviews were also favour-
able; they were written by Lorine Pruette in *The New York Herald-
Tribune* ('One wonders how any young person could know so much
about the lonely hearts of men, women and children too'[14]) and by
Ben Ray Redman in *The Saturday Review of Literature* ('An extraordinary novel in its own right, considerations of authorship
apart').[15] One of the most enthusiastic and perceptive reviews was
that of Richard Wright, the Negro novelist whose popular autobiographical novel, *Native Son,* was published the same year. He
wrote in *The New Republic*:

> Her quality of despair is unique and individual; it seems to me
> more natural and authentic than that of Faulkner . . . To me
> the most impressive aspect of *The Heart Is a Lonely Hunter* is
> the astonishing humanity that enables a white writer, for the
> first time in Southern fiction, to handle Negro characters with as
> much ease and justice as those of her own race.[16]

Negative opinions were expressed by L. B. Solomon in *The
Nation* and (when the novel appeared three years later in England)
by the anonymous reviewer of *The Times Literary Supplement,* who
wrote:

> It is not a novel of any real imaginative power or distinction . . .

14   9th June 1940, Book Review Section, p. 11.
15   8th June 1940, p. 6.
16   5th August 1940, p. 195.

At present Mrs McCullers, besides being too obviously deriva-
tive in manner, relies almost entirely upon what is strange and
passes comprehension to produce an effect of profundity. This
lends itself merely to impenetrable mystification. Make your
characters, after all, sufficiently singular, enigmatical and even
freakish, and you can easily claim vast and unexplored significance for what they say.[17]

Clifton Fadiman, then doyen of *The New Yorker*'s reviewing staff,
complained: 'She writes without humor, and reveals no special gift
for story telling. She might be a flop at handling ordinary human
beings.'[18] (He added, however, that he was willing to place 'a small
bet' on Mrs McCullers's future.) The popular book reviewer of *The
Boston Transcript*, Lewis Gannett, called it 'a strange and uneven
book, at times almost breathtaking in its concise intensity, at times
baffling.'[19] While praising the quality of the writing, *The Catholic
World* deplored its author's 'free use of very coarse language' and
'defeatist philosophy.'[20] And Robert Littell, in *The Yale Review*,
called it 'a queer sad book that sticks in the mind' and suggested
that Mrs McCullers study Huckleberry Finn and Chekhov.[21]

Reviewing these opinions, one is impressed by how few of the
critics—even the most enthusiastic of them—seem to have understood that Mrs McCullers was writing allegorically: most of the
praise was for the skill with which she handled the devices of
realism, while most of the censure was for her choice of improbable characters and far-fetched situations. Richard Wright, who
frankly confessed 'I don't know what the book is about,' nevertheless came closer to the truth than all the others:

The naturalistic incidents of which the book is compounded
seem to be of no importance; one has the feeling that any string
of typical actions would have served the author's purpose as well,
for the value of such writing lies not so much in what is said
as in the angle of vision from which life is seen. There are times
when Mrs McCullers deliberately suppresses the naturally
dramatic in order to linger over and accentuate the more
obscure, oblique and elusive emotions.[22]

17 27th March 1943, p. 153.
18 8th June 1940, p. 69.
19 5th June 1940, p. 13.
20 November 1940, p. 252.
21 Autumn 1940, p. viii.
22 Op. cit., loc. cit.

58 CARSON MCCULLERS

Today, more than two decades later, and with the remainder of her work to assist us, it is easier to make a more accurate appraisal of Mrs McCullers's first novel. For Granville Hicks, who (like F. R. Leavis) likes novels that criticize existing social values and institutions, it is the best of McCullers. And some of the most recent critics have defended it against the charge of formlessness. Thus, taking issue with Ihab Hassan's comment ('Its failure of form can be clarified, I think, with reference to a statement that Mark Schorer has made in *Society and Self in the Novel*: "The novel must find a form that will hold together in some firm nexus of structure the individual human being and the social being." '), Irving Malin declares: 'I think the novel does have form . . . *The Heart Is a Lonely Hunter* has what Robert M. Adams has called "open form", or, better yet, "suspended form".'[23] Nevertheless, the book is uneven stylistically: some scenes are rendered with a realism that Flaubert himself might have envied, while others have a shadowy, abstract, Kafka-like quality, and it is no wonder that the critics were confused. The extended incident in Part Two involving Bubber's shooting of Biff's niece, Baby, has no real connection with the main narrative on either a realistic or an allegorical level; it is a story—and a very entertaining one—in its own right. The insistence on local colour and on social justice tend to date the work somewhat from the point of view of realism, while allegorically the attempt to make of Singer a Christ figure and of Antonapoulos a mystery is not entirely successful. Nevertheless, *The Heart Is a Lonely Hunter* remains an impressive achievement. Singer, the mute symbol of spiritual eloquence, is one of the most unforgettable characters in recent fiction, and the book of which he is the protagonist is probably the most elaborate treatment in American literature of the theme of spiritual isolation. The fact that it is a first novel makes it, of course, all the more extraordinary.

23 *New American Gothic* (Southern Illinois University Press, 1962), p. 113. See also Lubbers' elaborate analysis (op. cit.) of the structure of *The Heart Is a Lonely Hunter*.

CHAPTER FIVE

'NOT EVEN THE HORSE IS NORMAL'

In 1939, during the interval between the acceptance of *The Heart Is a Lonely Hunter* and its publication, Mrs McCullers began her second novel. She and Reeves were living in Fayetteville at the time —in the second floor apartment of a huge old brick house which, like so many in the South, had seen better days but which had now become 'rental property' and was beginning to be badly in need of repair.

It was a trying time for both of them, in contrast to the idyllic months during which she had worked on the first novel. Carson began to perceive that she had idealized Reeves out of all resemblance to his real self: he was charming, yes, and good company, but he was not, and would never be, she realized sadly, the kind of intellectual and spiritual companion that she had always longed for and needed. The attraction she felt for him had come to be chiefly physical: she could still admire him as she might have admired an object of art—he was, as has been said, uncommonly handsome—but as time went on she became conscious of certain defects in his character to which, previously, she had been blinded by his charm. (He was spoiled, for one thing—as very handsome people frequently are). She had ceased to remind him of his literary plans, and he himself seldom referred to them any more. Reeves belonged to that species of men, not exactly uncommon in American society, who are prevented by their sensitiveness from functioning happily in the competitive world of business yet who lack the creative power, the dedication and the drive, of the genuine artist.

The disillusionment was not all on her side, of course. It was during the months in Fayetteville that Reeves made the discovery, to which he was never able to adjust, that Carson's work meant more to her than anything else in the world—himself included. Probably, also, the very sincere love he had for her at this time did not exclude, on the unconscious level, a certain amount of envy, mingled—as he saw the interest publishers were beginning to take in her work

—with a new respect. With one novel accepted and another nearing completion, she had succeeded (or so it must have seemed to him) where he had failed—and failed to the extent that, in spite of their agreement, he had not been able to produce so much as a single line of fiction.

Nothing of this troubled domestic background is visible in the high polish of *Reflections in a Golden Eye*. (The title this time was of her own choosing.) It is the least subjective of all her books: having written, so to speak, a Russian novel (the resemblances to Dostoevsky have been pointed out in the last chapter), she now turned her hand to a French one, and it was Flaubert who was her model, at least as involves technique, rather than Balzac, Zola, Stendhal, de Maupassant, or even Proust. The objectivity with which the story is told recalls *Madame Bovary*, as do also the economy and brilliance of the style, the swiftness of the action, and the inevitability of the tragic outcome. Where the actual circumstances of the novel are concerned there is, of course, a more obvious parallel with D. H. Lawrence's famous story, 'The Prussian Officer'. Mrs McCullers had read this story, and it is possible that it was in the back of her mind when she plotted her novel; she did not, however, borrow from it consciously, and the resemblances, though striking, are rather superficial.

There is another, less obvious influence, and that is Faulkner. *Reflections in a Golden Eye* is a Gothic novel, and the so-called Gothic school of Southern writers may be said to have begun (if we except Poe) with the publication, in 1934, of *Sanctuary*, which had a kind of *succès de scandale*. Voyeurism, it will be remembered, plays an important part in Faulkner's novel, as it does in Mrs McCullers's. Faulkner was probably the first of the Southern novelists to concern himself with this aberration, just as Mrs McCullers was the first of them to write openly about homosexuality. (There has since been such a plethora of novels, especially Southern novels, concerning homosexuality that it is easy to forget this.) Mrs McCullers had read and admired *Sanctuary*, and I think it is quite possible that in *Reflections in a Golden Eye* she was striving for an effect of shock similar to that which Faulkner's novel had been so successful in producing. She wanted to do more than that, however, for she did not want her book to be merely sensational.

The immediate source of the novel was an actual incident at Fort Bragg, related to her by Reeves, which involved a Peeping Tom. From her visits to the Tuckers Mrs McCullers was familiar with life on an army post, at least superficially, and Reeves—who had lived on one—was also helpful in supplying her with some of the details that make her description of it lifelike and authentic. And the setting is important, for the monotony of peacetime army life encourages the neuroses of the various characters at the same time that it allows them the leisure in which to express them.

Of these characters, the most neurotic is Captain Penderton. Algolagnia is his dominant defect, but he is also, though unconsciously, homosexual, and (as if these were not enough!) is something of a kleptomaniac and amateur drug addict as well. He is intelligent, though there is nothing original about the quality of his intelligence, and bookish: his function on the post, which he performs with an efficiency that earns him the respect of his superiors, is to teach military tactics. His wife, Leonora, is a stupid, sensual woman, passionately fond of riding and eating; she drinks her whiskey straight, and at night her dreams centre about plump, well-stuffed turkeys. They have an odd marital history: 'When she married the Captain she had been a virgin. Four nights after their wedding she was still a virgin, and on the fifth night her status was changed only enough to leave her slightly puzzled.' Leonora is beautiful, however, and has no difficulty in obtaining satisfaction elsewhere; she has had a series of lovers, in fact, and we are told that her husband has a 'sad penchant' for becoming enamoured of them. The latest in this series is Major Langdon, a rather brutish fellow—fond, like Leonora, of the simple pleasures of the bed and the table, and, like her, a fine horseman. They carry on their affair under the Captain's nose, but the latter does not seem to mind ('He carried his cuckoldry with a cynical good grace that was respected on the post') and even feels a certain affection for the Major.

Alison, Major Langdon's wife, is a frail hypochondriac who becomes a semi-invalid when her daughter—a malformed child who lives only a few months—dies. The knowledge that her husband is having an affair with Leonora aggravates her illness to the point of actual lunacy, and there is a shocking scene of self-mutilation in which she cuts off her nipples with a pair of garden shears. She soothes her pride by promising herself she will divorce the Major, but her constitutional weakness, together with a tendency to procrastination, prevent her from taking this step.

Alison has only two friends on the post. One of them is Lieutenant Weincheck, a bachelor of about fifty who is about to be retired because of his eyesight: his army career, as indicated by his rank, has been a failure, and he is unpopular with his fellow officers. Weincheck's hobby is playing the violin, and Alison, in wistful little sessions, occasionally accompanies him on the piano. Her other friend is Anacleto, the houseboy whom she and Major Langdon brought with them from the Philippines. Anacleto worships his mistress and makes no secret of his aversion for the Major. With his brilliantly coloured jackets, his half dozen or so French phrases, and his reportory of ballet steps (he once went with Alison to see a ballet and was never the same afterwards), this monkey-like little creature, who anticipates Cousin Lymon in *The Ballad of the Sad Café*, causes a sensation on the post: his devotion to Alison is the subject of many spiteful jokes, among them one to the effect that 'the little Filipino thoughtfully scented Alison Langdon's specimen of wee-wee with perfume before taking it to the hospital for a urinalysis.' Anacleto introduces a note of comedy into the novel, but it is comedy of a wry sort, and strangely mingled with pathos.

The remaining character, the one who precipitates the tragedy, is Private Williams. He is a primitive of the kind that Lawrence was fond of portraying—a creature of instinct and impulse rather than of reason. (Years ago, in an argument involving a wheelbarrow of manure, he killed a Negro and successfully concealed the crime.) Because of his understanding of horses he is ideally suited for his job as stable boy. Again and again Mrs McCullers underscores the animalism of his nature: 'In his eyes, which were a curious blend of amber and brown, there was a mute expression that is found usually in the eyes of animals.' His affinity with horses is extraordinary, and there is even something a little unnatural about the relationship which this man of nature enjoys with the beasts in his charge:

> His horse was an ordinary plug horse which, with anyone but Private Williams, could sustain only two gaits—a clumsy trot and a rocking-horse gallop. But with the soldier a marvelous change came over the animal; he cantered or single-footed with stiff elegance. The soldier's body was of a pale golden brown and he held himself erect. Without his clothes he was so slim that the pure, curved line of his ribs could be seen. As he cantered about in the sunlight, there was a sensual, savage smile on his lips that would have surprised his barrack mates. After such outings he came back weary to the stables and spoke to no one.

The passage has an amorous quality that is unmistakable, as does also the following:

> As the soldier passed between the stalls he heard the placid breath of the horses, a sleepy snuffle and a whinny. Dumb, luminous eyes turned towards him. The young soldier took from his pocket an envelope of sugar and soon his hands were warm and

sticky with slaver. He went into the stall of a little mare who was about ready to drop her foal. He stroked her swollen belly and stood for a long time with his arms around her neck.

But Private Williams's favourite horse is Firebird, a magnificent thoroughbred belonging to Leonora. This horse plays an important part in the story: he symbolizes the vital principle, the part of man that does not submit willingly to discipline (it is significant that Leonora has great difficulty in training him). And it is interesting to note that just as the author has been at pains to ascribe certain animal qualities to Private Williams, she has likewise ascribed to Firebird some of the qualities of a human being:

But now this brief daily struggle had a theatrical, affected air—it was a jocular pantomime performed for their own amusement and the benefit of spectators. Even when the froth showed in his mouth, the horse moved with a certain fractious grace as though aware of being watched. And after it was over he stood quite still and sighed once, in much the same manner as a young husband would sigh laughingly when giving in to the will of a beloved and termagent wife.

Between Private Williams, the man of animal grace and freedom, who never looks 'right' in his army uniform, and Captain Penderton, the man of will, there develops a curious relationship that reminds one of that between Billy Budd and the First Mate, Claggart, in Melville's novel, and between the soldier and the officer in the abovementioned story by Lawrence. Everything about Williams irritates the Captain, but at the same time he is conscious of a sense of attraction and goes out of his way to arrange encounters between them. As Williams is not his orderly he cannot submit him to the punishments and humiliations that Lawrence's officer inflicts upon his inferior, but satisfies himself with an occasional reprimand on the rare occasions when he can find a pretext. It should be added that the tension is all on the Captain's side: Williams, so far from returning his resentment, is not—a bit improbably, perhaps—even aware of it:

To this young Southern soldier the officers were in the same vague category as Negroes—they had a place in his life, but he did not look on them as being human. He accepted the Captain as fatalistically as though he were the weather or some natural phenomenon. The Captain's behavior might seem unexpected, but he did not identify it with himself. And it did not occur to

him to question it any more than he would question a thunder-
storm or the fading of a flower.

On one occasion, when Captain Penderton attempts to ride Firebird, the horse tries to throw him, then dashes off on a mad gallop
through the forest while the terrified Captain, his face lashed by
twigs and branches, clings desperately to the saddle. When Firebird,
exhausted, finally stops, the Captain whips him savagely, then throws
himself on the ground, sobbing with rage. While he is in this
position Private Williams comes up, surveys the situation, and without a word leads the animal away. After this humiliating incident
Captain Penderton becomes obsessed with the idea of revenging
himself upon the soldier, and finally he receives his opportunity in
an unexpected way.

One evening, passing the Penderton house, Private Williams
happens to see Leonora's nude body outlined against the lighted
window. The sight upsets him, and he cannot get it off his mind.
The thought of Leonora comes to obsess him as the thought of the
soldier obsesses her husband: he takes to watching the house after
dark, and learns the habits of its occupants. It is the Captain's
custom, after his wife goes to bed upstairs (they occupy separate
bedrooms) to continue working in his study. One night, very late,
the soldier slips into the house, climbs the stairs noiselessly, and
enters Leonora's room, where, crouching by her bedside, he remains for several hours watching her while she sleeps; then, just
before daybreak, he steals out. He repeats this extraordinary performance several times, and on one occasion is sighted by Alison.
(The Langdons and the Pendertons live in adjacent houses.) She
goes to the Captain's study, and tells him that someone is in his
wife's room: he, thinking that her mind is unhinged, does not bother
to investigate but escorts her back to her house; the Major calls a
medical officer, and it is decided that the time has finally come to
place Alison in an institution. Accompanied by Anacleto, she is
accordingly packed off. On her second night at this place, Alison
dies of a heart attack, and Anacleto disappears.

Shortly after this, the Captain, again seated in his study, hears a
sound in the hall and sees the soldier creeping upstairs to his wife's
room. He picks up his revolver, goes upstairs, switches on the light,
and kills Private Williams with two expert shots that leave a single
hole in the soldier's chest. Thereupon Leonora wakes up; Major
Langdon, who has heard the shots, rushes in; and the Captain
slumps against the wall looking like 'a broken and dissipated monk'.
Even in death, Mrs McCullers observes, the soldier's body has 'the

look of warm, animal comfort. His grave face was unchanged, and his sun-burned hands lay palm upwards on the carpet as though in sleep.'

2

The image likening Captain Penderton to a monk is peculiarly apt, for there is something essentially ascetic in his nature; he represents, as has been said, the man of will in contrast to Williams, the man of nature, and in contrast also to his wife and Major Langdon, who are sensual and easy-going types. His sadistic tendencies are balanced, as is often the case in algolagnia, with tendencies of exactly the opposite sort—that is, masochistic. As a child he worshipped the bully who beat him up, and the satisfaction he derives from Major Langdon's company—the situation with respect to Leonora being what it is—is definitely masochistic. Moreover, he imposes all manner of penances upon himself:

> The Captain, who was keenly sensitive to luxury and a finicky dresser, wore only the coarsest sleeping garments. He had on now a wrapper of rough black wool that might have been bought for a recently widowed matron of a jail. His pajamas were of some unbleached material as stiff as canvas. He was barefooted although the floor was now cold.

And again: 'The Captain had always been afraid of horses: he only rode because it was the thing to do, and because this was another of his ways of tormenting himself.'

As his emotional involvement with Private Williams increases, Captain Penderton becomes irritated with the furnishings of his house, which are of Leonora's choosing and reveal a distinctly feminine taste:

> The room had an air of flossiness that the Captain abhorred . . . the feminine, cluttered impression made by the room as a whole so exasperated the Captain that he stayed out of it as much as possible. With deep secret longing he thought of the barracks, seeing in his mind's eye the neat cots placed in a row, the bare floors, and stark curtainless windows.

His asceticism is thus seen to be associated with the homosexual side of his nature, and increases with the aversion which he has come to feel for his wife and for women generally. There is a striking resemblance (which nevertheless seems to have escaped the notice of critics) between the situation here and that in *The Heart*

Is a Lonely Hunter, where Biff Brannon, another character who is sexually ambiguous, fastidiously removes all traces of feminine occupation from the bedroom he has shared with his late wife: 'The bedroom was done over. His entirely now. Before it had been tacky and flossy and drab. There were always stockings and pink rayon knickers with holes in them hung on a string across the room to dry.'

One of the most interesting consequences of the Captain's passion is that it causes him, in his daydreams, to take a curious pleasure in imagining himself an ordinary soldier like Private Williams:

> Suddenly in the silent room three words had come unbidden to his tongue: 'Private Weldon Penderton'. And these words, with the associations they engendered, aroused in the Captain a perverse feeling of relief and satisfaction. Instead of dreaming of honor and rank, he now experienced a subtle pleasure in imagining himself as an enlisted man. In these fantasies he saw himself as a youth, a twin almost of the soldier whom he hated—with a young, easy body that even the cheap uniform of a common soldier could not make ungraceful, with thick glossy hair and eyes unshadowed by study and strain. The image of Private Williams wove itself through all these daydreams. And the background of all this was the barracks: the hubbub of young male voices, the genial loafing in the sun, the irresponsible shenanigans of camaraderie.

These fantasies, which evoke the atmosphere of a *palaestra* rather than of a monastery, are not merely masochistic; they suggest a desire on the Captain's part to escape from the cell of his very being —to identify himself in some way with the object of his love. Psychologically speaking, what the Captain does is strive to create the conditions under which he imagines that he and the soldier would be free to love each other as equals, though in fact it would be as impossible for him to 'lower' himself to Williams's level as it would be for the soldier to 'raise' himself (even if he wished to, which he does not) to the Captain's. On the spiritual level, what he does is what every lover does, and that is to seek something which will connect him with the love-object.

There is more to it than that, however. Mrs McCullers writes of Captain Penderton: 'In his balance between the two great instincts, toward life and toward death, the scale was heavily weighted to one side—to death. Because of this the Captain was a coward.' To the Captain, Private Williams symbolizes that which is natural, courageous, and *alive.* This is the real source of his irritation with the soldier, who by his very presence reminds him of his own in-adequacies (he senses his fearlessness, and resents it) and it is the source also of the strange fascination that Williams has for him, for he is envious of what he takes to be the soldier's healthy and active engagement with life. Thus viewed, his fantasies and even his sexual feelings may be considered as a projection of his desire to establish contact with life, however provisionally and vicariously, thereby enabling the 'heavily weighted scale' of his personality to achieve a normal balance. According to this interpretation, his en-counters with the soldier acquire a special significance:

> For a long time now he had ceased to attribute his feelings for Private Williams to hate. Also he no longer tried to find justifi-cation for the emotion that had so taken possession of him. He thought of the soldier in terms neither of love nor hate; he was conscious only of the irresistible yearning to break down the barrier between them. When from a distance he saw the soldier resting before the barracks, he wanted to shout to him, or to strike him with his fist, to make him respond in some way to violence.

The Captain, of course, is mistaken about Williams. Courageous he certainly is, and, up to a point, perhaps even 'natural', but he is not *healthy*: a tendency to voyeurism is scarcely an attribute of the Noble Savage, and neither is the sort of consciencelessness that Williams exhibits in the matter of the Negro he has murdered. The healthy man may, under extreme provocation, commit a murder, as do Melville's Billy Budd and the German orderly, but not in an argument over a wheelbarrow, and without a twinge of subsequent remorse. As for Williams's attitude toward women, it is, in its way, as warped as the Captain's own; he is thus, as John B. Vickery has observed,[1] a delusory symbol, and stands in somewhat the same re-lation to Captain Penderton as Antonapoulos does to Singer, and as the latter does to *his* admirers, in *The Heart Is a Lonely Hunter*. The situation thus possesses the kind of complication and irony of which Mrs McCullers is so fond, and which gives to her story a dimension that is lacking in Melville's and Lawrence's, where the men of nature are truer to type.

The horse, Firebird, is of such importance to the story that we are almost justified in considering him as a character in his own right. In her first paragraph, Mrs McCullers writes: 'The partici-pants of this tragedy were two officers, a soldier, two women, and a

[1] Op. cit.

horse'; and we have seen how she has suggested a human identity for him. More emphatically than Williams, and certainly more appropriately, this animal symbolizes and objectifies the vital principle, and the scene where the Captain attempts to ride him represents his attempt to come to terms with life, and if possible to master it. This is the reason why the Captain takes his failure so hard; on a realistic level his reaction (of throwing himself on the ground and sobbing) is out of proportion to the provocation, and it is obvious that something more is involved here than the mere rebellion of an animal which he has been unable to ride gracefully.

The author has heightened the drama of the scene by causing the soldier to witness the Captain's defeat: of all people in the world, he is the one whom Captain Penderton would like least to be looking on. 'Out in the forest there,' she writes, 'the Captain looked like a broken doll that has been thrown away.' The image again is marvellously just: the Captain, because of his lack of life, is a mere imitation of a man. In this connection it is interesting to note that the two characters with whom Firebird is associated throughout, and with whom he feels most at ease, are Williams and Leonora. His wife's success in taming the horse thus represents a victory not only over the animal but over her husband as well; for all her mindlessness, Leonora is closer to life than he. The Captain's insignificance in the vital realm is suggested as early as the first page, where we are told: 'Standing alone in the woods he was a small man.'

The incident involving Captain Penderton and Firebird is capable of yet another interpretation. It is barely conceivable that the Captain, without realizing it, may have identified the horse's lawlessness with the lawlessness of the passion which he feels for Private Williams. It is certainly true that the struggle which is going on in the Captain's heart, and the effort involved in refusing to admit to himself the real nature of his feelings toward the soldier, combine to make him miserable. Though a coward, Penderton is nevertheless a man of will, and it is possible that he may feel the necessity for asserting it in this crisis. To give in to his passion would be to invite permanent disgrace and ruin, and it is doubtful that the Captain could endure these, since, in spite of his idiosyncrasies, he is essentially a conventional man and acknowledges the values of his associates. That he occasionally questions those values, however, is manifested in a dialogue between him and Major Langdon, and it could be argued that the unexpected position he takes in this conversation is proof that he has been inwardly debating the advantages of conformity, where his relationship to the soldier is concerned, for some time:

> 'Anacleto [it is the Major speaking] wouldn't have been happy in the army, no, but it might have made a man of him . . . It always seemed to me terrible for a grown up man twenty-three years old to be dancing around with music and messing with water-colors. In the army they would have run him ragged and he would have been miserable, but even that seems to me better than the other.'
> 'You mean,' Captain Penderton said, 'that any fulfilment obtained at the expense of normalcy is wrong, and should not be allowed to bring happiness. In short it is better, because it is morally honourable, for the square peg to keep scraping about the round hole than to discover and use the unorthodox square that would fit it?'
> 'Why, you put it exactly right,' the Major said. 'Don't you agree with me?'
> 'No,' said the Captain, after a short pause. With gruesome vividness the Captain suddenly looked into his soul and saw himself. For once he did not see himself as others saw him; there came to him a distorted doll-like image, mean of countenance and grotesque in form. The Captain dwelt on this vision without compassion. He accepted it with neither alteration nor excuse. 'I don't agree,' he repeated absently.
> Major Langdon thought over this unexpected reply, but did not continue the conversation.

This dialogue takes place after the scene in which the horse runs away with the Captain: that Mrs McCullers intends us to connect what he says here with that incident is suggested by the fact that the image which he forms of himself (as a doll) is, as we have seen, the very same one used by the author to describe him in that scene. His unsuccessful attempt to subdue the animal may therefore represent his attempt, equally unsuccessful, to subdue the passion he feels for the soldier, and in whipping the horse he may, in a symbolic sense, also be whipping himself—an action which, in view of his personality, has a certain appropriateness. I offer this interpretation tentatively; it has value, I suspect, only to the extent that it may be possible to reconcile it with the more obvious one.

Though dissimilar in a formal sense to *The Heart Is a Lonely Hunter*, *Reflections in a Golden Eye* repeats the frustration pattern in that novel—a pattern which can be traced as far back in Mrs McCullers's work as the very early story, 'Sucker'. The characters are prevented, whether because of their natures or external circumstances, from achieving the kind of happiness that results from

mutual love: the Captain burns with an impossible love for the
soldier, and the soldier nourishes an equally impossible longing for
the Captain's wife. The only successful relationship is the one between Leonora and Major Langdon, and this is successful only in a
physical sense—a mere mating of animals. Mrs McCullers seems in
fact to be saying that physical love has the greatest chance of success
where the spiritual potential is slightest, and here, as elsewhere in
her work, spiritual love (where the potential for it exists) compensates for the failure of love on a physical level: thus, the
Captain's interest in Private Williams is testimony to the farce of
his marriage; and Alison's attachment to Anacleto is in direct ratio
to her husband's indifference to her, just as the Filipino's devotion
to her is in similar ratio to the difficulty which, as a grotesque, he
might expect to encounter in his search for a satisfactory physical
relationship. There is no evidence that Alison feels anything except
friendship for Lieutenant Weincheck, but the spiritual kinship between them is very strong, and, in the absence of her husband's love,
is a source of comfort to her as it is to him. The spiritual attach-
ments which Alison forms are at least reciprocal, and in this respect
she is more fortunate than the Captain, though, as we noted in our
analysis of *The Heart Is a Lonely Hunter*, reciprocity is not a
requisite for romantic (that is, ideal) love; and the Captain, though
he lacks the spiritual stature of Singer, is, like the mute, a typical
romantic lover. As such, he idealizes his beloved by ascribing to him
qualities which, as we have seen, the soldier does not really possess
—any more than Antonapoulos possessed the wisdom with which
Singer credited him. The Captain has more complication as a lover
than the mute, however, since his emotion is ambivalent: he both
loves and hates the soldier, and it is a subject for speculation
whether his hatred is a mere device for masking his love, or whether
it exists independently, as the complement to it.

Another compensation for the failure of normal love is seen in
the tendency of the various characters to indulge in impossible
dreams. Captain Penderton yearns to be a common soldier; Alison
dreams of buying a prawn boat and taking in Anacleto as her
partner in a fishing venture; and Anacleto imagines himself living
with Alison in a hotel (his idea of earthly paradise) or running a
linen shop in Quebec, where he can enjoy the feel of fine fabrics
and see all the snow he wishes.[2] These dreams remind us of Mick's
futile ambition to become a concert pianist and of Madame Zilensky's fantasy involving the 'King of Finland': illusions, the author

2 On the matter of snow symbolism in Mrs McCullers's work, see Chapter I.

is saying, are necessary to enable human beings to endure the reality of life.

The tendency to associate sexual health with primitivism is profoundly romantic; it recalls Lawrence, as does also the association which Mrs McCullers makes between love and pity. In Lawrence's story, 'The Horse Dealer's Daughter', the protagonist, a country doctor, saves a young woman from drowning and thereafter, moved by pity over her situation (she is *not* pregnant), unexpectedly falls in love with her; and readers familiar with *The Idiot* of Dostoevsky will remember that pity is the dominant element in Myshkin's love for Nastasya Filipovna. A similar mixture of love and pity characterizes the relationship of Singer and Antonapoulos in *The Heart Is a Lonely Hunter* and of Alison and Anacleto in *Reflections in a Golden Eye*, of Miss Amelia and Cousin Lymon in *The Ballad of the Sad Café*, and of Martin Meadows and Emily in the short story, 'A Domestic Dilemma'.

The title of the novel requires a word of explanation. Anacleto, painting water-colours at Alison's bedside, suddenly has an inspiration for a picture:

> 'A peacock of a sort of ghastly green. With one immense golden eye. And in it these reflections of something tiny and—'
> 'Grotesque,' she finished for him.
> He nodded shortly. 'Exactly.'

We are intended to associate the golden eye with the mirror of art (one is reminded of Stendhal's dictum, 'A novel is a mirror carried along the highway'), and it is significant, as Mr Hassan has observed,[3] that this eye does not *see;* it merely *reflects,* thereby symbolizing the objectivity with which Mrs McCullers wishes to render her effects. To see would be to feel—and the hearts, as one reviewer commented, have been left out of this particular deck of cards. At the moment when Anacleto and Alison share this inspiration Mrs McCullers is very close to them, for this too is her intention in the novel: to depict a world that is lacking in moral dimension but which is strange to the point of freakishness. This view of life reminds us that Mrs McCullers's connection with the naturalistic tradition is not merely a matter of style; it is almost as pessimistic as Stephen Crane's in 'The Blue Hotel': 'One viewed the existence of man then as a marvel, and conceded a glamour of wonder to these lice which were caused to cling to a whirling, fire-smitten, ice-locked, disease-stricken, space-lost bulb.'

3   Op. cit., p. 318.

3

Reflections in a Golden Eye appeared serially in two instalments (October and November) of *Harper's Bazaar* in 1940, and was brought out in book form by Houghton Mifflin in February, 1941. It was a disappointment to many critics, who felt that it did not satisfy the expectations aroused by the first novel. Mr Fadiman, apparently relieved that there had been no takers to the 'small bet' he had been willing to place the previous year on Mrs McCullers's future, deplored what he referred to as her 'too obvious desire to create people and situations that are strange and startling.' While conceding that she had 'obvious talent', he added:

> It would grow more harmoniously if she could, right at this point in her development, give herself a humorous once-over. If she did, she might find something to laugh at in the grotesque and forced hallucinations of which *Reflections in a Golden Eye* is composed.[4]

And Robert Littell, who had prescribed for her a reading course in Mark Twain and Chekhov, noted sadly:

> *Reflections in a Golden Eye* is something for her admirers to forget as quickly as possible. This isn't easy, for traces of the talent are still here, and make the novel's inversions and mutilations and nastinesses stick in the mind like burrs.[5]

In the influential *New York Times,* Frederick T. Marsh declared the book 'vastly inferior' to *The Heart Is a Lonely Hunter*:

> Quite unlike the other, it suggests the youthful prodigy; and one suspects it was written first and universally pressed into service by the publishers to follow up the success of the first novel. Either that or it has been over-hastily written.[6]

But he too had a word of praise for the author—followed by a word of advice:

> No one can say, however, that Mrs McCullers has not succeeded in making her genuine talent felt, a talent which is less of subtlety than of infant-terrible insight expressed with quite grown-up precision, as yet unmellowed and unhallowed. It should not be forced in order to take advantage of a passing

4 *The New Yorker*, 15th February 1941, p. 67.
5 *The Yale Review*, pp. xiii-xv.
6 *The New York Times*, 2nd March 1941, Book Review Section, p. 6.

vogue, for it will surely crack up in the hurly-burly of competition. It is a brave talent; but not, I think, a very sturdy plant. It calls for gentle handling and careful cultivation.[7]

Rose Feld, who had reviewed the first novel enthusiastically in *The New York Herald-Tribune*, found the new one 'more tightly bound' and 'more carefully constructed', but was puzzled by the significance of the horse, Firebird, who, she wrote, 'in a way that is not entirely clear, is symbolic of her [Leonora's] strength and her husband's weakness.' Alison's gesture of self-mutilation she found 'as physically unnerving to the reader as anything that has appeared in print,' and thought the incident a regrettable lapse of taste on the author's part:

> Mrs McCullers has been compared to William Faulkner; here, indeed, she seems almost deliberately to be seeking something that could match him at his most morbid. Her success does not, however, add anything to her power as an artist. One is merely impressed with and offended by her arrogant and pitiless fear-lessness which besides giving an unpleasant effect, betrays her youth . . . *Reflections in a Golden Eye* is a literary adventure into an emotional underworld and, as such, interesting. But one still hopes that Carson McCullers will use her very real powers to write a book that does not depend completely upon the grotesque and abnormal for its effect.[8]

Edward Weeks, book editor of the conservative *Atlantic*, commented:

> You have seen an artist at work—but an artist who still has a good deal to learn about reality. For, if this is a fair sample of army life, and if the country is soon to pour itself into the army, then God save the Union![9]

Mr Weeks then went on to praise Booth Tarkington's *The Heritage of Thatcher Ide*, which corresponded rather better to his idea of contemporary reality. But poet-critic Hubert Creekmore, in *Accent*, even denied the artistry of the writing:

> The whole thing has the atmosphere of snickering in a privy. Most people know about the juicy items she displays, but one feels that Mrs McCullers has just been told—and by people

7 Ibid., loc. cit.
8 Book Review Section, 16th February 1941, p. 8.
9 April 1941, p. xx.

who failed to caution her that a small degree of art would be necessary in presenting such stories to the public. She ought to learn how to write, how to build characters that are more than a pathology diagnosis, how to move them for her story, and how to be interesting without the abnormal.[10]

It is interesting to compare Mr Creekmore's impression of the book with Otis Ferguson's, in *The New Republic,* as 'a brilliant piece of execution, hard, exact and graceful in likeness, a sort of cameo in fiction.' Mr Ferguson, who on the whole was kinder to the novel than any of the other popular reviewers, made the following interesting comment about the story in general and the Captain and the soldier in particular:

> If this quiet, subtle and thorough treatment of human passions seems a *tour-de-force* in spite of its atmosphere of strange-but-true, its etched background of army post, the customs, the look and feel of the weather, the key to it is in these two principals. They are ranged against each other by such extreme peculiar-ities of temperament and moved by such dumb, obscure forces, that almost anything could be made logically to happen to either. Whereas in the sense of the dramatically inevitable, nothing *has* happened by the ending, in release or final ex-pression, vengeance or atonement. The reader is never identi-fied with anyone in the book; and it seems that the price of such perfection in having everything come out exact and even is that you have to play with a special deck of cards, deliberately leaving the hearts out of it.[11]

I have said that this is an interesting comment: one of the things that make it so is the fact that the last sentence might also have been written about *Madame Bovary.*

The charge of heartlessness was also made by Basil Davenport in *The Saturday Review of Literature,* but he also added:

> It is instantly plain that the book is by someone who can *write,* with a haunting power and suggestiveness that can be felt at once; but it all too soon becomes clear that the story is a vipers'-knot of neurasthenic relationships among characters whom the author seems hardly to comprehend, and of whose perversions she can create nothing.[12]

10 Autumn 1941, p. 61.
11 3rd March 1941, p. 317.
12 22nd February 1941, p. 12.

When the novel appeared in England the following year (1942), *The Times Literary Supplement,* echoing the prevailing opinion in America, remarked anonymously:

> There is, in the carefully plain style of the narrative, some quality of tension or mystery that continually promises more than is apparent. The promise comes to very little, however. You are left at the end with the feeling that everybody is frustrated in one way or another, but for the rest there seems insufficient point in this collection of arbitrary psychological vividness.[13]

Most of these critics, it will be seen, object to what they take to be Mrs McCullers's excessive preoccupation with abnormality. There was a strong hint of this preoccupation in the first novel, but as that was longer and more complicated, it did not loom so large in proportion to the whole. The objection is, I think, valid up to a point; at the same time, it is evidence that many reviewers were again guilty of reading Mrs McCullers on a merely realistic level. On this level, of course, the story is implausible, even a little absurd —a *grotesquerie* or a *tour-de-force* at best. Its bizarre situations and warped characters can scarcely be accepted as lifelike in any except a symbolic sense: the story is not intended to be of the slice-of-life type that James T. Farrell, for example, sometimes writes so skilfully, but few reviewers seemed to understand this at the time the book made its appearance. To complain of Anacleto, as did Mr Fadiman, that he is 'one of the most preposterous characters I have met in modern fiction,' and to observe, as did Mr Weeks, that the novel does not 'present a fair sample of army life,' is therefore perhaps more revealing of the *naiveté* of these critics than of any inadequacy in the author.

One reason why the critics may have been misled is that Mrs McCullers's language in this novel is realistic rather than abstract. There is thus a *surface* realism—uneven, to be sure, for the parable manner does show itself on occasion—which has the power to deceive the hasty or the impatient reader who, dissatisfied with that much, does not take the trouble to determine whether there may not be more of a different kind. This problem, which I shall discuss more fully in later chapters, and which involves more than the matter of language and style, has prevented Mrs McCullers's work from being appreciated as widely and as fully as it deserves to be. Also, because the abnormalities in *Reflections in a Golden Eye* are psychological

13   30th May 1942, p. 269.

rather than physical, the characters are less obviously striking *as symbols,* so that it is tempting to consider them as mere case histories out of, say, Krafft-Ebing—which, as we have seen, is exactly what happened in the case of many reviewers.

Subsequent critical judgments have been kinder to this book. The process began in 1950, when Tennessee Williams, in his Introduction to the New Directions reprint of it, claimed that *Reflections in a Golden Eye* represented an improvement over the first novel: 'Discerning critics should have found it the opposite of a disappointment since it exhibited the one attribute which had yet to be shown in Carson McCullers's stunning array of gifts: the gift of mastery over a youthful lyricism.'[14]

Mr Williams also praised the austerity and 'Grecian coolness' of the book, and the 'lapidary precision' of its style. Comparing the author to Joyce and Faulkner, he declared: '*Reflections in a Golden Eye* is one of the purest and most powerful of those works which are conceived in that Sense of the Awful which is the desperate black root of nearly all significant modern art, from the *Guernica* of Picasso to the cartoons of Charles Addams.'[15]

A series of revaluations followed throughout the decade of the Fifties, establishing that *Reflections in a Golden Eye* is primarily an allegory and that, although in form it is wholly unlike the first novel, the two have an identical theme: the spiritual isolation of the individual.[16] In 1958, Frank Baldanza suggested that the structural division of the novel into animalistic love and spiritual love recalls the myth of the two horses pulling the chariot of the soul in *Phaedrus*:

> Now in this myth, as in most of his other pronouncements on the subject in *Symposium, The Republic,* and other dialogues, Socrates specifically exalts the spiritual aspect of love, and while he never overlooks the physical aspect, he invariably sees it as a deterrent and a distraction, a vitiating tendency within the experience which needs to be resisted wholeheartedly. Carson McCullers, too, invariably focuses on the spiritual—and, in a sense, the asexual—relation, without, however, ignoring or denying the patently sexual basis from which the experience stems. This is the curiously disturbing synthesis of ideas which gives her writing the haunting flavor that one finds so hard to isolate in

14 p. xix.
15 Ibid., p. xviii.
16 See my article, 'The Theme of Spiritual Isolation in Carson McCullers,' *New World Writing No. 1,* 1952, p. 297.

analysis. In this book, the heartily sensual relation of Mrs Penderton and Major Langdon receives hardly more than passing mention, whereas the relations of Mrs Langdon and the houseboy and Captain Penderton and Private Williams (the latter carried on exclusively by means of significant glances) are delicately and poetically explored.[17]

Two years later another critic, John B. Vickery, analyzed the novel in terms of the author's concept of love. In Mrs McCullers's work, he says, love is less a matter of sex than it is 'the measure of the heart's desire, the goal of man's quest, and the image of the world he lives in.' The main characters therefore have a triple role —as lover, as quester, and as dreamer: 'However dissimilar they are and however different the object of their love, there is an essential kinship between Mick Kelly, the adolescent; Blount, the radical; Berenice, the Negro housekeeper; and Penderton, the army major [sic] with homosexual proclivities. For each of them pursues a dream in a world that is impatient with dreams and dreamers.'[18]

Still a third interpretation of the novel was made by Ihab Hassan in his interesting essay, 'Carson McCullers: the Alchemy of Love and Aesthetics of Pain'. Mr Hassan views the spiritualization of love in this author's work as the result of her Protestant-Gothic imagination:

> Being Gothic, which is to say Protestant—for the Gothic may be conceived as a latent reaction to the Catholic hierarchy under God—being both Protestant and Gothic, her imagination derives its peculiar force from a transcendental idea of spiritual loneliness . . . The Gothic insists on spiritualization, the spiritualization of matter itself . . . It should not be difficult to see how the mysticism of Suso and Eckhart, the idea of prayer in Luther, the experience of spiritual horror without sensible correlative in Poe, and the Gothic nightmare in the fiction of Carson McCullers fall into a somber sequence.[19]

He goes on to say that the need to suffer which characterizes Mrs McCullers's lovers conceals 'the fearful powers of the death wish' of which Denis de Rougemont wrote in *Love in the Western World*, and maintains that, contrary to Mr Williams's assertion that what

[17] Op. cit., p. 158. Mr Baldanza, however, is guilty of misreading the novel: he is evidently under the impression that the Captain, after shooting Private Williams, also shoots himself. It is difficult to see, unless he misinterprets the word *slumped* ('The Captain had slumped against the wall'), how he arrives at this impression, and the error may be merely a *lapsis memoriae*.

[18] Op. cit., p. 13.

[19] Op. cit., p. 312.

the book reveals is the 'underlying dreadfulness' of modern life, it is instead the absence of life. In *Reflections in a Golden Eye,* love, he observes, 'dispensing with its object, reaches the dead end of Protestant isolation.' Whether one agrees with what Mr Hassan says about the Protestant-Gothic imagination of the Western world (Dostoevsky's characters are also haunted by the need to suffer, but the quality of Dostoevsky's imagination is neither Protestant nor Western), his examination of the novel is nevertheless serious, thorough, and, in places, keenly perceptive.

Within the last three years, three fairly detailed analyses of *Reflections in a Golden Eye* have appeared in the U.S.A. and one in Germany: Chester E. Eisinger's, in *Fiction of the Forties*; Irving Malin's, in *New American Gothic*; Mark Schorer's, in *The Creative Present*; and Klaus Lubbers's in *Jahrbuch für Amerikastudien*. Mr Eisinger, who believes that Mrs McCullers's purpose in the novel is to show the incompleteness of human beings,[20] makes an interesting comment concerning the polarization of the six characters:

> They divide evenly into two groups. One is made up of Leonora Penderton, Major Morris Langdon, and Ellgee Williams. These people live in nature, enjoying (in the literal sense) life at the creature level. They illustrate the principle of healthy animality. For the first two especially the appetitive life—food, drink, sex, and sport, all of them equally attractive—is all-encompassing. They are insensitive and unintelligent. They are incapable of asking any questions about life. The other group is made up of Captain Weldon Penderton, Alison Langdon, and Anacleto, a Filipino houseboy. These people are cut off entirely from the world of nature. They represent the sensitive feminine principle of culture, that is, the cultivation of the mind and the arts. They are full of self-doubts and adept at self-torture. The two groups, even though they are moored to their separate spheres of being, destroy each other. No one succeeds in making himself whole, in borrowing from the other group what is lacking in his own personality.[21]

Mr Malin, who fits the novel into the tradition of modern American Gothic, which he maintains is dominated by the spirit of narcissism, observes: 'In *Reflections in a Golden Eye* we meet many

[20] The same belief is expressed by Wayne D. Dodd in connection with *The Member of the Wedding* (see Chapter 8) in 'The Development of Theme through Symbol in the Novels of Carson McCullers', *The Georgia Review,* Summer 1963, p. 209.

[21] Op. cit., p. 252.

more narcissists. Leonora Penderton, a bit feebleminded, loves her body and prances naked through the living room; Alison loves her illness; Private Williams is so withdrawn that he walks in a 'trance'; and the Major delights in his wit and adultery.'[22]

Mr Malin's analysis of Captain Penderton's character is especially penetrating, and among Mrs McCullers's critics he is unique in preferring this novel to all her other works, even *The Ballad of the Sad Café*, which he places second: '*Reflections in a Golden Eye* is inevitable, while *The Ballad of the Sad Café* is somewhat more contrived.'[23]

Mr Schorer makes the curious statement, untenable in the light of the existing interpretations of the story, that 'here Mrs McCullers has abandoned her theme of love and loneliness, or rather, she has given us its inversion, writing now of people whose self-engrossment, malice, contempt, or sheer stupidity have for all their desperation, put them ouside the possibility of feeling either loneliness or love.[24] But perhaps the least successful of the four analyses is that of Mr Lubbers, who finds the ending mysterious: 'The veil that surrounds tho last scene can never quite be lifted.'[25] Unless he has been misled by the construction which Mr Baldanza (whom he lists among his sources) places upon this scene (see note 17, this chapter), I do not understand his meaning, for the dénouement could scarcely be less ambiguous. On the whole he seriously under-estimates the book.

Viewing Mrs McCullers's second novel from a distance of more than twenty years, it is easier, therefore, for us to appreciate its excellences and to see how it fits into the total pattern of her work. In some respects it has worn rather better than the first one, which, as it involved issues of a more contemporary nature (I am thinking of the socialism of the Thirties), has now, on a realistic level, become slightly dated.

I am not suggesting that the charm of *Reflections in a Golden Eye* is timeless: the impact of Freudianism, which nearly knocks the book off its feet, tends to date it too, but in a somewhat different way, for here it is not so much a question of the material itself as the attitude the author takes toward this material and the interpretation she makes of it.

For Mrs McCullers to make her allegorical point it was scarcely necessary for her to construct so complete a chamber of horrors: is

22 Op. cit., p. 23.
23 Op. cit., p. 159.
24 Op. cit., pp. 88-89.
25 Op. cit., p. 194.

it not sufficient that Captain Penderton be a homosexual, an algo-
lagnist, and a drug addict without also being a kleptomaniac? Even
the insensitive Major Langdon is made to lie on the analyst's couch:

> On the surface the Major naively believed that his wife knew
> nothing about his affair. However, this soothing thought had
> become increasingly difficult for him to hold on to; the strain of
> not realizing the truth had given him hemorrhoids and had
> almost upset his good digestion.

Insights such as this, if they occurred less frequently, would perhaps
be welcome, but in a context already overladen with Freudian signifi-
cances they seem gratuitous and ill-advised, and suggest that the
author has let herself be carried away by the knowledge, too recently
acquired and not sufficiently assimilated, that ailments can be psychosomatic. This lack of control in the interpretation of her material
contrasts oddly with the marvellous discipline which Mrs McCullers
exercises in the organization and presentation of it, and results in a
certain unevenness that is disturbing. It is as if Flaubert, by an
anachronism involving a difference of fifty years, had made the discovery of Freud and had placed il his technical resources at the
command of that ingenious intelligence—as resistless before it as
was his heroine, Emma Bovary, before the temptation of luxury.

The packing of so many aberrated characters (one reader remarked that in this book not even the horse was normal!) into
so short a novel not only reduces the plausibility of the
story on a realistic level, so that the fusion in it between realism
and allegory is unsuccessful and it is acceptable *merely* as allegory;
it also, as we have seen, has had the unfortunate effect of causing
certain critics to classify Mrs McCullers as a sensationalist, a seeker
after cheap effects—a pornographer, so to speak, of terror. It is this
book which, for better or for worse, earned for its author the label
of Gothic—and the label has continued to stick. But Gothic horror
is horror for its own sake (as we sometimes find in Poe, for example),
and in the best of Mrs McCullers's work there is always a justification for it on other grounds. Granted that it lacks the maturity of
her later novels, *Reflections in a Golden Eye* established Mrs Mc-
Cullers as a virtuoso writer of the very first rank, and proved that
she had, in an incredibly short time, acquired a formidable command of technique. This is the more remarkable when we consider
how quickly and how easily she wrote the book, and that, contrary
to the impression which the story gives of having been carefully
calculated, it formed itself in the author's mind as she went along.

'When I began,' she has said, 'I had no idea who was going to shoot whom.'

In the first novel Mrs McCullers was still, formally, finding her way, and there was naturally a certain amount of fumbling: here the pattern, though simpler, is admirably sharp and clear. Part One—with the exception of the melodramatic scene in which Leonora, standing nude on the staircase, taunts her husband ('Son, have you ever been collared and dragged out on the street and thrashed by a naked woman?')—is a superb piece of writing, as perfectly unfolded as anything in recent American fiction. Not a word is wasted; the first paragraph plunges us deeply into the story, and our interest, thus secured, is not allowed to flag for a single instant. *Reflections in a Golden Eye*, for all its faults, accomplishes a very great deal in a very short space, and its theme is exactly the same as that of the first novel. Here too the characters strive for release from their isolation by means of love—love which differs according to the nature of the lover. And here too the outcome is frustration and tragedy.

* * *

CHAPTER SIX

FEBRUARY HOUSE

By the summer of 1940 Carson was convinced that her marriage had been a mistake. She and Reeves were living in New York now, in a Manhattan apartment, but she was planning to divorce him eventually. This year the circumstances were very different from those under which she had made her first trip to the city five years ago: then she was an unknown small-town girl from Georgia; now she was a publisher's 'find', with one successful novel already in print and another awaiting publication. One of her new friends was George Davis, then editor of *Harper's Bazaar*, who it seemed knew everyone in the New York literary world, and this friendship was the beginning of what was to become one of the most extraordinary intellectual *ménages* since the Brook Farm experiment in the 1840's.

Everything about this *ménage* was sensational, including the way its headquarters came to be chosen. George Davis, a bachelor, had for some time been dissatisfied with his apartment. One night he dreamed he was living in a huge old brownstone house in Brooklyn Heights: the dream was so vivid and it haunted him so persistently that the next day he took a subway to Brooklyn, walked about the neighbourhood, and, after a brief search, actually succeeded in finding the house he had dreamed about! The two were identical down to the smallest detail—and the real one was to let. Excitedly he telephoned Carson, who by this time had definitely decided to leave Reeves and was also looking for a place to live; she was delighted with it, so the two friends took prompt possession.

The British poet Wystan Hugh Auden was also in New York at this time, looking for a place to settle. Carson and George invited him to stay with them: he accepted, and so a third 'charter member' was added to the establishment. In time they were joined by Benjamin Britten, the composer; by his friend Peter Pears, the operatic tenor who has sung his work innumerable times; by poets Louis MacNeice and Chester Kallman; by novelists Christopher Isherwood and Richard Wright; by historian Golo Mann (Thomas

Mann's second eldest son); by the composer and novelist-to-be Paul Bowles and his wife, Jane, who was a novelist and future playwright; by Oliver Smith, the stage designer; and, of all people, by Gypsy Rose Lee, the strip-tease artist—surely the first of her profession to cultivate intellectual company on such a level. (Her collection of surrealist paintings later became one of the finest in America.) All of these people, to be sure, did not occupy the house simultaneously—when one of them went away another would sometimes take his place—but they all considered themselves charter members and continued to live there off and on, when there was room, for the next five years or so.

There were, over the years, dozens of house guests and hundreds of callers, among them some of the most impressive names in literature, art, and music during the War years: composers Virgil Thomson, Aaron Copland, Marc Blitzstein, and Leonard Bernstein; surrealist painters Pavel Tchelitchew, Eugene Berman, and Salvador Dali (accompanied by his wife and model, the fabulous Gala); ballet critic and patron of the arts Lincoln Kirstein; and author Denis de Rougemont,[1] to name only a few. It was the nearest thing to a genuine salon this side of Paris, and the house that George Davis had seen in his dream became famous all over New York. In the monumental diary which she has been keeping since childhood (and which Henry Miller says 'will take its place beside the revelations of St Augustine, Petronius, Abelard, Rousseau, Proust and others'), Anais Nin, the avant-garde surrealist novelist, noted that most of the prominent members of the ménage had been born under the sign of Pisces, and christened it 'February House'. (It was known more generally as Seven Middagh Street.) Co-operative living arrangements were fairly common in the United States in the late Thirties and early Forties, especially among those of the intelligentsia who had leftist leanings, but what distinguished February House from all other such establishments was the really extraordinary talent of its occupants, most of whom were relatively unknown at the time.

It was not the most tranquil place in the world: people came and went continually; the piano (with three talented performers and a singer in the house) was rarely silent; Tchelitchew did a whole set of murals on the walls. But the activity was stimulating, and there was an abundance of what had been lacking heretofore in Carson's

[1] Of de Rougemont's introduction to this ménage, René Micha (op. cit.) has written: 'C'est là que Denis de Rougemont la rencontra, un jour de 1941, dans une sombre maison de quatre étages où l'avait conduit, l'un des fils de Thomas Mann; des écrivains, des peintres, des musiciens, des chorégraphes y menaient "la vie de Bohème"—parmi eux W. H. Auden, Benjamin Britten, Paul Bowles; il semble qu' on buvait extraordinairement.'

life—the company of intellectual equals. Some of the people she met at this time, like Auden and Gypsy Rose Lee, have remained her close friends throughout the years. But her favourite of them all, Annemarie Clarac-Schwarzenbach, was destined to die shortly thereafter. Annemarie was a good friend of Thomas Mann's daughter Erika—whom Auden had married. Both Erika and her brother Klaus were constantly at February House, and it was through them that Carson met Annemarie. Young (in her late twenties), stunningly beautiful, a talented writer of fiction and poetry, Annemarie had also a glamorous and exciting background: she had operated a kind of secret shuttle between Austria and Switzerland, and had saved the lives of many German refugees. Carson formed a deep emotional attachment to her, and when *Reflections in a Golden Eye* appeared, Annemarie's name was on the dedication page. When Annemarie went back to Europe, and later to Africa, Carson continued to correspond with her. The news of her sudden death in a bicycle accident (according to Gypsy Rose Lee, she was accident-prone) in Zurich, when she was only thirty, reached Carson in 1943 at Yaddo, where she was working on *The Member of the Wedding*, and was a traumatic experience from which she was slow in recovering.

It was not the first time that Brooklyn had witnessed intellectual activity. In the middle of the nineteenth century a number of liberal writers and thinkers made it their home, and it became notorious as a centre for abolitionists. Walt Whitman worked on the *Daily Eagle*, where he wrote the anti-slavery editorials that eventually lost him his job; Henry Ward Beecher preached regularly at the old Plymouth Church; John Greenleaf Whittier stayed frequently at the old Cooper home. In the present century, Hart Crane used to spend hours roaming the Sand Street area, gathering material for his epic poem, *Brooklyn Bridge*, while on Cumberland Street another important modern poet, Marianne Moore, settled with calm dignity in an austere apartment to write many of the poems that have since made her famous.

February House stood on a quiet street lined with maple trees: in the autumn children would rake the leaves and make bonfires of them. It was a big, comfortable house with a back yard, and the neighbourhood had something of the quality of a small town. Mrs McCullers has described this period of her life in an article entitled 'Brooklyn Is My Neighbourhood' (*Vogue*, March, 1941). 'It is strange in New York,' she wrote, 'to find yourself living in a real neighbourhood.' It did not take her long to become acquainted with her neighbours—especially Mr Parker, the garrulous druggist on the corner, whose mind was 'a rag bag of odd scraps of information'. On her right lived an eccentric old lady who, it was rumoured, had once been jailed for smashing the windows of a saloon in a temperance demonstration. She collected stray dogs, kept a pet monkey, and was said to be very rich and very stingy.

Another eccentric was 'Miss Kate', the antique dealer on nearby Fulton Street from whom Mrs McCullers bought most of her furnishings. Miss Kate suffered greatly from the cold, and hovered constantly over a little coal stove in the rear of her shop. She permitted herself the luxury of a bath only once a year—in the summer, naturally. 'She has one of the handsomest and dirtiest faces I can remember,' Mrs McCullers wrote. 'She sleeps every night wrapped in a Persian rug and lying on a green velvet Victorian couch.'

One of Carson's favourite strolls was along Sand Street, which stretched from Brooklyn Bridge to the Navy Yard. Lined with bars, with shops selling navy uniforms, and with cheap hotels and rooming houses, it was a tawdry place by daylight, though there was always the excitement of the salt sea air. But at night it underwent an extraordinary metamorphosis: there was a never-ending flow of sailors and streetwalkers, and the lights of the bars glittered with a feverish gaiety. This was the street which, only a decade earlier, Hart Crane used to prowl in his lonely search for unorthodox love, and these were the bars in which he would carouse until dawn with the sailors of his choice.

Carson noted with amusement the deference that was paid in these establishments to some of the older prostitutes ('vivid old dowagers of the street' as she has called them) who had been Sand Street fixtures for years—colourful characters, often heavily tattooed. (There was a tattoo shop on the street, too.) They went by such names as The Duchess and Submarine Mary, and scorned to hustle drinks at the bar like the younger girls, but, relying on the widespread publicity of their reputations, sat as demurely as society dowagers until they were approached by their clients; one of them even used to bring her knitting with her. The one whom they called Submarine Mary was particularly imposing: her prestige, which perhaps partly owed itself to the fact that every tooth in her head was filled with gold, was enormous, and she reigned it like a queen in the bar that she was fondest of: in fact, her admirers also referred to her, rather blasphemously, as the Queen of Heaven, for there was a saying among the sailors that when they died they wanted to go to Sand Street. Carson, who would occasionally drop into this bar with George or Wystan, noticed that the Queen's favourite companion— the Royal Consort, so to speak—was a little hunchback who, as she wrote in 'Brooklyn Is My Neighbourhood', 'strutted in every evening and was petted by everyone, given free drinks, and treated as a sort of mascot by the proprietor.' Readers of *The Ballad of the Sad Café* will have little difficulty recognizing in this character the model for Cousin Lymon.

When Gypsy joined the group, who had been taking their meals mainly in restaurants, she found a cook for them, and, as they became more numerous, other servants were added. Each occupant paid his share of the cooking and housekeeping expenses. Paul Bowles recalls, 'It was full of people always, and Auden ran it and paid for the servants and food, and we all paid him regularly on a co-operative basis, and it worked very well except for a few terrible rows, which were inevitable.'

Though the neighbourhood had, as has been said, something of the quality of a small town in the sense that its residents knew one another, sometimes intimately, and visited back and forth frequently, it was fortunately lacking in the inquisitiveness, the tendency to pry and to meddle, that are so often characteristic of a small town environment. In this respect it was thoroughly metropolitan: New York is at once the most tolerant as it is the largest of all American cities, and Brooklyn, because of its ethnic and cultural variety, is perhaps the most tolerant of all New York neighbourhoods. If Carson's neighbours found anything strange in the fact that a young, apparently single woman should be sharing a house with so many young people, chiefly male, or that dozens of people came and went at all hours of the day and night, they never betrayed their surprise by so much as a word or a gesture; nor did they allow it to affect the cordiality with which they welcomed her to the neighbourhood. The good people of Brooklyn did not expect one to be like everybody else; they were respectful of differences, and for this Carson was grateful. Though unconventional in her habits and in certain of her attitudes, she has never flaunted these publicly: believing that everyone is entitled to a certain amount of privacy in his personal life, and believing also (with Captain Penderton) that it is folly to force square pegs into round holes, she is herself one of the most tolerant of persons.

Carson loved Brooklyn and February House, and continued to make them her headquarters for the next four or five years (she received her divorce from Reeves late in 1940), interspersed with periods spent at Yaddo, the writers' colony at Saratoga Springs in upstate New York whose director, Elizabeth Ames, became one of her most intimate friends, and in Columbus, where she was forced to retreat from time to time for reasons of health. But something happened in Columbus that was distinctly unpleasant. One day, shortly after the publication of *Reflections in a Golden Eye,* she received an anonymous telephone call from someone representing himself as a member of the Ku Klux Klan and telling her that unless she got out of town immediately he was coming with his friends to 'get her' that very evening. 'We know from your first book that you're a nigger-lover,' the voice said, 'and we know from this one that you're queer. We don't want queers and nigger-lovers in this town.' Mr Smith sat all that night on the front porch with a loaded shotgun in his lap, but nothing came of the threat.

On the whole she felt safer in Brooklyn. But satisfying in so many ways as was the life at February House, the late hours, the irregular meals, and the general over-stimulation of the place began to have an adverse effect upon her health, which had always been delicate. The only way in which it was possible for her to stay on—without suffering a total collapse—was therefore to spend a few weeks or months out of every year with her family in the house on Starke Avenue where life was smoothly ordered and as different from the other as could well be imagined. She overtaxed her strength severely in the winter of 1940, and when she was in Columbus recuperating she suffered the first of the three strokes which have combined to cripple her so seriously. The source of these strokes, as it is now known, was a damaged heart caused by rheumatic fever, misdiagnosed when she was a child. This first attack, like the others, might possibly have been averted had she avoided strain and over-exertion, but she had always lived a very active life and had had no reason to suspect an impairment of the heart. For a short time after this first stroke she could not see well enough to read, and could not even make out the numerals on the face of a clock. She thought she was going blind, and knew several days of terror before improvement gradually began to set in.

It took Mrs McCullers two months to recover from this experience—two agonized months during which she wondered if the dazed state of her mind was going to be permanent, and if she would ever be able to write again. She was only twenty-three years old! Fortunately her mother and father were there to reassure her and to watch over her until she was strong enough to get about once more. But none of her subsequent strokes frightened her as badly as this one.

CHAPTER SEVEN

* * *

TREES, ROCKS, AND CLOUDS

In the period of depression that followed her first stroke, Mrs McCullers wrote what many readers think is the best of her short stories: 'A Tree, a Rock, a Cloud'. First published in *Harper's Bazaar* (November, 1942), it was promptly chosen by Herschel Brickell for his annual anthology, *O. Henry Memorial Prize Stories of 1942*. This story holds a very special place in the author's affections, for it proved emphatically to her that she had not, as she had feared, lost her ability to write.

Both in its own right and in its relation to the rest of her work, 'A Tree, a Rock, a Cloud' is such an important story that it deserves to be analyzed in some detail. Early one rainy morning a newsboy, about twelve years old, whose route is almost finished, enters an all-night café for a cup of coffee. The owner of the café is a man named Leo, who the author tells us is 'bitter and stingy', and there are, besides the boy, six customers in it: three mill workers, two soldiers, and a tramp who is 'long and pale with a big nose and faded orange hair'. The tramp is drinking beer: he motions for the boy to join him, and when he does so declares simply, 'I love you.' He then shows him two photographs of his wife, who he says left him for another man ten years ago, and, in a manner reminiscent of the Ancient Mariner, unfolds to the astonished boy, who thinks him drunk, the story of how, through the years, he has come to acquire a mastery of the 'science' of love. From time to time his recital is interrupted by exclamations of contempt from Leo, who clearly has no use for him, but the tramp carefully ignores him and concentrates all his attention upon the boy.

He had always, he tells him, been a person who experienced things intensely, but before meeting his wife he had never succeeded in assimilating these experiences properly; it was as though they were 'laying around loose in him':

What happened was this. There were these beautiful feelings

88

and loose little pleasures inside me. And this woman was something like an assembly line for my soul. I run these little pieces of myself through her and I come out complete.

When his wife, whom he had thought happy, deserted him, he was inconsolable. Giving up his job as railroad engineer, he travelled about the country for two years searching for her; then he let himself go to the dogs, indulging in every form of wickedness :

I was a sick mortal. It was like smallpox. I confess, Son, that I boozed. I fornicated. I committed any sin that suddenly appealed to me. I am loath to confess it but I will do so. When I recall that period it is all curdled in my mind, it was so terrible.

For three more years he drifted purposelessly, and then in a sudden flash of illumination his 'science' came to him. He perceived that most men make a mistake when they fall in love for the first time : 'Without science, with nothing to go by, they undertake the most dangerous and sacred experience in God's earth. They fall in love with a woman.' He goes on to say that, because they start at the 'wrong end' of love, at the climax instead of at the beginning, most of them are doomed to failure. Instead, they should start with 'a tree, a rock, a cloud' and work their way gradually upward. As soon as he realized this profound truth, he began to teach himself the new science : 'I meditated and I started very cautious. I would pick up something from the street and take it home with me. I bought a goldfish and I loved it. I graduated from one thing to another.' Now, after six years of perfecting his technique, he says he has become a master : he has reached the point where he no longer has to 'think about it'—he can love anything and anybody : 'I see a street full of people and a beautiful light comes in me. I watch a bird in the sky. Or I meet a traveler on the road. Everything, Son. And anybody. All stranger and all loved.'

With the final injunction, 'Remember I love you,' the tramp finishes his beer and leaves the café. The boy then asks Leo his opinion of the man—is he drunk, a dope fiend, or merely a lunatic?—but Leo, beyond denying that he is either drunk or doped, surlily refuses to make any further comment. Whereupon the boy says wonderingly, 'He sure has done a lot of traveling,' and goes out.

The setting of the story, and its external pattern, are reminiscent, as Mr Baldanza has observed,[1] of Hemingway's by-now classic story, 'The Killers'. With the exception of a single important scene in the latter (the one in which Nick goes to Ole Andreson's room to

[1] Op. cit., pp. 155-6.

tell him the hoodlums are 'tailing' him) the action in both cases occurs in a cheap restaurant and involves a proprietor with a tough, matter-of-fact air and a youth who is just beginning to acquire experience of life and whose innocence contrasts with the worldliness of his elder. The endings are very similar: both stories conclude with a dialogue in which these two characters discuss a third, and the final speech, uttered in each case by the youth, registers the impact that this experience has had upon him.[2]

The correspondence between Hemingway's story and Mrs McCullers's is, however, merely structural. 'The Killers' is a triumph of naturalistic technique, while Mrs McCullers, writing as usual on the symbolic level, has deliberately made her characters abstract: except for the proprietor, she does not even give them names. And while 'The Killers' presents the spectacle of a man trapped by his past—a strong man suddenly rendered helpless—'A Tree, a Rock, a Cloud' presents the spectacle of a man who, through repeated effort, succeeds in learning the most difficult lesson that life has to teach and thereby attains the highest wisdom. As for the effect upon the youths of their separate experiences, in Nick's case it is, as Brooks and Warren correctly maintain, one of terror at the realization of the evil that exists in the world, while in the case of the newsboy it is mere bewilderment over what appears to him to have been an utterly senseless monologue.

From the point of view of theme, 'A Tree, a Rock, a Cloud' bears a closer resemblance to another Hemingway story, 'The Snows of Kilimanjaro', though the patterns are reversed: in the latter, a man loses the ability to love and dies of a gangrenous wound that symbolizes the spiritual decay which began with that loss; in the former, a man escapes the fate of death-in-life by acquiring the ability to love through a systematic process of self-training. The implication in both these stories is that life without love is meaningless and amounts to death-in-life.

The most perfect analogue to 'A Tree, a Rock, a Cloud', however, is found in neither of these two stories but in Coleridge's poem, *The Rime of the Ancient Mariner*. The theme of both the prose and the verse narrative is salvation through love—not necessarily love

2 This should not be taken to mean that the youth, in the case of either story, is the protagonist. (See my article, 'The Protagonist of Hemingway's "The Killers",' in *Modern Language Notes*, December, 1958, p. 589.) There is even less reason for believing that the newsboy is the protagonist of 'A Tree, a Rock, a Cloud' than for believing, as do Cleanth Brooks and Robert Penn Warren, who began this influential heresy in 1943 (see *Understanding Fiction*, pp. 316-24), that Nick is the protagonist of 'The Killers'. Mr Baldanza evidently accepts the Brooks-Warren interpretation of the story.

of one's fellow man but of all objects that exist in nature:

> He prayeth best who loveth best
> All things both great and small;
> For the dear God who loveth us,
> He made and loveth all.

The structural similarity is obvious: in both cases a man of eccentric manner and appearance buttonholes a bewildered stranger and unburdens himself of a story the first part of which is a confession of evil and the second an account of restoration to grace by means of love. The tramp's taking the goldfish home with him is the turning point, the moral climax of the story, and corresponds to the moment at which the Ancient Mariner feels a gush of love for the watersnakes:

> O happy living things! no tongue
> Their beauty might declare:
> A spring of love gushed from my heart
> And I blessed them unaware ...
>
> The selfsame moment I could pray;
> And from my neck so free
> The Albatross fell off, and sank
> Like lead into the sea.

Finally, both narratives end with an injunction, or exhortation, from the speaker to the listener, and with an account of the effect that the experience has produced upon the listener. The tramp's 'Remember I love you' reminds one of the Mariner's parting words:

> Farewell, farewell, but this I tell
> To thee, thou Wedding Guest!
> He prayeth best, who loveth well
> Both man and bird and beast.

In Coleridge's poem the listener 'went like one that hath been stunned/And is of sense forlorn'; in Mrs McCullers's story, the newsboy is similarly bewildered.

Implicit in both the poem and the story is the Neo-Platonic doctrine of the relation of the individual soul to the World Soul (Plotinus's Primal Nature), which both contains the individual soul and is itself partially contained by it—a doctrine, incidentally, in which

Whitman[3] was also much interested—as well as the concept of a chain of love which connects all objects in the natural universe: as Robert Penn Warren puts it in his essay on *The Rime of the Ancient Mariner*, 'The human love . . . must be understood in the context of universal love and only in that context achieves its meaning.'[4] Coleridge's Neo-Platonic studies probably account for the presence of these ideas in his poem, but Mrs McCullers had had no such exposure to them. She was, of course, familiar with the poem, and had read the Platonic dialogues. It is also possible that her conversations with Auden, who was concerned at this time with the problem (in a social context) of the relation of individual love to universal love, may have interested her in the subject. Auden had written, the year previously:

> The error bred in the bone
> Of each woman and each man
> Craves what it cannot have,
> Not universal love
> But to be loved alone.[5]

That there is a 'science' of love which can be mastered by practice is also the theme of two of Yeats's better known poems. In 'Adam's Curse' the couple have fallen out of love because they lack this science, and the speaker muses sadly:

> It's certain there is no fine thing
> Since Adam's fall but needs much labouring.

And in 'Brown Penny' the poet says of love that it is such a difficult thing that one cannot begin the study of it too soon:

> O love is the crooked thing,
> There is nobody wise enough
> To find out all that is in it,
> For he would be thinking of love
> Till the stars had run away
> And the shadows eaten the moon.

3   Eisinger observes: 'This mystical and monistic idealism, so suggestive of Whitman, is the happiest view of love Mrs McCullers gives us, although this conviction that love is all comes to us from a broken man,' p. 256.

4   Robert Penn Warren, ed., *The Rime of the Ancient Mariner: a Poem of Pure Imagination* (New York, Reynal & Hitchcock, 1946), p. 144.

5   'September 1, 1939'. See also his essay, 'The Stone and the Shell', in *The Enchafèd Flood* (New York, Random House, 1950).

Ah, penny, brown penny, brown penny,
One cannot begin it too soon.

Mr Baldanza, in discussing the Platonism of the story, cites the passage from *The Symposium* wherein Socrates quotes Diotima :

> And the true order of going, or being led by another, to the things of love, is to begin from the beauties of earth and mount upwards for the sake of that other beauty, using these as steps only, and from one going on to two, and from two to all fair forms, and from fair forms to fair practices, and from fair practices to fair notions, until from fair notions he arrives at the notion of absolute beauty, and at last knows what the essence of beauty is.

The tramp's 'science of love', he maintains, is the same as the 'single science, which is the science of beauty everywhere' spoken of in *The Symposium*; the only difference is that Socrates begins his progression where Mrs McCullers leaves off: in *The Symposium* individual human beauty is the lowest rung of the ladder, while in Mrs McCullers's story it is the highest, so that she plays the same theme 'a whole octave lower'.[6]

It is also true that the situation in 'A Tree, a Rock, a Cloud' resembles that in a typical Platonic dialogue. 'One thinks,' Mr Baldanza says, 'of Socrates' session with the slave boy on the Pythagorean theorem', and declares that the questions which the tramp asks the newsboy make of him 'a typical Socratic stooge who must give the predetermined answers to further the progress of the dialogue'. This is to state the case rather strongly, but I think I should be willing to concede his general point. It seems to me, however, that Mr Baldanza's claim that 'Plato's allegory of the cave stands behind the story too' is merely ingenious :

> But after the tramp's departure with a final 'Remember . . . Remember I love you,' the newsboy himself becomes the Socratic gadfly and proceeds to quiz Leo; the latter denies that the man is either a drunkard, a dope addict, or a maniac. Now we see in Leo's obvious embarrassment that Plato's allegory of the cave stands behind the story too. The tramp was a true philosopher who had been vouchsafed escape from the cave of the bondage of the senses; he had seen the sun of spiritual reality, and when he returned to the cave to tell of the sun he had seen, men were simply embarrassed at his divine fervour. The capstone is the closing sentence, which the newsboy intends

6 Op. cit., p. 155.

as an equivocal remark, but one that fits well with a Platonic interpretation : 'He sure has done a lot of travelling.'

Now the newsboy's closing remark is certainly to be taken symbolically, as indicating that the tramp has come a long way in his search for final wisdom (this is the reason Mrs McCullers has made him a *tramp*), but in order to do this it is scarcely necessary to think that his journey corresponds to that of Plato's adventurer. The tramp's journey, on the literal level, was an aimless and prolonged wandering that culminated accidentally in a revelation, while on the spiritual level there were *two* journeys, the first (preceding the moment of revelation) unsystematic and the second (following that moment) systematic and deliberate. The pattern of Plato's allegory is simpler and involves both a going and a *return*. Moreover, Leo is not at all like Plato's skeptics, who were merely unenlightened. Mrs McCullers has given him a bad character in the very first paragraph : 'a bitter and stingy man'. The word that best describes Leo's attitude is not *embarrassment;* he actually hates the tramp with a hatred that is the measure of his envy. When the tramp reaches the climax of his recital, and describes how he perfected his technique, here is Leo's reaction :

'Aw shut up!' screamed Leo suddenly. 'Shut up! Shut up!'

It is a cry of rage. Had he thought the tramp's claim merely an idle boast, he would not have expressed himself so strongly. It is not because he doubts the tramp's story but because he believes it that he reacts as he does. Plato's returned wanderer is believed to be mad by his former friends; Mrs McCullers's tramp is hated because a man who we have been told is 'bitter and stingy' recognizes his moral superiority. It should also be noted that when Leo is given the opportunity to say that the tramp is 'crazy', in answer to the boy's direct question, he says nothing.

What then is Leo's function in the story? That he is intended as a foil to the tramp is obvious enough, so that we associate him with the principle of hatred rather than of love. It is no accident that he is 'stingy'; his penury contrasts with the lavishness of the tramp's love—while the latter 'can love anything', Leo can love nothing. This is why he is 'bitter', whereas the tramp seems 'very happy'. Leo's experience of life excludes the spiritual or ideal aspect of love, though it does not exclude its physical aspect, so that to the tramp's opening remark to the newsboy ('Son, I love you'), made in complete innocence, he is quick to give a sinister interpretation and says warningly, 'He's a minor.'

Leo is not the only one who is conscious of the tramp's moral superiority: the tramp realizes it also, and this explains the serenity with which he is able to ignore the proprietor's insulting interruptions. Only once does he betray annoyance, and then it is not so much with annoyance as with an air of weary and dignified patience that he addresses Leo: 'Please do not be vulgar. Besides, I was not speaking to you.' Part of the effectiveness of 'A Tree, a Rock, a Cloud' lies in the fact that it dramatizes in the simplest possible terms the abstract struggle between love and hatred and demonstrates the superior strength of good over evil. As in the best work of Tennessee Williams (such as *A Streetcar Named Desire*), one is conscious of the clashing of elemental, abstract forces, and senses—perhaps even without quite realizing consciously what these forces are—that the conflict is important.

The setting of the story must be understood in relation to its theme, which, as has been suggested, is universal. We have seen how, from the various realistic particulars that help to make her story interesting on a narrative level (a *tramp* with a *big nose* and *faded orange hair* who has had an *unsuccessful marital history* and is *drinking beer*, a boy who *sells papers* and *orders a cup of coffee*, a proprietor *named Leo*), Mrs McCullers has abstracted the essential situation: a (wise and good) master attempts to teach a valuable lesson to an innocent youth while a (wicked) bystander tries to interrupt.[7] Likewise the café, a remodelled streetcar with its row of stools, its beer mugs and coffee cups, its pink strips of bacon frying on the grill, is more than a *particular* place: the scene of a conflict that is eternal and universal, it too must be abstracted, and becomes not only *any* place but *all* places—in short, the world itself. The concept of café as microcosm is found in two other works by Mrs McCullers: *The Heart Is a Lonely Hunter*, where the function of the proprietor is quite different, and *The Ballad of the Sad Café*, where it is different again. In *The Member of the Wedding* the kitchen substitutes the café as the scene of the allegory, but the setting is equally important and has the same significance. Mr Baldanza, in discussing the relation of setting to theme in the novels of Carson McCullers and Truman Capote, observes:

> Two of these themes are almost monotonously reiterated in the other works of these two authors—the concept of the café, of a place or a context that is congenial for conversations and confidences (like the spot beneath the plane-tree in *Phaedrus*); and the theme of love as an absolute, abstract force that overrides all

7   In a sense they may be thought of as wrestling over the boy's soul, though (since it is doubtful the lesson has been understood) the efforts of both may be wasted.

barriers of age, sex, time, and distance and that manifests itself in an endless variety of ways.
In fact, the concept of place is fundamental to the latter one of love. The whole society of these novels is a microcosm. The clearly defined hierarchy of Southern society gives cohesion to this world, while its local, economic, and climatic isolation give it color and character.[8]

I think Mr Baldanza is mistaken when he maintains—as he goes on to do—that the microcosm is *a* world rather than *the* world, especially in the case of Mrs McCullers, but he is correct when he points out that 'the whole society of these novels is a microcosm'.

An interesting fact remains to be noted about 'A Tree, a Rock, a Cloud': its protagonist anticipates by almost a decade the type of saintly tramp (or 'holy barbarian', as Lawrence Lipton has called him), contemptuous of possessions and filled with an other-worldly sort of wisdom, whom the writers of the so-called Beat movement in the United States have until quite recently been so busily occupied in glorifying; one thinks of Dean Moriarty in Jack Kerouac's *On the Road,* and, still more pertinently, of Albert Ancke, in Clellon Holmes's *Go.* I do not insist on a connection, since it is generally acknowledged that the prototype of the Beat hero is the wandering Zen sage, but if the circumstance is accidental it is all the more interesting. Leo, by contrast, is the man with petty commitments and possessions; he is the *owner* of the restaurant, and it is ironical that, though he dispenses physical nourishment, his own soul is in a state of starvation.

The lesson, finally, which 'A Tree, a Rock, a Cloud' teaches is that there is a science of love which can be learned—and learned by beginning, not with the most complex and highly organized of natural forms, but with the simplest and lowliest. Obviously it is ideal love with which Mrs McCullers, here as in her other work, is concerned, and this love is entirely selfless: it does not require reciprocation, merely an object, and the object can be anything—or anyone—in the universe. The chief value of love is to the lover, on whom it has the power to bestow the blessing of happiness.

8 Op. cit., p. 156.

* * *

CHAPTER EIGHT

THE 'WE' OF ME:
THE WORLD OF F. JASMINE ADDAMS

1

After Carson divorced him, Reeves re-entered the army, where, partly because of his previous training at Fort Benning and partly because of his superior natural abilities, he was quickly given a commission. The United States entered World War II in 1941, and men of Reeves's calibre were very much in demand. He was made a company commander in the Second Ranger Battalion. (The Rangers, like the Commandos, were an outfit of men specially selected for physical toughness and were given some of the most difficult and dangerous assignments in the army.) During the rigorous training period which he and his men underwent prior to going overseas, he and Carson resumed their correspondence. The divorce had been her idea; Reeves worshipped her still, and the thought that she might never see him again after he left the country was disquieting. So she answered all his letters, and even met him several times when he was able to arrange a furlough—a dangerous thing to do, for she was still uncertain of her feelings. From Columbus she wrote to their old friend Edwin Peacock, who was now in the Navy:

> Reeves was here, on his furlough, last month. He is now with the Rangers. He is in good shape, in every way. But oh, Edwin, it was sad—thinking back over the old days and realizing that a certain kind of relation which we once had is a thing of the past, and that we must each of us face life alone.

In the autumn of 1943, Reeves and his company received their orders. They were sent to the port of embarkation centre at Fort Dix, just outside New York, and Carson, who had received a Guggenheim fiction fellowship as well as a thousand-dollar award from the American Academy of Arts and Letters, and who was in Columbus working on *The Member of the Wedding*, went up to visit

him for a week just before he left for the European Theatre. On
November 15th she wrote to Edwin:

> He is in splendid trim, and a wonderful soldier . . . Reeves is so
> handsome, it fills me with a sort of horror to look at him and
> to know the danger he must face. I am very glad, though, that
> we had this visit together. We have been through such sorrow
> together, such ties of mutual destruction, and somehow those
> last days made all those dreadful doings seem far away. He was
> so glad to have me. So proud for me to see his company, and
> meet the men he has been training with. I have always loved
> him so tenderly. Now, knowing the Rangers will see so much
> action ahead of them, it will be very hard to wait between
> letters. God help him.

Before Reeves left, Carson made a date to meet him at the end of
the war on the terrace of New York's Brevoort Hotel.

In the same letter, Mrs McCullers wrote: 'I have had and am
having a struggle with this book, and the end is nowhere yet in sight.'
The book she was referring to was *The Member of the Wedding*,
which she had started soon after finishing her second novel. It was
originally a short story, with the title 'The Bride of My Brother'.
Carson worked on this book for five years before she was fully
satisfied with it, (an award of $1,000 from the American Academy
of Arts and Letters, in addition to the Guggenheim, helped to tide
her over this period) interrupting it only once to write her novella,
The Ballad of the Sad Café, which she published in *Harper's Bazaar*
for November, 1943. The characters, drawn from her own childhood,
had been in her mind for some time, but she had not been able to
arrange them in any sort of satisfactory relationship. One Thanks-
giving at February House, after everyone had eaten the big turkey
dinner and were sitting down before the fire with brandy and coffee,
they heard the sound of a fire engine. Gypsy Rose Lee rushed out to
look; Carson followed, and then, in a flash of illumination, the idea
of the book suddenly became clear to her. Catching Gypsy's arm,
she shouted over the noise of the fire engine: 'Frankie is in love
with her brother and his bride and wants to become a member of
the wedding.' 'Gypsy,' she recalls, 'stared at me as though I had lost
my mind.'

Written during the years of the war, echoes of which are present
in the background, *The Member of the Wedding* avoids both the
social tensions of *The Heart Is a Lonely Hunter* and the Freudian
obsessions of *Reflections in a Golden Eye*. Even more than her first

novel it is autobiographical—an attempt, as she has said, to re-capture the experience of her own troubled adolescence—but here the material is under firmer control than in the earlier and more ambitious book. The formal discipline she had acquired in the writ-ing of her second novel now served her to good advantage, and many critics regard *The Member of the Wedding* as Mrs McCullers's best work to date.

Had it not been for the distraction caused by the war and by her worries over Reeves's safety, the book would doubtless have been finished earlier. But it was a difficult period, and with nobody certain what kind of news the next day was to bring there was a tendency for the stay-at-homes to live feverishly in the present, and to try to forget their worries as best they could. On June 25th, 1944, Carson re-ceived a cable from the War Department saying that Reeves had been wounded in action in France, and that details would follow. By the time she received them Reeves was back in action again; the wound, fortunately, had been a slight one. But she lived in an agony of suspense, and every time she saw a Western Union messen-ger she would tremble with fear.

The loss of her father this same year was a further source of de-pression: the Smith family, as has been said, were very close to one another, and Carson knew for the first time the experience of bereavement with which she was later to become so familiar. Following his death Mrs Smith sold the jewellery store and went to Nyack, where she and her two daughters (Rita was now working in New York as fiction editor of *Mademoiselle*) took an apartment at 127 South Broadway, whose back yard overlooked the Hudson River. It was a comfort to Carson to be with her mother and sister, and she also had at this time the consolation of five very dear friends: Henry Varnum Poor, the painter who lived at nearby New City; his wife, the novelist, Bessie Breuer; Elizabeth Ames, director of the Yaddo colony at Saratoga Springs, where Carson was a frequent guest; Gypsy Rose Lee, at whose house in Highland Mills, just outside New York, she also stayed occasionally; and novelist Kay Boyle, whose own husband was serving overseas and who lived with her three children in the city. Mrs Boyle, who because of her own experience well understood the torment that Carson was under-going at the time, dedicated to her her most recent book, a collection of poems (*American Citizen*).

Late in 1944, when staying at Yaddo, Carson received reassuring news of Reeves from his brother, Thomas McCullers, who had been shipped back to the States for hospitalization because of a stomach condition and who was able to give her a first-hand report: he had seen Reeves in England just before leaving, and he was in excellent shape. Nevertheless, she continued to worry. Just after this meeting with Reeves's brother, Carson wrote to Edwin from Yaddo:

> Here I am living in the same cabin I had one winter up here . . .
> The tension about Reeves is of course simply awful. But I have a superstitious feeling about this cabin, that helps me a little. It was here, that dreadful winter, that I first got the news about my friend Annemarie's death. And somehow I can't help remembering that lightning never strikes twice in the same place. So I feel better living here than I would elsewhere.

In December, Carson received another cable. Reeves had been wounded again, and once more she had to endure the suspense of waiting for the details.[1] His hand and wrist, she finally learned, had been smashed in a barrage on December 9th, and he had been sent to a hospital in England. Now they wrote to each other every day. Late in January she received a wire from him which almost made up for the many months of uncertainty and worry: it said merely MAY BE HOME, but the three words acted upon her like a charm, and she was able to work with a better will on *The Member of the Wedding*. In the evenings she read Henry James. 'I'd never realized how really good he is,' she wrote Reeves from Nyack. 'One is quite willing to stumble through pages of ambiguities for those sudden exquisite lines, those almost unexpected revelations . . . I want us to read "The Beast in the Jungle" together.' And in another letter:

> I'm making a pact with myself to finish this monstrous story[2] by March 15. This morning I worked several hours. But it's one of those works that the least slip can ruin. Some parts I have worked over and over as many as twenty times. I must finish it soon and get it out of my system—but at the same time it must be beautifully done. For, like a poem, there's not much excuse for it otherwise.

She continued:

> The Henry James could be very disheartening at this point. Some of the *nouvelles* are among the best I have ever read. I gawk over them like a child watching the trapeze lady at the fair. They are really supreme achievements.

[1] Though his injuries were minor, Reeves McCullers was actually wounded three times in 1944, so that this was the third time Carson endured the ordeal of waiting for the particulars.

[2] *The Member of the Wedding*.

In February, 1945, Reeves returned to the States. His wrist bones had not yet knitted properly, and the army doctors said that he would never be able to scramble in and out of fox-holes again. Carson was relieved to learn that he would be taken off combat duty, and shortly after he returned to keep their date at the Brevoort, she remarried him. On March 26th she wrote to Edwin:

> Reeves and I are asking for your blessings again. We were married legally this last time in New City.[3] There was no Edwin playing the Bach concerto on the gramophone: we were married in a court house by a black-robed judge. But we were happy again anyway.

By an extraordinary coincidence, one of the characters in *The Heart Is a Lonely Hunter* (Biff Brannon's sister, Lucile) also marries the same man a second time: what makes it so extraordinary is that this novel was written at least seven years before Reeves and Carson appeared before the 'black-robed judge' in New City, so that in a sense she was herself acting out the part she had assigned to Lucile in the book—a curious case of the fact's following upon the fiction. In the novel, Biff lectures his sister as follows:

> You married this certain party when you were seventeen, and afterwards there was just one racket between you after another. You divorced him. Then two years later you married him a second time. And now he's gone off again and you don't know where he is. It seems like those facts would show you one thing —you two are not suited to each other.

The passage is strangely prophetic, and Mrs McCullers would have been wise to ponder Biff's opinion.

2

The feeling of being excluded from something joyous and exciting is evident in both of Mrs McCullers's autobiographical novels: *The Heart Is a Lonely Hunter*, where, as has been shown, it figures only secondarily, and *The Member of the Wedding*, where it is central and all-pervading. The feeling can perhaps be traced back to an extremely early childhood experience which Mrs McCullers has described in an article in *Esquire* (December, 1959):

> When I was a child of about four, I was walking with my nurse

3 Near Nyack, in Rockland County—where her friends the Henry Varnum Poors lived.

past a convent. For once, the convent doors were open. And I saw the children eating ice-cream cones, playing on iron swings, and I watched, fascinated. I wanted to go in, but my nurse said no, I was not Catholic. The next day, the gate was shut. But year by year, I thought of what was going on, of this wonderful party, where I was shut out. I wanted to climb the wall, but I was too little. I beat on the wall once, and I knew all the time that there was a marvelous party going on, but I couldn't get in.

The attempt to 'get in', to join the 'marvelous party', is the real subject of *The Member of the Wedding*. 'I bet they have a good time every day,' says Frankie Addams enviously of her brother and his fiancée, just before their marriage.

Frankie is a gawky twelve-year-old tomboy who 'belonged to no club and was a member of nothing in this world . . . an unjoined person who hung around in doorways.' Doorways: that is, always on the threshhold of things, but never really inside them. For in adolescence the sense of isolation is very strong: one is no longer a child nor yet an adult, and even one's sexual identity is ambiguous (one remembers Biff Brannon's musings about Mick Kelly in the first novel). Adolescents do not *belong* anywhere, and thus constitute excellent symbols of spiritual loneliness. Frankie and Mick are symbols, just as are Singer, Antonapoulos, and Captain Penderton.

The story begins in late August, towards the end of a summer that has seemed 'like a green sick dream, or like a silent crazy jungle under glass'—a summer of infinite boredom which Frankie has spent hanging around the kitchen talking with Berenice Sadie Brown, the Negro cook, and John Henry, her six-year-old cousin. These are the only two companions she has in the world, as her mother is dead and her father spends most of his time at the jewellery shop:

> This was the summer when Frankie was sick and tired of being Frankie. She hated herself, and had become a loafer and a big no-good who hung around the summer kitchen: dirty and greedy and mean and sad.

The boredom is suddenly ended on the last Friday of the month, when her brother, Jarvis, an army corporal who has been stationed in Alaska, comes home to marry Janice, a girl from the nearby town of Winter Hill, and brings his fiancée to the house for dinner. This event produces an extraordinary effect upon Frankie; the wedding is to take place the following Sunday at Winter Hill, and she cannot put it out of her mind. She immediately packs her suitcase, and talks of nothing else. She is struck by the coincidence that Jarvis, after his stint in Alaska (which she imagines as being perpetually covered with snow) should marry a girl from a town named Winter Hill, and that both their names begin with the letters *Ja* Frankie decides that she too must have a name beginning with these letters, and finally hits upon F. Jasmine Addams, which has a glamorous sound to her. Though she does not realize it at the time, she is already seeking to identify herself with the pair. And very shortly after this decision concerning her name, realization does occur:

> Yesterday, and all the twelve years of her life, she had only been Frankie. She was an *I* person who had to walk around and do things by herself. All other people had a *we* to claim, all other except her. When Berenice said *we,* she meant Honey and Big Mamma, her lodge, or her church. The *we* of her father was the store. All members of clubs have a *we* to belong to and talk about. The soldiers in the army can say *we,* and even the criminals on chain-gangs.[4] But the old Frankie had had no *we* to claim, unless it would be the terrible summer *we* of her and John Henry and Berenice—and that was the last *we* in the world she wanted. Now all this was suddenly over with and changed.

Struck by this discovery of her new identity, she scarcely hears John Henry, who has asked in his 'high child voice': 'You want me to eat supper with you?' Though she has already invited him, she says shortly, 'No.' Her relationship with John Henry has suddenly become a thing of the past: 'For it was just at that moment that Frankie understood. She knew who she was and how she was going into the world. Her squeezed heart suddenly opened and divided. Her heart divided like two wings.' It is at this point that she conceives the fantastic notion of accompanying her brother and his bride on their honeymoon, and after that 'to whatever place they will ever go'.

When Frankie gets up the next morning, which is the day before the wedding, the world seems completely changed:

> Because of the wedding, F. Jasmine felt connected with all she saw, and it was as a sudden member that she went around the town . . . It was the day when, from the beginning, the world seemed no longer separate from herself and when all at once she felt included.

4 The chain gang as symbol is discussed in Chapter IX.

She feels strangely light-headed and giddy. The feeling of happiness is so strong within her that she has to share it, and she walks about confiding to strangers, who listen to her with astonishment, the news of the wedding and her plan to join the bride and groom. Among these strangers is a red-headed soldier whom she agrees to meet at nine o'clock that night in the Blue Moon Café. She spends the afternoon at home and eats dinner as usual with John Henry and Berenice, who warns her that her plan is doomed to disappointment. 'Two is company and three is a crowd,' she says, but Frankie declares that she will shoot herself if her brother and Janice refuse to take her with them. In the evening, excited at the thought of having a 'date', she goes out to meet the soldier. He invites her to accompany him to his room over the Blue Moon: she does so, but when he attempts familiarities she hits him over the head with a pitcher of water and escapes.

Sunday, the day of the wedding, Frankie accompanies her father, Berenice, and John Henry on the bus to Winter Hill, where things turn out even worse than Berenice predicted. She is treated like a child by the bride's parents and by the other guests, and has no opportunity to say what is in her heart:

> She stood in the corner of the bride's room, wanting to say: I love the two of you so much and you are the we of me. Please take me with you from the wedding for we belong to be together. Or even if she could have said: May I trouble you to step into the next room, as I have something to reveal to you and Jarvis? And get the three of them in a room alone together and somehow manage to explain. If only she had written it down on the typewriter in advance, so that she could hand it to them and they would read! But this she had not thought to do, and her tongue was heavy in her mouth and dumb.

After the ceremony she plants herself and her suitcase in the couple's car and causes a scandal by refusing to move:

> You are the we of me, her heart was saying, but she could only say aloud: 'Take me!' And they pleaded and begged with her, but she was already in the car. At the last she clung to the steering wheel until her father and somebody else had hauled and dropped her from the car, and even then she could only cry in the dust of the empty road: 'Take me! Take me!' But there was only the wedding company to hear, for the bride and her brother had driven away.

During the bus ride home Berenice and John Henry try to console her, but she refuses to let herself be comforted. That night, when everyone is in bed, she steals out of the house with her suitcase, planning to board a freight train. But the train is not due until two in the morning, and she wanders disconsolately about the deserted streets, finally going into the Blue Moon Café. Meanwhile her father (whom John Henry, seeing her leave the house, has awakened) alerts the police, who find her in the café.

Several weeks elapse between this incident and the final scene. There have been many changes: little John Henry is dead, after a ten-day struggle with meningitis; she and her father are moving to a house in the suburbs; Berenice is leaving to marry her fourth husband. And we meet a new Frankie, recently turned thirteen—a young lady who calls herself Frances, who insists that Berenice say 'braids' instead of 'pigtails', who is 'just mad about Michelangelo', who is uncertain whether she shall become a great poet or the world's foremost authority on radar, and who has a friend at last, Mary Littlejohn, with whom she is planning to travel around the world some day.

3

In Mrs McCullers's work, love is the means by which men attempt to escape from the bondage of the self: Frankie's longing to identify herself with her brother and his bride, to become a *we* person, reminds us of Captain Penderton's yearning to identify himself with the young soldiers in the barracks. Here, as in the earlier novels, fantasy compensates for reality. Frankie is, with all the awkward intensity of her age, seeking a love-object, but, just as Captain Penderton is only semi-conscious of the truth about his sexual nature, Frankie is also largely unconscious of the implications of her search. In her innocence, the possibility of love as a physical experience does not even occur to her, and her reaction, when the soldier tries to force his attentions upon her, is both swift and violent. This is the purpose of the incident in which he figures, an incident which, except for its humour, must otherwise appear rather pointless—to dramatize the difference between the meaning which love has for him, who thinks of it exclusively in physical terms, and the meaning which it has for the young girl, whose interest in it excludes whatever is not spiritual. All their encounters are expressive of this difference: while she speculates in the Blue Moon about the exciting foreign places to which he may be sent, he watches her, unhearing, with 'a peculiar expression' on his face—an expression she is still too young to recognize.

Parallelling the desire to escape from the prison of the self and to become identified spiritually with others is the desire to escape from familiar surroundings to places that are remote and exotic, so that in Mrs McCullers's novels spiritual love frequently has associations of high adventure, glamour, and excitement. Mick, in *The Heart Is a Lonely Hunter,* resentful of the lack of privacy in her parents' boarding house, creates an 'inside room' in her imagination, and dreams of giving concerts in foreign countries. In *Reflections in a Golden Eye* Captain Penderton, avoiding the flossy, cluttered living room which Leonora has decorated, thinks longingly of the enlisted men's barracks, of 'the hubbub of young male voices, the genial loafing in the sun, the irresponsible shenanigans of camaraderie.' And Frankie, in *The Member of the Wedding,* bored almost beyond endurance by Berenice and John Henry and by the 'ugly old kitchen' which is the scene of their conversations, keeps her suitcase packed in anticipation of the glamorous doings at Winter Hill and the voyages that she imagines are to follow.

But though she is sick to death of the 'ugly old kitchen', she is nevertheless reluctant to leave it for very long, as it is inhabited by the only two companions she has in the world. Again, more is meant here than meets the eye. Frankie's dependence on companions who bore her, who for one reason or another are unequipped to give her the release she desires, is actually the situation of most men, forced into an unhappy compromise between the ideal romantic relationships for which they long and those humdrum and unsatisfactory substitutes that are available to them. And for *kitchen,* read *world*—a monotonous and sordid world from which there is no escape for most of us. 'They sat together in the kitchen, and the kitchen was a sad and ugly room. . . And now the old kitchen made Frankie sick. The name for what had happened to her Frankie did not know, but she could feel her squeezed heart beating against the table edge. "The world is certainly a small place," she said.' Berenice asks her, 'What makes you say that?' and she cannot explain. But it is clear that Frankie here has connected the kitchen with the world: both are small places, and both are 'sad and ugly'. And from both of them there is no escape. (There is a certain superficial resemblance between the situation in this novel and that in Sartre's play, *Huis Clos* (*No Exit*), where three characters are condemned to bore one another throughout eternity in a single comfortably furnished room—an unorthodox but oddly convincing concept of Hell.) It is because Mr Eisinger fails to see how the microcosm of the kitchen corresponds to the macrocosm of the world that he objects, 'The limitations of the novel are in its focus on the child's self-centred world in which the macrocosm plays no part.'[5]

Though she is unconsciously seeking a love-object, it is not to a particular person that Frankie wishes to be joined; it is to something not only outside herself but also bigger than herself and more inclusive. She does not wish to be joined to a person but to *that which joins all people*—to the *we* of people. For this, a wedding is of course exactly the right symbol. And what she has fallen in love with is an *idea*, the idea of the wedding. Berenice, whose wisdom is of the earth, remarks: 'I have seen many a peculiar thing in my day. But one thing I never knew and never heard tell about . . . I never in all my days heard of anybody falling in love with a wedding.' But Frankie is seeking nothing less than the common denominator of all humanity. Elsewhere she says: 'All these people and you don't know what joins them up. There's bound to be some sort of reason or connection. Yet somehow I don't know.' And Berenice answers her: 'If you did you would be God. Didn't you know that?'

What Frankie experiences on the day before the wedding, when she is conscious of a 'connection' between herself and people she has never seen before, is also what the tramp in 'A Tree, a Rock, a Cloud' has experienced: 'I meet a traveler on the road. Everything, Son. And anybody. All stranger and all loved!' As Mr Baldanza comments:

> What Frankie learns, and what Berenice knows only very fleetingly, is a nearly mystical conviction of 'connections' with all sorts of random people seen casually on the street—precisely what Walt Whitman feels on the Brooklyn ferry and what Virginia Woolf's Mrs Dalloway feels in her meanderings on London streets. In Platonic terminology, she has begun to experience love as an absolute.[6]

Frankie's desire to identify with the world at large assumes the proportions of a monomania. She wants to donate a quart of blood to the Red Cross every week so that it 'would be in the veins of Australians and Fighting French and Chinese, all over the whole world, and it would be as though she were close kin to all of these people.' When she is turned down because of her age, she is heartbroken. Her fantasies come to a climax in a scene towards the end

5 Op. cit., pp. 255-256.
6 Op. cit., pp. 160-161.

of Part Two, when, envisioning her future life with Jarvis and Janice, she works herself into a perfect frenzy of anticipation :

> We will have thousands of friends, thousands and thousands and thousands of friends. We will belong to so many clubs that we can't even keep track of all of them. We will be members of the whole world. Boyoman! Manoboy!

Heroically Frankie hammers against the walls that threaten to confine her. In an early scene, after the pair have come for dinner and gone away again, she follows them in her mind :

> She could feel them leaving her. She could feel the two of them together on the train, riding and riding away from her. They were them, and leaving her, and she was her, and sitting left all by herself at the kitchen table.

Later, she asks Berenice :

> Doesn't it strike you as strange that I am I, and you are you? I am F. Jasmine Addams. And you are Berenice Sadie Brown. And we can look at each other, and stay together year in and year out in the same room. Yet always I am I, and you are you. And I can't ever be anything else but me, and you can't ever be anything else but you.

Patiently Berenice explains that everyone is 'caught' in some way : 'We all of us somehow caught. We born this way or that way and we don't know why. But we caught anyhow.' She goes on to say that she is less fortunate than Frankie, for she is caught in two ways : first, 'as all human beings is,' and, secondly, because she is a Negro. 'When I was with Ludie,' she reminisces about her first husband, 'I didn't feel so caught,' and in this statement the reader will recognize at once the familiar McCullers thesis that only love has the power to free men from the cells of their being.

But love not only enables men to escape the fate of isolation, so that for the time they love they are happy, even though they may be unloved in return—it is also their only means of acquiring an individual identity. Paradoxically, it is only by identifying themselves with something outside themselves that they acquire selfhood. This is a paradox which Mrs McCullers explores more fully in *Clock Without Hands,* but she has been concerned with it from the beginning of her career. When Antonapoulos dies, Singer loses his identity; the death of his physical self is merely anticlimactic. Similarly, for as long as Frankie remains an 'I' person she lacks identity;

the moment she thinks of herself as having a 'we' she begins to know 'who she is' and 'where she is going.' When she tells Berenice of her plan to change her name, Berenice objects that names are not to be taken lightly, that 'things accumulate' around them, and Frankie asks: 'But what has accumulated around my old name? Nothing!' Berenice reminds her that she finished in the B section of the seventh grade and found the golden egg at the Baptist Easter Hunt, but Frankie interrupts her impatiently: 'But those things are nothing. See? They're not worth while. Nothing ever happened to me.' Now, on the other hand, something is about to happen to her, something that will give her an identity: she will become a member of the wedding.

In the past, Frankie has from time to time assumed a number of false selves. She would sit at her father's work-bench wearing his glasses with the jeweller's loupe attached and pretend for the benefit of passers-by that she understood the art of watch repairing. Or she would wear a sombrero and go around pretending that she was a Mexican:

> Me no speak English—Adios Buenos Noches—abla pokie peekie poo, she had jabbered in mock Mexican. Sometimes a little crowd of children gathered and the old Frankie would swell up with pride and trickery—but when the game was over, and she was home, there would come over her a cheated discontent.

Now these games of her childhood are finished, and she is consumed with a desire to be known for her true self.

The urgency of Frankie's desire to become a 'we' person may be measured by her refusal to dwell for a single moment on the possibility that Jarvis and Janice will not wish to share their honeymoon with her. This possibility is so dreadful that, in spite of Berenice's warnings, she simply cannot acknowledge that it is a possibility at all—much as Mick, up until the moment she is obliged to go to work at the dime store, clings pathetically to her dreams of the concert hall, and as Madame Zilensky cherishes her fantasy involving the King of Finland. When the reality of the situation finally forces itself upon her, it is all the more painful for the resistance with which she has opposed it.

Both *The Member of the Wedding* and *The Heart Is a Lonely Hunter* involve the initiation of an adolescent into adulthood, and in both novels the ritual accompanying the initiation ends in failure. One remembers the party which Mick Kelly plans so carefully, a party she is determined shall be 'grown-up', and which nevertheless ends in a free-for-all. Frankie's elaborate preparations for the wedding—the silver slippers and orange satin evening gown—recall the high-heeled pumps and the rhinestone tiara (which gets lost in the fight) that Mick dons for her party. But whereas Mick, in the excitement of the scuffle, is able to revert to her old adolescent self and forget her festive encumbrances, Frankie, whose spiritual investment is more extravagant, is left stranded.

The theme of social justice, which loomed so large in the first novel, is in this one merely suggested, and here, as in the other, Negro-white relations provide the context. Berenice's foster brother, Honey, a 'sick, loose person' who has been physically broken by labour in a gravel pit and rejected by the army, acquires a drug habit, and the source of his supply, the 'pusher', is a white man, a druggist. One night, after he has been smoking marijuana, he breaks into the white man's shop in a desperate attempt to steal more drugs. When last we hear of him he is being held incommunicado in the local jail while Berenice bustles about trying to raise money to see a lawyer.

Yet another theme, one which will become increasingly prominent in Mrs McCullers's work (it appears in the short story, 'The Sojourner', in the play *The Square Root of Wonderful,* in miscellaneous poems written between 1948 and 1952, and in the latest novel, *Clock Without Hands*) is that of time. Its relation to the theme of identity is obvious, and we have noted how, even as a child, she wondered whether 'the *I* of the tree and the August afternoon would be the same *I* of winter, firelight, and the Christmas tree.' But Frankie is the first of Mrs McCullers's characters to ponder consciously the enormous problem:

> I wonder if you have ever thought about time. Here we are—right now. This very minute. Now. But while we're talking right now, this minute is passing. And it will never come again. Never in all the world. When it is gone it is gone. No power on earth could bring it back again. It is gone. Have you ever thought about that?

4

Berenice and John Henry represent the two worlds (of experience and innocence respectively) between which Frankie darts uncertainly back and forth, feeling at home in neither. Berenice, whose resemblance to Portia in the first novel is immediately obvious,[7] is the

[7] Mrs McCullers has said that both of them, though composite portraits of Negro servants in the Smith household, have an affinity with Dilsey, in Faulkner's *The Sound and the Fury.*

mouthpiece for Mrs McCullers's theory: she is the Socrates of the novel. She has a bright blue glass eye, and, as Mr Baldanza has commented, her spiritual vision is the keener for this physical defect—just as the spiritual eloquence of Singer, the mute, is greater than that of any other character in *The Heart Is a Lonely Hunter*. One of the things her experience has taught her is that anyone, no matter how unattractive he may seem to others, can be the object of love—that, as Mrs McCullers says in *The Ballad of the Sad Café*, 'the value and quality of any love is determined by the lover himself'. Berenice tells Frankie:

> I have knew mens to fall in love with girls so ugly that you wonder if their eyes is straight. I have seen some of the most peculiar weddings anybody could conjecture . . . I have knew womens to love veritable Satans and thank Jesus when they put their split hooves over the threshold. I have knew boys to take it into their heads to fall in love with other boys.

Another thing Berenice has learned from her experience is that a love which is completely successful can never be duplicated or repeated. Though she has had three husbands, the first (Ludie) was the only one who brought her happiness. Ludie's thumb had been mashed in a hinge, and the year after his death, when Berenice was sitting in church, she noticed a man whose thumb resembled Ludie's: 'I felt drawn to him on account of the thumb. And then one thing led to another. First thing I knew I married him.' But nothing else about her second husband resembled Ludie, as she discovered too late, when he 'went crazy' and she had to leave him. After Ludie's death Berenice had sold his clothes to a second-hand dealer in order to pay for the funeral, and one day, after she left her second husband, she saw a man in the street who was wearing Ludie's old coat:

> He had chanced to buy Ludie's coat and he was built on the same shape as Ludie. And from the back view it looked like he was Ludie's ghost or Ludie's twin. But how I married him I don't exactly know, for to begin with it was clear that he did not have his share of sense.

Berenice has insight (or rather hindsight) into her situation, for she explains to Frankie:

> I loved Ludie and he was the first man I loved. Therefore, I had to go and copy myself forever afterward. What I did was to marry off little pieces of Ludie whenever I came across them.

It was just my misfortune they all turned out to be the wrong pieces. My intention was to repeat me and Ludie.

Mr Baldanza, characteristically, interprets Berenice's behaviour from the point of view of Platonism, maintaining that it is 'a direct duplication of the essentials of Aristophanes' speech in *Symposium*' :

> It will be remembered that Aristophanes maintains that at one time each human being was a double creature with two heads, four arms and legs, and the like; and that Zeus, in a moment of fury, punished mankind by splitting each creature in two; Aristophanes interprets the frenzied search of humans for love simply as a pursuit of one's other half-soul; as a consequence, obviously, success and failure in love are dependent on whether or not one actually finds the other half of his soul in the beloved. Thus love is synonymous, almost mathematically, with wholeness. Berenice extols her ecstatic first marriage to Ludie Freeman as a transfiguring experience. After his death, however, repeated attempts to duplicate her relation failed . . . She was reversing the Platonic theory by continuing the search after Ludie's death because supposedly once she had found the other half of her soul in Ludie, there would be no second chance, short of reincarnation.[8]

This is yet another element which romantic love inherits from Platonism : the idea that for every lover there is one (and only one) individual who is uniquely qualified to be loved by him—to be, quite literally, his 'soul mate'. Berenice here sets the pattern which old Judge Clane will follow several years later in *Clock Without Hands*: when his wife, whom he has loved passionately and who has sung in a choir, dies, he frequents various churches looking for choir singers who resemble her in particular ways. Berenice's present suitor is T. T. Williams, who owns a coloured restaurant, and Frankie, tired of always receiving advice and never giving any, urges her to accept his offer of marriage : 'I think you ought to quit worrying about beaus and be content with T.T. I bet you are forty years old. It is time for you to settle down.' But Berenice bristles : 'I got as much right as anybody else to continue to have a good time so long as I can. And as far as that goes, I'm not so old as some people would try to make out. I can still ministrate.' T. T., she says, is 'a fine upstanding colored gentleman. But he don't make me shiver none.'

As for John Henry, his immersion in the fantasy world of childhood is demonstrated by his refusal to abide by the rules of the

8   Op. cit., pp. 159-160.

card games with which the three characters while away the long
hours in the kitchen. 'He is a child!' Frankie exclaims despairingly
when he refuses to sacrifice his jack to her queen. 'He don't
even follow the beginning laws. It is hopeless!' But John
Henry is as secure in his world as Berenice is in hers: it is
Frankie, torn between the two, who suffers. Hers, as Mr Vickery
observes, are 'the contradictory emotions of the adolescent who
wishes both to explore the alluring mysteries of the adult world and
to retain the comprehensible familiarities of childhood.'[9] A case in
point is her adventure with the soldier, who, as we have seen, represents the physical aspect of love. Mr Baldanza shrewdly suggests that
Frankie's choice of a new friend of her own sex (Mary Littlejohn)
at the end of the book may be interpreted as a recoil from this experience:

> The aura of physical passion is represented by the drunken
> soldier with whom F. Jasmine becomes innocently involved on
> the eve of the wedding; her perilously close escape from seduc-
> tion crystallizes later into a vague awareness of the meaning of
> desire, and almost as in a revulsion against the knowledge, she
> finds a new friend, Mary Littlejohn, to whom she becomes
> strongly attached.[10]

A similar aversion to the physical aspect of love is seen in her
reluctance to accept the knowledge, passed on to her by neighbourhood children, of the 'facts of life' (which she labels 'nasty lies').

Besides the soldier, two other minor characters are of special
interest: the Portuguese bartender and the monkey man. The bartender—the third such whom we have met in Mrs McCullers's
fiction—more nearly resembles Biff Brannon than the sinister fellow
in 'A Tree, a Rock, a Cloud'. Unlike Biff, however, he is not an
active participant but *merely* an observer. Also, while Biff is a sympathetic character, and the other bartender is antipathetic, the Portuguese remains an enigma. We know Biff's thoughts because Mrs
McCullers enters his mind, and we know what the proprietor of the
diner is like because of his speeches and actions, but the Portuguese
bartender is inscrutable, a mystery to the end. What is his reaction
to Frankie's recital? Is he bored? Is he amused, cynically or otherwise? Does he have, like Biff, a protective feeling towards her?
There is no way of knowing; we are told merely that he looks
'startled'. He is associated, of course, with the Blue Moon, and the

9   Op. cit., p. 22.
10   Op. cit., p. 159.

café here does not have the same symbolic function that it does in *The Heart Is a Lonely Hunter* and *The Ballad of the Sad Café*, where it is a microcosm of the world at large. Here it is *a* world rather than *the* world, a sleazy, dimly-lit world of loud juke music, drunken conversations, and illicit sexual encounters—a world, in short, of evil. And yet towards Frankie the proprietor of this world seems polite, even attentive, and obviously harbours no ulterior motive. The reader, it is true, does feel slightly apprehensive about Frankie when she is in his company, but the feeling is justified only because of the appearance and reputation of the place—not because of anything the bartender says or does. It ought perhaps to be pointed out, in passing, that it is not always easy to justify the existence of Mrs McCullers's minor characters merely in terms of what we know about them; the reader will sometimes feel they belong in the book without quite knowing why. (Another example of this in *The Member of the Wedding* is the monkey man.) On the other hand, where major characters are concerned, a reluctance to define them can—as we have seen in the case of Antonapoulos—be ill advised.

The remaining main characters are Frankie's father, Royal Quincy Addams, who is allowed only a few speeches (they are addressed to Frankie and are mainly of an admonitory character) and Big Mama, the ancient Negro fortune teller whom Frankie consults about her future and whose chief function, apart from supplying a touch of the supernatural and a bit of local colour, is to predict the outcome of Frankie's trip to Winter Hill. It is to her that Frankie confides the dream she has had earlier in the summer, and which has haunted her ever since: of a door opening slowly. Big Mama interprets it, accurately enough, as meaning there will be a 'change' in her life.

5

Any discussion of *The Member of the Wedding* would be incomplete that did not mention its musical elements. These are not merely a matter of structure, though it is true that here, as in the first novel, themes are suggested, stated, and restated in the manner of a sonata or a symphony and the story contains a coda—the short scene which, occurring several months after the main action, introduces us to the young lady whose name is Frances. More than this, the whole atmosphere of the book is charged with musical meanings. The dialogue is full of strategic repetitions which suggest refrains in music, and the total effect is reminiscent of the group-singing of certain folk ballads in the South. Again and again the speeches are likened to songs, or chants. 'They talked,' writes Mrs McCullers, 'and their voices tired down into a little tune and they said the same things over and over . . . So that now the words were like an ugly little tune they sang by heart.' Berenice speaks with a 'dark jazz voice that was like a song', and when she begins the recital of her love life 'the words flowed one into the other and her voice began to sing.' When she talks about the sorrows of her race 'her voice was a strong deep song that soared and sang in beautiful dark tones leaving an echo in the corners of the room that trembled for a long time until silence.'

Sometimes, instead of talking, the three main characters actually do sing together:

> Often in the dark, that August, they would all at once begin to sing a Christmas carol, or a song like the Slitbelly Blues. Sometimes they knew in advance that they would sing, and they would agree on a tune among themselves. Or again, they would disagree and start off on three different songs at once, until at last the tunes began to merge and they sang a special music that the three of them made up together. John Henry sang in a high wailing voice, and no matter what he named his tune, it sounded always just the same: one high trembling note that hung like a musical ceiling over the rest of the song. Berenice's voice was dark and definite and deep, and she rapped the offbeats with her heel. The old Frankie sang up and down the middle space between John Henry and Berenice, so that their voices were joined, and the parts of the song were woven together. Often they would sing like this and their tunes were sweet and queer in the August kitchen after it was dark.

That Frankie's voice should sing 'up and down the middle space' is, of course, appropriate in view of her relationship to the other two characters.

Other incidents involving specific musical sounds occur throughout the novel. The most important of these is the piano-tuning episode in Part Two. While Frankie and Berenice and John Henry are in the kitchen having their supper, they hear the nerve-racking sound of an 'August piano' being tuned by Mr Schwarzenbach,[11] the local specialist:

> In a dreaming way a chain of chords climbed slowly upward like a flight of castle stairs: but just at the end, where the

11   It may be a coincidence that this is also the name of the friend to whom Mrs McCullers dedicated *Reflections in a Golden Eye*. (See Chapter V.)

eighth chord should have sounded and the scale made complete, there was a stop. This next to the last chord was repeated. The seventh chord, which seems to echo all of the unfinished scale, struck and insisted again and again.

Over and over the performance is repeated, until even little John Henry winces and Frankie says, 'It almost makes me wonder if he does that just to torment us.' The emphasis given to this scene suggests that it is intended to have a symbolic meaning, and indeed the monotonous-sounding chords which ascend without reaching a climax or a resolution are like the experience of the whole 'green and crazy summer' which Frankie is so anxious to leave behind her: she too is mounting towards a climax which, in this scene, has not yet occurred, and she is waiting for it with the same feeling of suspense with which she waits for Mr Schwarzenbach to complete his scale. Earlier, in Part One, she listens to the sound of a Negro playing a blues tune on a horn. In this scene Mrs McCullers directly connects the music with the 'green and crazy summer' which Frankie is so anxious to leave behind her: it is, she writes, 'like the telling of that long season of trouble.' And here too the tune is left uncompleted:

> Just at the time when the tune should be laid, the music finished, the horn broke off. All of a sudden the horn stopped playing . . . The tune was left broken, unfinished.

The function of the music which the monkey man plays on his organ is less easy to analyze. It—and he—are somehow associated with Frankie's childhood and with the season of summer (he goes south to Florida in the winter). But this summer she has not seen him, and when at last she hears the organ it strikes her as appropriate that they should meet again on what she imagines is her last day in town. On the level of symbol it is therefore with the purpose of bidding him (and what he represents) a final farewell that she searches for him as she does. There is also about the monkey man a slight suggestion of fantasy that is appropriate if we accept him as a reminder of childhood—a sort of Pied Piper, possibly, with even, perhaps, a touch of Pan about him, and this latter identity seems all the more plausible when we consider that he is present at her meeting with the soldier who personifies the carnal principle.

It has been mentioned that the speeches of the characters, with their curious repetitions, have the quality of a folk ballad, and in this connection one cannot fail to be impressed by the frequency with which the number three (a favourite with ballad-makers) occurs throughout. There are three main characters; the book is divided into three parts; the main action occupies three days; the protagonist has three successive identities (Frankie, F. Jasmine, Frances); Berenice has been married three times; when Berenice says to Frankie, 'I can see right through them two gray eyes of yours like they was glass,' John Henry says 'Gray eyes is glass' three times; and in the same scene the three characters sigh three times: 'F. Jasmine took her fingers from her ears and breathed a long sigh. When she had sighed, John Henry sighed also, and Berenice concluded with the longest sigh of all.' The dominance of this number, in addition to enhancing the ballad-like quality of the novel, makes for an unusual symmetry in it as well, and helps to give definite form to a story that, from a purely narrative point of view, may occasionally appear to ramble.

6

Almost exactly a year after Mrs McCullers remarried Reeves, the book which she had written largely in his absence—and which, as we have seen, gave her such difficulty—made its appearance. It was dedicated to her friend Elizabeth Ames at Yaddo, where it had been partly written. Eagerly they awaited the reviews, nor, for the most part, were they disappointed. In a full-page article in *The Saturday Review of Literature*, George Dangerfield wrote enthusiastically:

> While there are quite a few writers who unfortunately resemble Mrs McCullers, she fortunately resembles no one else. She is unique . . . Nothing occurs here, and yet every page is filled with a sense of something having happened, happening, and about to happen. This is in itself a considerable technical feat; and, beyond that, there is magic in it . . . This is, to my mind, a marvelous piece of writing. Not merely does it sustain the interest all the way through, but it does so under circumstances which demand the utmost delicacy and balance from the author . . . It is a work which reveals a strong, courageous and independent imagination.[12]

Comparing the author with Thomas Wolfe, Isa Kapp, in *The New York Times*, was scarcely less enthusiastic. 'Rarely has emotional turbulence been so delicately conveyed,' she exclaimed. 'Mrs McCullers's language has the freshness, quaintness and gentleness of a sensitive child.'[13] Richard Match, in *The New York Herald-*

[12]   30th March 1946, p. 15.
[13]   24th March 1946, p. 5.

Tribune, while praising the writing for its intensity, suggested that it lacked breadth, and objected that the kitchen setting produced a 'static effect'.[14] In *Commonweal*, Francis Downing wrote approvingly: 'That Mrs McCullers is writing about the central fact of life— the problem of human loneliness—is as overt as this hinting writer ever makes anything overt.'[15] But Diana Trilling, in *The Nation*, felt that the author had identified herself too closely with the protagonist, and did not keep the proper aesthetic distance between her and her characters as did Proust in *Swann's Way*, Mark Twain in *Huckleberry Finn*, and Elizabeth Bowen in *The Death of the Heart*.[16]

The strongest negative verdict on the u.s. side of the Atlantic, however, was rendered by none other than Edmund Wilson, who, in an extraordinary review in *The New Yorker*, committed what must surely be one of the biggest blunders in a generally distinguished career. There is, he wrote, 'no element of drama at all' in the book: 'The scenes have no internal structure and do not add up to anything. The whole story seems utterly pointless.'[17] In justice to Mr Wilson, however, it should perhaps be pointed out that, as though a bit uneasy about this judgment, he added: 'I hope that I am not being stupid about this book.' That he did not read it very carefully, even on the level of fact, is evident from his objection that we never learn the fate of the soldier whom Frankie hits over the head with the water pitcher: 'The reader assumes that the man must have survived or something would have been heard about him.' Something, of course, *is* heard about him—just enough to let us know he has 'survived', for Mrs McCullers does this sort of thing delicately and the soldier in any case has served his purpose. In the Blue Moon Café, when Frankie is waiting for her father to come for her, we are told:

> A soldier banged the screen door and walked through the café, and only the distant stranger in her recognized him; when he had climbed up the stairs, she only thought slowly and with no feeling that a curly red head such as that one was like cement.

Only one critic, this time, revived the old charge of obsession with abnormality—a charge which, as I have shown in earlier chapters, proceeds primarily from an ignorance of Mrs McCullers's intentions. Nothing more unwholesome than the growing pains of adolescence

14   24th March 1946, p. 5.
15   24th May 1946, p. 148.
16   6th April 1946, p. 406.
17   30th March 1946, p. 87.

is the subject of *The Member of the Wedding*, and it must have been depressing for her to read what Joseph Frank wrote in *The Sewanee Review*: 'Mrs McCullers is fascinated by the revolting and perverse to an almost morbid extent . . . John Henry is a monster . . . Frankie herself . . . is not exactly one's idea of an average American girl, even an adolescent.'[18] Mr Frank, however, found Berenice a 'profoundly impressive character' in spite of 'all her absurdity' and added benevolently: 'If Miss McCullers can continue to create similar ones, and, like Dostoyevsky, place them in a situation where their very grotesqueness takes on symbolic value, then American literature may find itself with a really important writer on its hands.'

It was in England, oddly enough, that the new novel received its worst reviews—a circumstance that may partly be accounted for by the fact that the rhythms of Southern speech which Mrs McCullers reproduces so faithfully in the book and upon which it depends so heavily for its effect (a very large part of it consists of dialogue) are unique and indigenous; they do not transplant readily to British soil. Wrote *The Times Literary Supplement*:

> Two previous novels by Miss McCullers met with exclamatory and disproportionate praise both in America and in this country.[19] The story has its humorous felicities, even though they are a shade too deliberately contrived, but too seldom leaves an impression of considered imaginative experience . . . Her unusual exploration of doubtful depths and her addiction to the prettily whimsical both tend in this instance to falsify character.[20]

D. S. Savage, in *Spectator*, was even less charitable:

> I wish I could say that this was a 'sensitive' study, but it appears to me to be remarkably insensitive, written in a clogged and turgid prose reminiscent of the worst of Faulkner and Gertrude Stein, with not a single clear visual image or pure emotional perception.[21]

Although his opinion of the book was generally unfavourable, Robin King, in *The New Statesman and Nation*, made an interesting comparison between it and Coleridge's *Rime of the Ancient Mariner*:

18 Summer 1946, p. 537.
19 A sampling of the British reviews, from some of which I have already quoted, scarcely supports this assertion.
20 15th March 1947, p. 113.
21 7th March 1947, p. 250.

One has learned to expect anything in the way of precocious children from America, but Frankie Addams is surely the strangest little monster who ever opened her eyes to a bottle of coca-cola . . . she loses all probability and becomes, instead, a female version of the *Ancient Mariner*. She goes about the town 'stopping one in three'—a Portuguese bartender, a lady cleaning her steps, a tractor man, and a red-haired soldier—and proceeds to tell these people about the wedding. One almost expects an albatross. What Miss McCullers is driving at is hard to understand, and where she will end up is hard to say.[22]

The resemblance between Coleridge's poem and Mrs McCullers's short story, 'A Tree, a Rock, a Cloud', has been discussed in the preceding chapter; it is, of course, much greater than in the case of the novel. Nevertheless, Mr King is on the right track, for Frankie, like the Ancient Mariner—and like the tramp in the above-mentioned story—has, on the morning that she becomes conscious of a 'connection' binding her to others, become joined to that which, in Neoplatonic doctrine, joins all men to one another and to God.

What was by far the most thorough and perceptive review of *The Member of the Wedding*—in England or America—appeared in the distinguished literary quarterly, *The Kenyon Review*,[23] in the winter of 1947. Written by Marguerite Young, a brilliant young poet, critic and novelist with an academic background in philosophy as well as literature, it represents the first really serious full-scale attempt to analyze Mrs McCullers's artistic intentions and to estimate what was at that time her total achievement.[24] In this essay, entitled 'Metaphysical Fiction', Miss Young first disposed of the charge of sensationalism:

> Mrs McCullers, sometimes depicted as a sensationalist revelling in the grotesque, is more than that because she is first of all the poetic symbolist, a seeker after those luminous meanings which always do transcend the boundaries of the stereotyped, the conventional, and the so-called normal.[25]

22   5th April 1947, p. 242.

23   Published at Kenyon College, Gambier, Ohio.

24   Because it was not so widely read as Tennessee Williams's defence of Mrs McCullers in his Introduction to the New Directions reprint of *Reflections in a Golden Eye*, in which he acclaimed her as a major talent, this is not generally realized. But Miss Young's appreciation was published three years before Mr Williams's.

25   Winter 1947, p. 153.

She followed this by a discussion of Mrs McCullers's characteristic technique:

> Though its themes are romantic, their working out is classically controlled. There is no wilderness for the reader to get lost in, and if he is lost, it is perhaps because this writing does not weep, groan, wail, shout, wear its heart on its sleeve. It is rather like a chess game, where every move is a symbol and requires the reader's counter-move. Many modern poems[26] are of this order.

Miss Young was the first critic to perceive that Mrs McCullers is essentially a didactic writer, and to suggest comparisons with Bunyan and Sterne:

> Narrative and allegory are the two-headed flower growing from one stem, and if this is a Pilgrim's Progress backward to the cold and unintelligent and unintelligible universe suggested in Matthew Arnold's popular poem, it is still a pilgrim's progress, modernistic, aware of no simple definition of good and evil. The argument, though veiled by diverse imagery, is never lost. The imagery is functional. In fact, if there is any one statement to define Mrs McCullers's position as a writer, it is not that she is merely the sensationalist but that she is also, like Sterne, the preacher, concerned with theories of knowledge—though the by-play of wit does not entice her away from the main theme. The framework is always visible.

She also shrewdly located the reason why many critics found it difficult to accept this author's vision of life:

> People want to be told what they already believe, and Mrs McCullers, in this case, is not telling most people what they already believe. Rather, she is continually questioning a great many complacent assumptions as to what is what, for she is too closely skeptical and analytical a writer to suppose that in accepted platitudes lies truth. She weighs, she measures. Wild idealism does not carry her beyond the boundaries of a rigorous common sense world, partly for the reason that she finds the world itself a sufficient phantasmagoria of lost events. Her attitude towards human nature is patient, behaviorist, clinical. Her writing, brooding and exploratory though it is, remains for these reasons as formal as a problem in geometry, though the perspectives bewilderingly and constantly shift. She sees life as

[26] That Mrs McCullers, while writing *The Member of the Wedding*, thought of it as a poem is evident from the letter to Reeves, quoted earlier in this chapter.

an impressionist, but she herself is not the impressionist. She is a logician in an illogical realm.

Perceiving an analogy between the 'illogical realm' of life and the game which the three characters attempt to play with missing cards, she declared:

> Some of the cards are, though they do not know it, missing from the very beginning, maybe like those cards which God threw down at creation—and maybe that is why nothing ever turns out right, why there are expectation and disappointment.

In fact Miss Young's chief service to Mrs McCullers, apart from establishing the fact that she is a serious writer employing the allegorical mode, has been to define the nature and the quality of her pessimism:

> Is there a given pattern in the nature of things, a music of the spheres, or was it all, as Mrs McCullers implies, accident and chaos and fragment to begin with? Mrs McCullers, speculative like her characters, dreams of an omniscient pattern but finds that such a pattern is rather more man's project than God's and that its realization may comprise another chaos.

The idea that 'some of the cards are missing' in the world as Mrs McCullers views it has more recently been expressed by Wayne D. Dodd, who, writing of *The Member of the Wedding,* said:

> The characters talk about how each would remake the world if he were God. Each would fashion it from his limited point of view, so that seen from any other point of view it would be grotesque. All this, when paralleled with the fact that Honey Brown is described as only partially finished ('The Creator had withdrawn His hand too soon. God had not finished him.') and that the continuing tuning of the piano is never completed, so that Frankie and Berenice are always left hanging, just short of the finished scale, establishes the thematic significance of this motif: the world is somehow unfinished, incomplete. Thus once again we can see a reason for the inability of men finally to communicate.[27]

7

The general feeling among critics was that *The Member of the Wedding* was Mrs McCullers's most 'wholesome' book. It is true

27 *The Georgia Review*, Summer 1963, p. 209.

that her main character is more 'normal', say, than Captain Penderton, but is not this merely another way of saying that adolescence is
a more socially acceptable badge of isolation than homosexuality?
Frankie, at any rate, is perfectly conscious of her affinity with the
freaks at the Fair Grounds—the Half-Man, Half-Woman; the Pin-
head; the Midget; and so on: 'She was afraid of all the Freaks, for
it seemed to her that they had looked at her in a special way and
tried to connect[28] their eyes with hers, as though to say: We know
you. She was afraid of their long Freak eyes.' Because of her height,
which is excessive for her age, Frankie is afraid that she too will
grow up to be a freak.

Other allusions to abnormality occur throughout: Frankie has
committed, in the spring, a 'queer sin' with Barry MacKean in the
MacKeans' garage, and Berenice tells Frankie about the strange
case of Lily Mae Jenkins, the Negro who, 'to all intents and purposes', changed his sex and turned into a girl. But these allusions
are carefully controlled; they are, moreover, by no means irrelevant,
for they serve as reminders that Mrs McCullers is writing, here as in
her earlier work, about the condition of isolation. One might expect
to find them, for that matter, even in the ordinary slice-of-life type
of story, where the question would be merely one of proportion,
since the abnormal is certainly present in life.

Some critics also felt that, because Frankie recovers so quickly
from her disappointment, *The Member of the Wedding* ends on a
more 'positive' note and is generally more affirmative than the
earlier novels. But a thoughtful reader will wonder if Frankie at the
end of the story is not merely replacing one impossible ambition
with another: how likely are her dreams of becoming a great poet
or the world's 'foremost authority on radar'—or even of travelling
around the world with Mary Littlejohn—to be realized? Their resemblance to Mick Kelly's dream of becoming a concert pianist is
all too apparent; when they collapse, or when she outgrows them,
others will take their place, and so on. The materials of the dream
will change, but not the necessity for it, and this I take to be the
implication of the coda. Few things, as I have shown, are so typical
of Mrs McCullers's characters as this necessity to compensate, in
dreams and illusions, for the imperfections and dissatisfactions of
the real world.

As for the other characters, they fare even worse. John Henry dies
a peculiarly painful death which Berenice regards as a judgment on

---

[28] This kind of 'connection', which exists among outcasts, serves as a sort
of counterpoint to the connection theme which occurs later, in Part Two.

her from the Lord: when, at the beginning of his illness, he complained to her of a headache, she (who was worried about Honey at the time) did not take him seriously. It may be observed in passing that John Henry's death disturbed a good many readers, and even some critics have wondered whether or not it was 'necessary'. I suspect that this attitude (which is actually proof of the power with which Mrs McCullers secures her effect) is a form of emotional cowardice, and springs from a reluctance to accept what is painful in fiction—the implication being that while we are forced to submit to it in life we are not so obliged in fiction, where, if we wish, we can lay the book aside for one which is easier on the feelings. Nevertheless, it is not difficult to show that John Henry's death is consistent with the logic of the story: it emphasizes the sense of universal meaninglessness and chaos which, as Miss Young has pointed out, dominates the novel. It is precisely in order to make the reader ask 'Why?' that Mrs McCullers causes this child, who is one of the most sympathetic of all her characters, to die such a painful death. Berenice, in her simplicity, thinks that God is punishing her thereby; she must find a *reason* for the child's death, and it never occurs to her that there may be none. The brand of Mrs McCullers's naturalism here is very similar to that of Stephen Crane in 'The Open Boat':

> When it occurs to a man that nature does not regard him as important, and that she feels she would not maim the universe by disposing of him, he at first wishes to throw bricks at the temple, and he hates deeply the fact that there are no bricks and no temples.

And again:

> The boat was headed for the beach. The correspondent wondered if none ever ascended the tall wind-tower, and if then they never looked seaward. This tower was a giant, standing with its back to the plight of the ants. It represented in a degree, to the correspondent, the serenity of nature amid the struggles of the individual—nature in the wind, and nature in the vision of men. She did not seem cruel to him, then, nor beneficent, nor treacherous, nor wise. But she was indifferent, flatly indifferent.

Structurally, too, John Henry's death serves a purpose, since he is identified with Frankie's childhood, the period she has left behind her, so that the child's death parallels and dramatizes the death in her of this early identity.

Berenice also, her dream of finding another Ludie forever ended, is planning a compromise we have been led not to expect of her: a loveless marriage to T. T. Williams. It is thus difficult to accept the view that *The Member of the Wedding* avoids the frustration pattern of the first two novels; on the whole, it is easier to see the book as yet another parable dealing with the essential loneliness of man and the eternal futility of his escape.

The autobiographical element in *The Member of the Wedding* looms, as we have seen, larger than in any of the other novels: Frankie, like the youthful Carson, is too tall for her age; she is a tomboy; she yearns to go away, particularly to places where it snows; she puts on shows which she writes herself; she has a desertion complex; she longs for a glamorous identity; she even reads the same books. But though it is in this sense the most personal of all her novels, it also has universal value: Frankie is not merely Carson McCullers at the age of twelve, nor is she merely a successfully realized portrait of a type—she is a peculiarly eloquent symbol of human loneliness.

In this novel Mrs McCullers finally freed herself of her influences, and in none of her other books has she been so successful at fusing the realistic with the allegorical level: It is therefore, in this respect at least, the most nearly perfect of her works. Mrs McCullers never wrote more movingly than in the passage which describes, without a trace of sentimentality, the death of little John Henry, nor in that where we have our last glimpse of the faithful Berenice, sitting tiredly in the kitchen, Ludie's fox fur in her lap, and wincing when Frankie, with not quite unconscious cruelty, says to her apropos of Mary Littlejohn: 'There's no use our discussing a certain party. You could never possibly understand. It's just not in you.'[29] Berenice's usefulness to the Addams family, as this haughty young lady does not bother to conceal, is now a thing of the past—like the conversations the three of them had together in the 'ugly old kitchen' which is the world.

---

[29] Berenice's dislike of Mary Littlejohn probably has jealousy for its source. Whether or not one accepts Mr Baldanza's explanation of Frankie's 'crush' as an aversion to the fact of physical love (personified by the soldier), Berenice recognizes its intensity and bows before it.

* * *

CHAPTER NINE

THE SONG OF THE CHAIN GANG

1

During the first two years that Mrs McCullers worked on *The Member of the Wedding,* she thought frequently of the hunchback whom she and George Davis used to see in the Sand Street bars. For some reason she could not put him out of her mind—just as, years before, she had been haunted by the portrait of the Jew who provided her with the visual image of her first protagonist. She particularly remembered how (rather like Toulouse-Lautrec) he had been petted by the habitués of these dives, which were as low as any in the city, filled with misfits of various kinds. It was as if his physical deformity was a badge of his spiritual affinity with them, enabling them to recognize him as one of their own, and he strutted proudly among them scarcely condescending to acknowledge their homage, quite as if he owned the premises. The hunchback was a colourful character, certainly, as colourful as any about whom Mrs McCullers had written, but he was more than that: he was also valuable as a symbol, and in his relationship to the other patrons of the Sand Street establishments she gradually came to recognize a situation that was full of literary possibilities. Slowly at first, and then with increasing clarity, the outline of *The Ballad of the Sad Café* began to shape itself in her mind at those moments when it was not occupied with the longer work. Finally, when she was quite ready, she laid aside *The Member of the Wedding* temporarily and went to Yaddo. In six weeks' time the new story, a novella, was finished.

It will be remembered that, from the time of the publication of her first novel, certain reviewers had predicted that Mrs McCullers might some day produce a masterpiece if only she could succeed in conquering what they took to be her excessive interest in the grotesque. In writing *The Ballad of the Sad Café,* she very wisely proceeded to ignore all this well-meant advice, and in the process of ignoring it produced what most critics now, ironically, believe *is* her masterpiece. She knew instinctively the kind of materials that were

126

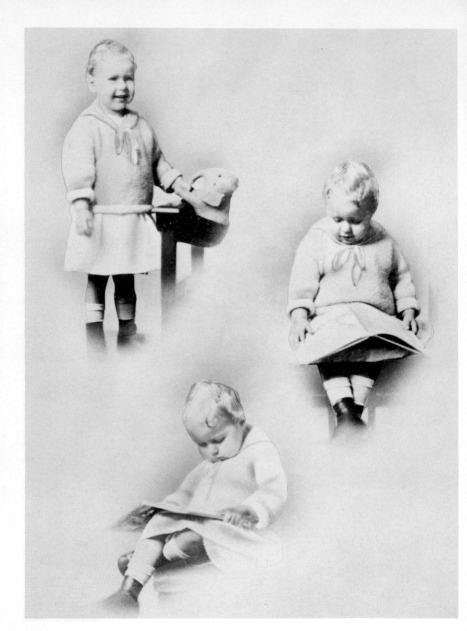

Carson as an infant

The artist as a young woman

The house at Bachvillers

With Reeves McCullers in Paris (1947)

With John P. Marquand and Alberto Moravia (1952)

With Tennessee Williams in Havana (1956)

~~The next minute happened and, or as you as it sounded, it was true~~
than the crazy House in the real
The next minute was like a minute in Milledgeville. Already
F. Jasmine had started for the door, for she could no longer stand
the silence. But as she passed the soldier he grasped her skirt and,
~~and pulled her toward the, and~~, limpened by fright, she was pulled
~~down on the bed beside him~~ down beside him on the bed. The next
minute happened, ~~but it it~~ but it was too ~~swift~~ crazy ~~for her~~ to be
~~to~~ realized. She felt his ~~arm~~ around her and smelled ~~and fist~~
his   *shut. A*
~~felt his~~ sweaty ~~chest,~~ his hand beneath her dress she felt
              in a second
also, and ~~something in~~ she was paralyzed by ~~unnamed horror.~~ *shock.*
She could not push away ~~and ×~~ , but she bit down with all her
might upon the crazy soldier's tongue,_ so that he screamed out
and she was free. Then he was coming toward her, ~~in the corner~~
~~by the window, and in the instant where and in that instant she~~
                blank
with an amazed, ~~and furious~~ face, ~~which concentrated a tent were forever~~
~~which had and it he×~~ and her hand reached the ~~cut~~-glass pitcher
and ~~hanged~~ brought it down upon his head. He ~~swayed~~ swayed a
second, then slowly his legs ~~buckled under him and~~ began to crumpled,
and slowly he sank ~~to~~ sprawling on the floor. The sound ~~had~~
                                                        silence
~~reminded her of××× been like××× like~~ was hollow like the hammer
on a ~~Christmas~~ coconut, and with it the ~~silence~~ was broken× at last.
He lay there there ~~with his face×××× freckled and× pale× the~~
              the
~~×××××ment freckened his×××f~~ still with ~~an~~ amazed expression on
                the was now pale ;
his ~~pale~~, freckled face, and a froth of blood showed on his mouth.
But his head was not broken, or even cracked, and whether he
                                              over
was dead or not she did not know. The silence was ~~broken~~ and it

Manuscript page, with the author's corrections, from *The Member of the Wedding* necessary for the sort of story she wanted to write. In her first two novels, and more particularly in *The Heart Is a Lonely Hunter*, the allegorical and literal levels struggle with each other for dominance (they achieve a nearly perfect balance in *The Member of the Wedding*, but this, of course, was not as yet completed). Now the tendency toward abstraction that is a condition of all allegory gained the upper hand, and it is clear from the very outset that in the *Ballad*, as in the best of Kafka, the characters are less interesting in their own right than they are as symbols: the sleepy Southern mill town in which the action takes place is here the merest of backdrops; the scene is Everywhere, and the protagonist is Everyman—Everyman with a hump on his back.

2

The story requires summary in some detail. 'The town itself is dreary,' begins the first sentence. 'If you walk along the street on an August afternoon there is nothing whatsoever to do . . . . The town is lonesome, sad, and like a place that is far off and estranged from all other places in the world . . . . These August afternoons when your shift is finished—there is absolutely nothing else to do; you might as well go down to the Forks Falls Road and listen to the chain gang.' The tone of boredom and loneliness is established from the very first sentence, and the chain gang (to which Mrs McCullers returns in a kind of epilogue or coda) is important in a way which I shall presently show. We are introduced to a Miss Amelia Evans, a woman who lives all alone in a large house of which all the windows but one have been boarded up, a woman with a face 'like the terrible dim faces known in dreams—sexless and white, with two gray crossed eyes which are turned inwards so sharply that they seem to be exchanging with each other one long and secret gaze of grief.'

But the house has not always been thus silent: it had originally been a kind of general store, run with an iron hand by Miss Amelia herself, a grim, masculine giantess with a habit of fingering her powerful biceps absent-mindedly. The town's richest woman, she was once married to Marvin Macy, a handsome ne'er-do-well whose love for her had had, in the beginning, a reforming influence upon his character. But Miss Amelia's motive in marrying had apparently been merely a desire for companionship, for when Marvin attempted to make love to her on their wedding night she repelled him furiously and thereafter, during the brief ten days he stayed with her, hit him 'whenever he came within arm's reach of her and whenever he was drunk.'[1] She finally turned him off the premises altogether. After putting under her door a letter threatening revenge, Marvin then left town, became a hardened criminal and at last was sent to the penitentiary.

In the meantime Miss Amelia receives a visit from a hunchbacked dwarf, Cousin Lymon, whom she has never seen but who claims to be a distant relation. The hunchback is tubercular and inverted sexually, but Miss Amelia falls in love with him from the very first. She closes her shop the day following his arrival, giving rise to rumours among the townspeople (who were certain that she would show the door to Cousin Lymon) that she has murdered him for something he was carrying in his suitcase. Actually Miss Amelia has given herself a holiday to celebrate the beginning of a new chapter in her life, and a delegation of mill workers, who come to investigate Cousin Lymon's 'death', finds him decked out in a lime-green shawl, 'the fringes of which almost touched the floor', and very much alive. Cheered by some of Miss Amelia's best liquor and amused by the antics of the dwarf, who is sociable in the extreme, the delegation stays on; and the session is so convivial that Miss Amelia decides to start a café on the premises.

For six years all goes well. Miss Amelia showers favours upon Cousin Lymon; he has the best room upstairs and nothing is too good for him. Though it is apparently unreturned, her love causes a gradual transformation of character in Miss Amelia: she loses much of her old grimness and becomes in every way more amiable. Then Marvin Macy, released from the penitentiary, returns. Miss Amelia is alarmed: now that she has found love she is vulnerable, and she knows it. And her alarm is justified, for the hunchback is fascinated by Marvin; though the latter treats him with contempt, Cousin Lymon dogs his footsteps, hangs upon his every word, plies him with Miss Amelia's liquor. In short, he falls in love with Marvin, thus becoming the instrument of the latter's revenge upon Miss Amelia. Night after night Cousin Lymon treats Marvin at the café, and even invites him to live with him upstairs, while Miss Amelia moves to a cot on the first floor. Miss Amelia endures all this because her love for the dwarf is large enough to include his love for Marvin, even though the latter is her deadly enemy. If she drives Marvin away she knows Cousin Lymon will leave too, and she cannot bear the thought of that: 'Once you have lived with another

[1] Captain and Leonora Penderton have a somewhat similar marital history: 'When she married the Captain she had been a virgin. Four nights after their wedding she was still a virgin, and on the fifth night her status was changed only enough to leave her slightly puzzled.'

it is a great torture to have to live alone . . . it is better to take in your mortal enemy than face the terror of living alone.'

Cousin Lymon, realizing the extent of her dependence upon him, exploits it to the utmost: he even mocks her publicly by imitating her walk, while Marvin looks on approvingly. 'There was something so terrible about this,' writes Mrs McCullers, 'that even the silliest customers of the café did not laugh.' Miss Amelia has resort to various stratagems (setting a lethal trap for him in the woods, poisoning his food), but none of them is successful. One day the mutual hatred of these two explodes in a scene which is as ludicrous as it is terrible: a slugging match between them which is witnessed by the whole town (who have sensed that it was imminent) and which Miss Amelia wins. But at the precise moment that she pins Marvin to the ground and is presumably about to throttle him, the hunchback alights on her back and claws at her throat, forcing her to let Marvin go. After that Cousin Lymon and Marvin disappear together, but not before they have destroyed Miss Amelia's still, wrecked her café, and stolen her private belongings (she has locked herself and her grief in her study) They even try to poison her, leaving on the café counter a plate of her favourite food 'seasoned with enough poison to kill off the county.' Thereafter Miss Amelia's hair turns grey and her eyes become increasingly crossed. For three long years she waits in vain for the hunchback to return; then, a broken woman, she hires a carpenter to board up the premises and becomes a recluse. The story closes on the same note of loneliness and boredom with which it began, and there is the same ballad-like use of repetition which we noted in *The Member of the Wedding* and which is here even more effective: 'Yes, the town is dreary. On August afternoons the road is empty, white with dust, and the sky above is bright as glass . . . . There is absolutely nothing to do in the town . . . The soul rots with boredom. You might as well go and listen to the chain gang.'

3

Near the beginning of *The Ballad of the Sad Café* there is a passage in which Mrs McCullers, momentarily abandoning the narrative vein for the expository, discourses briefly on the nature of love. The effect is that of a text at the beginning of a sermon, which is precisely the author's intention, though the sermon itself is presented in the form of the story—or parable—which follows. (Indeed, all of Mrs McCullers's books are parables in this sense.) She writes:

There are the lover and the beloved, but these two come from different countries. Often the beloved is only a stimulus for all the stored-up love which has lain quiet within the lover for a long time. And somehow every lover knows this. He feels in his soul that his love is a solitary thing . . . . Let it be added here that the lover about whom we are speaking need not necessarily be a young man saving for a wedding ring—this lover can be man, woman, child, or indeed any human creature on this earth. Now the beloved can also be of any description. The most outlandish people can be the stimulus for love . . . . The preacher may love a fallen woman. The beloved may be treacherous, greasy-headed and given to evil habits. Yes, and the lover may see this as clearly as anyone else—but that does not affect the evolution of his love one whit . . . . The value and quality of any love is determined solely by the lover himself.

She concludes:

It is for this reason that most of us would rather love than be loved. Almost everyone wants to be the lover. And the curt truth is that, in a deep and secret way, the state of being beloved is intolerable to many. The beloved *fears and hates* the lover [italics mine], and with the best of reasons. For the lover is forever trying to strip bare his beloved. The lover craves any possible relation with the beloved, even if this experience can cause him only pain.

There is seen here still another reason for Mrs McCullers's choice of 'outlandish people': not only do they serve as symbols of isolation, but they prove her thesis that 'the value and quality of any love is determined solely by the lover himself.' The more outlandish the characters and the more incongruous the matches which they make (one remembers Singer's love for Antonapoulos), the more eloquently they illustrate this thesis. Cousin Lymon is outlandish enough for anyone's taste: he is a dwarf, he is hunchbacked, he is tubercular, and he is homosexual. His relationship with the man-like Amelia constitutes one of the saddest and most grotesque situations in modern fiction. (Observe the initial care with which the author has selected these two personalities, whose association can only end in frustration: indeed, a physical union between them—as she is careful to make clear—is out of the question, which, of course, only adds to the poignancy of the situation.)

Love need not be reciprocal to benefit the lover: so much we learned from *The Heart Is a Lonely Hunter*. And now this concept has been developed even further: the beloved actually fears and hates the lover. Cousin Lymon despises Miss Amelia, and we are shocked by his treatment of her; it is not, however, in *spite* of her love for him that he despises her (as it somehow seems more congenial for us to imagine), but *because* of it. There is dreadful justice in the fact that in the past she has herself treated Marvin Macy in the same way and for the same reason. One can trace the beginning of this idea as far back as the very early story, 'Sucker' (see Chapter II). It occurs again in *The Heart Is a Lonely Hunter,* where Mick hated Biff Brannon, but with the important difference that she was not aware of his love for her: in the novel, moreover, it was merely suggested, and perhaps unconsciously at that, while here it is the very centre of the story, the melancholy burden of the ballad itself.

The Ballad of the Sad Café must be among the saddest stories in any language—not merely on the surface level of narrative, the level of 'realism', but also, and far more importantly (because it makes a generalization about mankind), on the level of parable. Love, it will be remembered, is the only means by which man can hope to escape his loneliness. In the early novels escape was still *possible,* even though their outcome showed how difficult it was of achievement. Escape was possible in theory, if not in actual practice, so long as the only obstacles were time and imperfect reciprocity (for *relatively* reciprocal relationships were, after all, still available). But now the difficulty is not merely that in any relationship one person must always love more than the other, nor is it that one of the persons may exhibit the indifference of an Antonapoulos. Now the obstacle is much more serious, so serious as to be in fact insurmountable: the beloved *hates* the lover. This, according to Mrs McCullers in *The Ballad of the Sad Café,* is the terrible law of nature that has sentenced man to a life of perpetual solitary confinement. There is no longer even a possibility of escape.

But although escape is impossible, there is still some advantage in making the attempt. The impulse to love is a good impulse, even though it is doomed to end in frustration. Singer's one-sided love for Antonapoulos sustains him so perfectly that the whole town is impressed by his air of poise and wisdom; Marvin Macy's early love for Miss Amelia has a brief refining influence upon his character; and Miss Amelia's love for Cousin Lymon transforms her whole personality: prior to his arrival she scowls constantly, and is forever suing, or planning to sue, somebody over something. It is true that these changes are temporary, but they are valuable while they endure. Some joy exists even in the midst of pain, though it is adulterated by the knowledge that it cannot last. (One is reminded of Keats's 'Ode on Melancholy': 'Aye, in the very temple of Delight/ Veiled Melancholy has her sovran shrine.') The lover realizes this intuitively, with the result that even such temporary escape as he contrives for himself must be imperfect: 'And somehow every lover knows this. He feels in his soul that his love is a solitary thing.' Love paroles man, and the tragedy is that he must return to his cell through no defection of his own.

In Miss Amelia's love for Cousin Lymon there is a strong element of pity. This is especially obvious in the scene of their first meeting, where the circumstances are such as to arouse it most successfully, and it characterizes her attitude to the dwarf throughout. Part of the terrible effectiveness of the story lies in the fact that Cousin Lymon returns the goodness of pity as well as the goodness of love with the evil of spite and hatred. Miss Amelia is able to pity the dwarf because her own abnormality affords her special insight into his predicament: he too is a deviate and suffers isolation. A freak herself, she feels for him the same kind of affinity that Singer feels for Antonapoulos (and that Biff, to a less degree, feels for Mick) in *The Heart Is a Lonely Hunter*. The same mixture of love and pity is also found, as we have seen, in the relationship between Anacleto and Mrs Langdon in *Reflections in a Golden Eye* and between Martin Meadows and Emily in the short story 'A Domestic Dilemma'.

Is is perhaps significant that the townspeople mistake Miss Amelia's intentions toward Cousin Lymon at the beginning. They are certain she has murdered him, when she has instead fallen in love with him. Love, as has been noted, is frequently misunderstood and even mistaken for its opposite in Mrs McCullers's work: one will remember Mick's attitude towards Biff Brannon, and Doctor Copeland's towards Jake Blount, in *The Heart Is a Lonely Hunter*. In this connection it should be noted that the author has been at some pains to give these suspicious neighbours the identity of a *group*:

> All at once, as though moved by one will, they walked into the store. At that moment the eight men looked very much alike— all wearing blue overalls, most of them with whitish hair, all pale of face and all with a set, dreaming look in the eye . . . . Except for Reverend Wilkin, they are all alike in many ways as has been said . . . all having taken pleasure from something or other, all having wept or suffered in some way. Each of them worked in the mill, and lived with others in a two or three room house for which the rent was ten dollars or twelve dollars a month. All had been paid that afternoon, for it was Sunday. So, for the present, think of them as a group.

These men are an abstraction: they are suspicion itself. But they are also surprisingly human for an abstraction, and Mrs McCullers has been careful to emphasize the normality, the *averageness* of them at the same time that she has used them as a symbol of suspicion. The inference is clear and characteristically melancholy. Most men *are* suspicious, quick to supply others with evil motives and slow to credit them with good ones, unable to recognize love when they see it; and this, of course, constitutes yet another obstacle to their escape. These townspeople are among the least sympathetic of all Mrs McCullers's characters. When Marvin Macy leaves town in disgrace after Miss Amelia repels his advances, we are told that 'the town felt the special satisfaction that people feel when someone has been thoroughly done in by some scandalous and terrible means.' And again: 'People are never so free with themselves and so recklessly glad as when there is some possibility of commotion or calamity ahead.' Passages such as these recall the misanthropy of the Mark Twain who wrote 'The Man that Corrupted Hadleyburg', of Chekhov in 'The New Villa', and of Flaubert in *Madame Bovary*. They also recall the scene in *The Heart Is a Lonely Hunter* where the chance meeting in Singer's room of the various characters ends, because each of them is obsessed selfishly with his own problems, in a total failure of communication.

The epilogue, simply and significantly entitled 'The Twelve Mortal Men', describes a chain gang at their back-breaking task of repairing a highway. The meaning here is richly symbolic. The work of the 'twelve mortal men' is hard work, and there is no escape from it as they are chained at the ankle. But while they work they sing:

> One dark voice will start a phrase, half-sung, and like a question. And after a moment another voice will join in; soon the whole gang will be singing. The voices are dark in the golden glare, the music intricately blended, both somber and joyful. The music will swell until at last it seems that it does not come from the twelve men on the gang, but from the earth itself, or the wide sky. It is music that causes the heart to broaden and the listener to grow cold with ecstasy and fright . . . . And what kind of gang is this that can make such music? Just twelve mortal men, seven of them black and five of them white boys from this county. Just twelve mortal men who are together.

The twelve mortal men represent all mankind, and they are prisoners because they cannot escape the fate of spiritual isolation. There is paradox and irony in the fact that *what joins them together is exactly what keeps them apart*: that is, the predicament of their loneliness. They escape temporarily through their singing (love), which it is significant that they do *together* in an attempt to resolve.

or rather dissolve, their individual identities; but their music is 'both somber and joyful' (love, that is, mixed with despair). The effect of this music of chained humanity upon the casual listener is also paradoxical, a mixture of 'ecstasy and fright'.

There is, of course, other symbolism as well. In this story the café, besides serving the microcosmic function we have noted in Mrs McCullers's earlier work (it is the scene of the fight between Miss Amelia and Marvin Macy, thus the stage for an elemental allegorical drama of love and hate), serves also as a refuge and a solace for the townspeople—a place of good cheer, it is a kind of bulwark against the impersonal and the inimical, and more nearly resembles Biff Brannon's establishment than the café in 'A Tree, a Rock, a Cloud' or the Blue Moon:

> Now this was the beginning of the café. It was as simple as that. Recall that the night was gloomy as in wintertime, and to have sat around the property outside would have made a sorry celebration. But inside there was company and a genial warmth. Someone had rattled up the stove in the rear, and those who bought bottles shared their liquor with their friends . . . . Nor did the opening of liquor on the premises cause any rambunctiousness, indecent giggles, or misbehavior whatsoever. On the contrary the company was polite even to the point of a certain timidity . . . . Even the richest, greediest old rascal will behave himself, insulting no one in a proper café. And poor people look about them gratefully and pinch up the salt in a dainty and modest manner. For the atmosphere of a proper café implies these qualities: fellowship, the satisfaction of the belly, and a certain gaiety and grace of behavior. This had never been told to the gathering in Miss Amelia's store that night. But they knew it of themselves, although never, of course, until that time had there been a café in the town.

The café in Mrs McCullers's novella serves, in this respect, exactly the same function that it does in Hemingway's well-known short story, 'A Clean, Well-Lighted Place': as a fortress[2] against loneliness and disorder, symbolized in both stories by the darkness outside.

Of the minor symbols, perhaps the most striking is the acorn which Miss Amelia picked up years ago and keeps (together with her kidney stones) in a glass-doored cabinet.

The other object she had added to the collection, the large

2   See also W. H. Auden's poem, 'September 1, 1939,' in which the 'dive on Fifty-Second Street' is likened to a fort.

acorn, was precious to her—but when she looked at it her face was always saddened and perplexed.

When Cousin Lymon asks her, 'What does it signify?,' she replies: 'Why, it's just an acorn I picked up on the afternoon Big Papa died . . . I mean it's just an acorn I spied on the ground that day. I picked it up and put it in my pocket. But I don't know why.' To this Cousin Lymon remarks: 'What a peculiar reason to keep it.' The acorn here symbolizes what the egg does in Sherwood Anderson's famous story, 'The Egg'—life itself, by which the protagonist in both stories is baffled. When we read that Miss Amelia's face was 'saddened and perplexed' when she contemplates the acorn, we remember that the one disorder which, in her role of amateur country doctor, she refuses to treat is a 'female complaint' ('Indeed at the mere mention of the words her face would slowly darken with shame, and she would stand there craning her neck against the collar of her shirt or rubbing her swamp boots together for all the world like a great, shamed, dumb-tongued child') and we remember also the fury with which she repels Marvin Macy on her wedding night. Her sadness and perplexity are caused by the realization of her failure to accept the vital principle, and the moment is analogous to that, in Anderson's story, in which the lunchroom proprietor, unable to perform the trick of forcing the egg through the neck of a bottle (symbolizing his inability to master life), throws it angrily at his customer and goes upstairs to weep in his wife's lap.

Another striking instance of symbolism is the fact that after the departure of Cousin Lymon and Marvin Macy, Miss Amelia's eyes become increasingly crossed 'as though they sought each other out to exchange a little glance of grief and lonely recognition.' The physical defect becomes more pronounced as the isolation which it symbolizes increases.

In order to give to her novella something of the authentic flavour of a traditional ballad, Mrs McCullers includes certain touches of the supernatural. On the day of Marvin's return all the pork in the county spoils, and a hawk with a bloody breast circles ominously over the town. There is even something a little mysterious about the way in which Cousin Lymon interferes in the fight:

> The whole town was there to testify to what happened, but there were those who doubted their own eyesight. For the counter on which Cousin Lymon stood was at least ten feet from the fighters in the corner of the café. Yet at the instant Miss Amelia grasped the throat of Marvin Macy the hunchback sprang forward and sailed through the air as though he had grown hawk wings. He

landed on the broad strong back of Miss Amelia and clutched at her neck with his clawed little fingers.

As in *The Member of the Wedding*, Mrs McCullers also makes extensive use of the magical numbers three and seven. There are three main characters; the introductory action (from the arrival of Cousin Lymon to the opening of the café) occupies three days and three nights; there are, the author tells us, 'three good persons in the town'; on the day of the fight three young boys come from Society City dressed in their Sunday best; Miss Amelia, after the fight, sits sobbing at her desk and knocks her fist three times on its top; and she waits three years for Cousin Lymon to return before she goes into seclusion. Marvin Macy is one of seven unwanted children, and on the disastrous day of his return Miss Amelia, as if warned by some premonition, invites cousin Lymon seven times to accompany her to Cheehaw and is seven times refused. The fight itself takes place at seven o'clock :

> Seven is a popular number, and especially it was a favorite with Miss Amelia. Seven swallows of water for hiccups, seven runs around the millpond for cricks in the neck, seven doses of Amelia Miracle Mover as a worm cure—her treatment nearly always hinged on this number. It is a number of mingled possibilities, and all who love mystery and charms set store by it. So the fight was to take place at seven o'clock.

Though there are echoes, in *The Ballad of the Sad Café*, of both 'A Clean, Well-Lighted Place' and 'The Egg', the story to which it bears the greatest resemblance is Faulkner's 'A Rose for Emily'. The similarity is partly in the setting, partly in the characterization of the protagonist. In both stories we are introduced, at the beginning, to a female recluse who lives in a dilapidated old house. In Faulkner's story, no one except an old Negro manservant has seen the interior of Miss Emily's house in ten years :

> Only Miss Emily's house was left, lifting its stubborn and coquettish decay above the cotton wagons and the gasoline pumps—an eyesore among eyesores. Now and then we would see her in one of the downstairs windows—she had evidently shut up the top floor of the house—like the carven torso of an idol in a niche, looking or not looking at us, we could never tell which.

Here is Miss Amelia :

The building looks completely deserted. Nevertheless, on the second floor there is one window which is not boarded; sometimes in the late afternoon when the heat is at its worst a hand will slowly open the shutter and a face will look down on the town . . . . It is a face like the terrible dim faces known in dreams . . . The face lingers at the window for an hour or so, then the shutters are closed once more, and as likely as not there will not be another soul to be seen along the main street.

Both Miss Emily and Miss Amelia are victims of a father complex, and both are proud and forceful women who believe themselves to be superior to the rest of the townspeople, who look up to them and accept them at their own evaluation of themselves. In fact, what Mrs McCullers writes of Miss Amelia might, in view of the outcome of Faulkner's story, apply with even greater accuracy to Miss Emily: 'When a person is as contrary in every single respect as she was and when the sins of a person have amounted to such a point that they can scarcely be remembered all at once—then that person plainly requires a special judgment.'

Revenge also occurs in both stories, and with the same provocation: Miss Amelia's refusal to accept her husband's advances corresponds to Homer Barron's refusal to marry Miss Emily, and it is only an accident that it is not accomplished by the same means, since, as we have seen, Marvin and Cousin Lymon do attempt to poison Miss Amelia. Granted these similarities, which after all are rather external, I think there can be no doubt that Mrs McCullers's is the better story. Though brilliantly written (technically it must belong in the very first rank of Faulkner's work), 'A Rose for Emily' is, in the last analysis, a Gothic story, in which the horror tends to become an end in itself. Cleanth Brooks and Robert Penn Warren make a gallant defence of this story in *Understanding Fiction*,[3] but the fact remains that Miss Emily is a madwoman. It is perfectly true, as these critics point out, that the quality of her madness, and the boldness and uniqueness of her revenge, are consistent with her firmness of character and with the distinction she enjoys among the townspeople, so that, as Mrs McCullers says of Miss Amelia, she may require 'special judgment'. Nevertheless, a story written on the literal level, as Faulkner's is, which requires that its protagonist be insane in order to render the outcome plausible is scarcely a story which can lay claim to universality: 'A Rose for Emily' is an unforgettable story, but in it Faulkner sacrificed the universal to the sensational. On the other hand, Mrs McCullers,

3 Op. cit.

whose purpose is didactic and whose treatment is allegorical, has
made her characters unique for a purpose: their eccentricities are
the badges of their isolation, and prove her point that even the most
grotesque individual can be the object of a love that is 'wild, extravagant, and beautiful as the poison lilies of the swamp.' In *The Ballad
of the Sad Café*, as elsewhere in her work, the abnormal is used
symbolically to dramatize what is true of the normal heart, and the
story thus possesses greater universality than one which treats of the
abnormal as such.

4

As has been mentioned, *The Ballad of the Sad Café* first appeared
in the November, 1943, issue of *Harper's Bazaar*. The following
year it was included by Martha Foley in her anthology, *The Best
American Short Stories of 1944*. In the spring of 1951, it was reprinted, together with Mrs McCullers's first three novels and six
short stories,[4] in a thick volume which was, in effect, a collected edition. The occasion was a momentous one in the history of American
publishing, for by this time the importance of Mrs McCullers's
talent, at least in the United States, had become rather generally
acknowledged and — though with some reluctance in certain
quarters—accepted. Critics were now enabled conveniently to survey
her total achievement, extending over a period of more than a
decade. In a front-page review in the Sunday *New York Herald-
Tribune*, Coleman Rosenberger exclaimed:

> What an impressive and unified body of work has been produced
> by Mrs McCullers at an age when many another writer has
> hardly started upon his career! For *The Ballad of the Sad Café*
> makes abundantly clear, which was not generally seen at the
> time of their separate publication, that *Reflections in a Golden
> Eye* and *The Member of the Wedding* broaden and extend the
> theme of her first book, as do the shorter pieces, so that each
> takes its place in an expanding structure in which each part aug-
> ments and strengthens the rest.[5]

Of the novella itself, he wrote:

> It is, however, in the title story, *The Ballad of the Sad Café*,
> that Mrs McCullers' achievement is seen at its most intense . . .
> It is condensed and brilliant writing, which carries the reader

4 'Wunderkind', 'The Jockey', 'Madame Zilensky and the King of Finland',
'The Sojourner', 'A Domestic Dilemma', and 'A Tree, A Rock, A Cloud'.
5 *Books,* Sunday, 10th June 1951, p. 1.

along so easily on the wave of the story that he may not at first be aware how completely he has been saturated with symbolism.

In *The Saturday Review of Literature*, Ben Ray Redman declared:

> Carson McCullers is one of the truly original writers of our time . . . With Defoe she shares the rare gift of knowing how to make her readers believe in the unusual and even the improbable; she sets her more freakish characters and incidents firmly in a frame of commonplace facts and details, which she enumerates precisely . . . It is too soon to guess whether or not Mrs McCullers' work will prove of lasting interest and importance; but it is possible to say with assurance that her novels and stories, now collected under the title of *The Ballad of the Sad Café*, are even more impressive on second reading than they were when first read. This is, I think, particularly true of the strange, fascinating tale of Miss Amelia and Cousin Lymon, which gives its title to the collection.[6]

Time pronounced with characteristic terseness:

> Taken together, the 791 pages pretty well establish novelist McCullers as one of the top dozen among contemporary United States writers . . . Her writing is part of an American tradition of mooning, the tradition represented by Sherwood Anderson, Thomas Wolfe, Eugene O'Neill, and, at his rare best, William Saroyan.[7]

Hubert Creekmore, who, in his review of *Reflections in a Golden Eye,* had deplored Mrs McCullers's lack of talent and the pedestrian quality of her style, now made the discovery that she had 'a specialized talent for a sharp, controlled, revealing style', and though he found the title story 'too attenuated', admired its 'queerly ingratiating tone'.[8]

Most enthusiastic of all the American reviewers was William P. Clancy, in *Commonweal*, who identified Mrs McCullers's work with a tradition which, according to Stephen Spender, is specifically and peculiarly American:

> It is a feeling of intense loneliness, Stephen Spender has written, which gives all great American literature something in common,

6   23rd June 1951, p. 30.
7   4th June 1951, p. 106.
8   *New York Times Book Review*, Sunday, 8th July 1951, p. 5.

and this feeling finds expression in its recurrent theme: 'the
great misunderstood primal energy of creative art, transformed
into the inebriate . . . the feeling ox . . . the lost child.' Spender's
insight seemed to me a particularly acute one when I first read
it. Surely one is haunted by loneliness and longing in Hemingway, in Fitzgerald, in Faulkner. When I was reading the collected novels and stories of Carson McCullers, his observation
struck me with new force. Here is a young American talent of
the very first order, and one leaves her work with an almost
terrifying sense of the tragic aloneness of man.[9]

Mr Clancy then proceeded to show how Mrs McCullers's best
work transcends the Gothic category:

> The art of Mrs McCullers has been called 'Gothic'. Perhaps it
> is—superficially. Certainly her day-to-day world, her little
> Southern towns, are haunted by far more masterful horrors
> than were ever conjured up in the dreary castles of a Horace
> Walpole. It seems to me, however, that the 'Gothic' label misses
> the essential point. Because Carson McCullers is ultimately the
> artist functioning at the very loftiest symbolic level, and if one
> must look for labels I should prefer to call her work 'meta-
> physical'.

This is very much the same point, it will be remembered, that Marguerite Young made in her critical study (published in *The Kenyon
Review*) of *The Member of the Wedding*. Mr Clancy went on to
stress an important truth about Mrs McCullers's freaks—that they
are used as symbols of the normal—[10] and to justify her use of them
on that account:

> Behind the strange and horrible in her world there are played
> out the most sombre tragedies of the human spirit; her mutes,
> her hunchbacks speak of complexities and frustrations which
> are so native to man that they can only be recognized, perhaps,

9 15th June 1951, p. 243.
10 In this he was anticipated by Paul Engle, who wrote in *The Chicago
Tribune* (10th June 1951, p. 5): 'The quality of Mrs McCullers' art is that, out
of the grotesque and the unreal, she creates the most accurate comments on
normal existence. One moves into a level of unreality which is simply an exaggerated form of that level on which we lead our daily lives.' Most recently,
the point has been made by Ihab Hassan ('The Character of Post-War Fiction
in America', in *Recent American Fiction*, ed. by Joseph J. Waldmeier, Boston,
Houghton Mifflin, 1963, p. 30): 'The grotesque . . . is perhaps the true, ironic
symbol of man in this century: Flannery O'Connor's Haze Mote, in *Wise
Blood*; Carson McCullers' Miss Amelia in *The Ballad of the Sad Café*; or
even Ralph Ellison's Invisible Man in the novel by that name. For in the
grotesque, the distortion of physical forms corresponds to that perversion of
mental states which is the malady of the age.'

in the shock which comes from seeing them dressed in the robes of the grotesque. They pass us on the street every day but we only notice them when they drag a foot as they go by.

Mrs McCullers's 'metaphysical fusion of horror and compassion', he concluded, represents 'an achievement equalled by few other contemporary American writers.'

The English edition of the book, identical except for the omission of *The Heart Is a Lonely Hunter,* was published by Cresset Press in 1952. British reviewers had previously been almost unanimous in their rejection of Mrs McCullers's work, and now for the first time there were murmurs of approval. In *Spectator,* Robert Kee compared her favourably with Hardy :

> There is in her style a distant Olympian dispassionatcncss which is designed to strengthen the violence of the human emotions with which she is often concerned. It is the same sort of effect which Hardy achieved for his characters in far more clumsily contrived sentences.[11]

The Times Literary Supplement, which, as we have seen, had until now been consistently unfavourable, at last conceded: 'Miss McCullers is in the first rank of the younger American writers.'[12]

It was V. S. Pritchett, however, who wrote the most enthusiastic review outside America. Commenting, in *The New Statesman and Nation,* that American writing had a 'limp democratic charm' but lacked individuality, he observed :

> What we look for is the occasional American genius—the Faulkner, for example—who will build his own original, imaginative or intellectual structures . . . Such a genius is Carson McCullers, the most remarkable novelist, I think, to come out of America for a generation . . . She is a regional writer from the South, but behind her lies that classical and melancholy authority, that indifference to shock, which seem more European than American. She knows her own original, fearless, and compassionate mind. The short novels and two or three stories now published in *The Ballad of the Sad Café*—the sing-song Poe-like title so filled with the dominant American emotion of nostalgia—make an impact which recalls the impression made by such very different writers as Maupassant and D. H. Lawrence. What she has, before anything else, is a courageous imagination; that is to say one that is bold enough to consider the terrible in human nature without

11 12th September 1952, p. 340.
12 25th July 1952, p. 481.

loss of nerve, calm, dignity, or love. She has the fearless 'golden eye' of one of her stories.[13]

While noting Mrs McCullers's talent for realism ('She is as circumspect as Defoe was in setting down the plain facts of her decaying Southern scene') and for creating strange and unusual characters, Mr Pritchett nevertheless perceived very clearly that it was neither of these which gave to Mrs McCullers's work its peculiar power and distinction:

> It may be objected that the very strangeness of the characters in a story like *The Ballad of the Sad Café* is that of regional gossip and, in fact, turns these characters into minor figures from some American Powys-land. They become the bywords of a local ballad. But the compassion of the author gives them their Homeric moment in a universal tragedy. There is a moment at which they become 'great'. A more exact definition of the range of her genius would be to say that human destiny is watched by her in the heart alone.

In summary, he declared:

> In her power to show the unconscious breaking surface, Miss McCullers is remarkable. She is a wonderful observer—this is rare in Anglo-Saxon writers—of the forms of love . . . She is a writer of the highest class because of her great literary gifts; but underlying these, and not less important, is her sense of the completeness of human experience at any moment.

Mr Pritchett's article proved extremely influential: British critics, though they naturally differ concerning the relative merits of Mrs McCullers's works (Mr Pritchett's own favourite is *The Member of the Wedding*) are now agreed almost without exception on the importance of her contribution to American literature.

5

Of all Mrs McCullers's writings, *The Ballad of the Sad Café* has elicited the greatest praise. Critics as diverse as Tennessee Williams, Mark Schorer, Ihab Hassan, Louis Rubin,[14] and Irving Howe, who called it 'one of the finest novels ever written by an American',[15]

[13] 2nd August 1952, p. 137.
[14] '*The Ballad of the Sad Café* is almost perfectly contrived, one of the really distinguished works of short fiction of our time.'—*The Sewanee Review*, Summer 1962, p. 509.
[15] *New York Times* Book Review, Sunday, 17th September 1961, p. 5.

have preferred it over all her other works. A young man with theatrical ambitions read it and conceived the idea of some day adapting it for the stage: his name was Edward Albee, and the idea has since become a reality.[16] Others, like the Chinese composer, Chou Wen-Tsung, have seen in it possibilities for a ballet in the modern manner.

There is a terrible finality about the vision of life which Mrs McCullers projected in The Ballad of the Sad Café: an eternal flaw exists in the machinery of love, which alone has the power to liberate man from his fate of spiritual isolation. There is no escape, and no hope of escape—one might as well go and listen to the chain gang. With this particular theme Mrs McCullers had now done all that she could possibly do—all, perhaps, that could possibly be done, for the pattern is a closed one, and no other American writer had embroidered it nearly so fully nor so perfectly.

[16] Mr Albee's dramatization of The Ballad of the Sad Café opened in October 1963, at The Music Box and ran until February 1964.

CHAPTER TEN

THE EYE AND THE SPARROW:

TRIUMPH ON BROADWAY

1

In the spring of 1946, in the guest room of a luxurious apartment just off Park Avenue, in Manhattan's lower Seventies, a young man lay in bed smoking and reading a novel. The hour was late, but of this he was oblivious. He did not stop reading until he had finished the book; then he laid it aside and, frowning slightly, puffed thoughtfully at his cigarette holder before switching off the bedlamp. It was a long time before he could get to sleep: for some time now he had been bothered by palpitations of the heart which caused him to break out in cold sweats; they were terrifying, and he had lately succeeded in convincing himself that his days were numbered. But tonight it was not his palpitations nor the neurotic fears which they invariably engendered that made him restless. The novel had awakened in him certain memories of his childhood—some disturbing, others pleasant—and his mind kept returning to these and to the book. It was a work of genius; there was no doubt about that. He could not remember when he had been so moved by a novel, and he made up his mind that he must meet the author.

The young man was Tennessee Williams, whose first successful play, *The Glass Menagerie,* had been the hit of the previous season on Broadway. The apartment was that of Miss Elizabeth Curtis, an elderly New York socialite and patroness of the arts, whom Mr Williams was then visiting with his young friend, Amado Pancho Rodriguez. And the novel was *The Member of the Wedding.* Despairing finally of getting any sleep, Mr Williams switched the lamp back on and reached for his dressing gown. Then he wrote a rather extraordinary letter to Carson McCullers in which he expressed his unbounded enthusiasm for her work: he felt, he said, that it had a strong affinity with his own, and he also said that, as he thought he had not much longer to live, owing to a heart condition, it would give him the greatest pleasure to meet the author of *The Member of the Wedding* before he died. Carson, who, though she had not seen *The Glass Menagerie,* had read and admired it, was saddened to learn that the famous young playwright was so ill, but was flattered by his praise and delighted at the prospect of seeing and talking with him.

A meeting was arranged, and the two writers took to each other at once. They had, to be sure, a very great deal in common: their small-town background in the Delta, their interest in depicting characters suffering from frustrations of various kinds, their precocity, their dedication. Williams was planning to spend the summer with Mr Rodriguez on Nantucket Island, where he had rented a cottage, and he invited Carson, who had just received another Guggenheim fellowship, to join them for a few weeks. She accepted, and, leaving Reeves in New York, set out for Nantucket. The weeks she spent there sealed her friendship with the playwright, a friendship that has continued unbroken over the years—yet another one of the intimate relationships which, as we have seen, Carson is capable of forming with certain individuals of either sex. As Williams himself has said:

From the moment of our first meeting, Carson, with her phenomenal understanding of another vulnerable being, felt nothing for me but that affectionate compassion that I needed so much and that she can give so freely, more freely than anyone I know in the world of letters.[1]

It was a productive period for them both. At the suggestion of Mr Williams, who was working with some difficulty on *Summer and Smoke,* Carson began a dramatization of *The Member of the Wedding.* She has always thought of herself—and very properly—as a novelist primarily, but now she was tempted by the dramatic possibilities which she, and Mr Williams, perceived beneath the surface of the book. These possibilities were not immediately obvious, for there was very little action or complication of the sort that, in the Forties (before the examples of Beckett, Williams and Albee) one was accustomed to seeing in the American theatre:

As soon as I was installed, Tennessee asked me, 'Why don't you make a play out of *Member*?' I was challenged in one malicious part of myself because *The New Yorker* in reviewing the novel said that I had many of the components of great writing, but the chief thing that I lacked was a sense of drama. Clifton Fadiman

[1] *Saturday Review,* 23rd September 1961, p. 14.

attacked the book because it 'was not dramatic'.[2]

It had to be, she realized, a *mood* play, as *The Glass Menagerie* had been, and its success would depend entirely upon the skill with which she created and communicated this mood, which is, of course, predominantly one of nostalgia. Would she be equal to the task? Not only did she lack experience in playwriting, except for the childish productions of her adolescence, acted out in the big back yard on Starke Avenue; but she had only seen six plays in her whole life—four in high school and two on Broadway.

She decided to try it. Her health was good, and she was happy on Nantucket. Unfortunately, it was the last year Carson was to know the happiness that comes of good health. 'It was,' she has said, 'a wonderful summer of sea and sun and friendship.'[3] In the mornings, she and Williams sat working at opposite ends of the same table ('For the first time I found it completely comfortable to work in the same room with another writer,' he has admitted[4]); in the afternoons they would bicycle to the beach; and in the evenings, over after-dinner drinks, they would read to each other what they had written. Williams gave her the benefit of his experience in the theatre, and she, for her part, encouraged him to finish a play that he had begun to fear was hopeless:

> When I told her that I thought my creative powers were exhausted, she said to me, wisely and truly, an artist always feels that dread, that terror, when he has completed a work to which his heart has been so totally committed that the finishing of it seems to have finished him too, that what he lives for is gone like yesterday's snow.[5]

In a few weeks the play was finished. There remained the problem of finding producers—not an easy one, as she was soon to discover. Leaving the manuscript with her agent, Ann Watkins, she and Reeves (to whom she had dedicated it) sailed in the autumn for Europe on the *Ile de France*. Truman Capote, a great friend of Rita's (she had published some of his earliest stories, such as 'Miriam', in *Mademoiselle*) who had been visiting the family in Nyack, accompanied the pair on the bus to New York. Reeves, he recalls,[6] was

2 Unpublished manuscript of Mrs McCullers.
3 Ibid.
4 Op. cit., p. 14.
5 Ibid.
6 Unpublished letter (dated 5th December 1953) from Janet Flanner to Carson McCullers.

jubilant. 'This is not just an ordinary bus,' he confided to the other passengers with his usual amiability. 'Oh no, this is no ordinary bus. It's the bus that's taking us to Paris.'

Carson's euphoria matched her husband's. During the voyage she was ecstatic. Her lifelong ambition—to cross the ocean and visit foreign places—was being realized at last, and the dreams she had had six years before, when she had wistfully watched the great liners arriving and departing in New York Harbour, were now actually coming true: the 'impossible voyages' were no longer impossible. When they disembarked she was bewildered, and Reeves, who had spent many months in France during the war and had acquired a smattering of the language, enjoyed to the fullest his role as guide and protector. In Paris they were enchanted with the suite of three rooms which Kay Boyle had taken for them in the attic of the old France et Choiseul near the Place Vendôme: Mrs Boyle was staying with her family at the same hotel. There were great cabbage roses on the wallpaper, and a charming open fireplace.

An amusing incident happened shortly after their arrival. One morning Kay Boyle strode into their suite and said to Carson, 'What's all this about your giving a lecture at the Sorbonne?' Carson did not know what she was talking about, and then Mrs Boyle showed her a printed announcement to the effect that Carson McCullers, leading American novelist, was scheduled to speak at the Salle Richelieu the following evening on the similarities and differences between the contemporary literature of France and the United States. Carson gasped, and then she remembered a charming little man who had paid her a visit several days before. She had understood nothing of what he was saying, but he seemed to be asking her something, and she had obligingly said 'Oui'—one of the very few French words in her possession—whereupon he had seemed greatly pleased and left.

In desperation Carson telephoned her friend John Brown, formerly her publisher at Houghton Mifflin and now a cultural attaché at the American Embassy in Paris. Mr Brown generously came to the rescue with an idea which, as things turned out, saved the evening: there would be no lecture but instead a panel discussion between himself, as spokesman for contemporary American literature, and his friend René Lalou, who would represent the modern French writers. Was there, he asked Carson, anything that *she* could do? She searched her mind frantically, then remembered a poem she had recently been working upon and had just finished. 'Suppose I recite my poem?' she suggested. Mr Brown looked startled, then consented. So Carson sat in the centre of the stage between the two men trying to look as if she understood what they were saying: when the appropriate moment came she recited her poem, and the evening went off smoothly enough.

These were happy days, but they were not to last. When her friends Wright and Edita Morris, who were also living in Paris and were going away for a few months, offered to lend their château to Carson and Reeves, they gladly accepted it, but they had scarcely become properly settled in it when (in June, 1947) she suffered a stroke which deprived her of the lateral vision in her right eye. It was similar to the one she had had in Columbus, when she was twenty-three, but more serious. Carson was also concerned about *The Member of the Wedding*, which was still looking for a producer. No one seemed willing to take a chance on it: it seemed terribly talky and static, and no one seemed to know what it was all about. One producer advised her to tear it up and write another play, and Miss Watkins wrote suggesting that she allow a 'drama specialist' to rework it. Carson reluctantly consented, but when she read the result she was appalled and refused to allow her name to be connected with it.[7] The evening following her reading of this revision—a nerve-wracking experience—she suffered the third and most serious stroke of all—the one which has left the left side of her body partially paralyzed ever since. It occurred in an apartment to which they had moved on the Morrises' return: Carson was alone at the time (Reeves was confined in the American Hospital with an infected leg), and had retired for the night after a day of unusually strenuous physical activity. Rising to get a glass of water she suddenly fell prostrate on the floor, her left side completely paralyzed, and lay for eight hours in this condition before she was discovered by a neighbour.

It is scarcely possible to overestimate the traumatic nature of this experience: when Carson speaks of it her voice, after all these years, still trembles with horror. The psychic shock was in fact almost as distressing as her physical disability. Fortunately, she was in capable hands: her friend Bob Myers, a physician connected with the American Hospital, where she lay for three weeks recuperating, was in constant attendance, and she had also, besides the company of Reeves, frequent visits from the Boyles and her old friend Richard Wright, who interrupted his vacation on the Riviera to visit her. Mr Wright cheered her considerably by telling her of a similar stroke which his mother once had had and from which she had made an almost total recovery.

7   Mrs McCullers was later sued, unsuccessfully, for $50,000 by this writer.

In December 1947, Carson was removed by ambulance from the American Hospital and flown to New York, where she entered the Neurological Institute at Columbia Presbyterian Hospital. It was then that Tennessee Williams came to the rescue. He persuaded his own agent, Audrey Wood, to read Carson's original manuscript, and, at their suggestion, Carson wrote a second version, dictating it from her bed. In 1949 Miss Wood found the necessary producers (Robert Whitehead, Oliver Rea, and Stanley Martineau), and the play was finally scheduled to open early in 1950.

2

Notwithstanding the delays and difficulties in its production (and the objection of talkiness, made by Miss Watkins and others), *The Member of the Wedding*, as is now generally realized,[8] provides an object lesson in the difficult art of adapting a novel to the dramatic medium. The dialogue is skeletal: the repetitiousness of which some reviewers complained in the novel is missing in the play, and when a speech is repeated (as when John Henry says, 'Gray eyes is glass' three times) it is always for a purpose that is dramatically justifiable. There are very few changes in the action. Perhaps the biggest difference is that the wedding, instead of taking place at the bride's home in Winter Hill, occurs at Frankie's house in a room joined by a hall to the kitchen, which (wisely) is the scene of the play throughout. We know what is happening on this occasion from remarks exchanged between Berenice and T. T. Williams, who watch the ceremony and the reception which follows it through a half-open door leading into the hall. Frankie, awkward and uncomfortable in her silver slippers and orange satin evening dress (which Berenice has told her makes her look like 'a Christmas tree in August'), makes several entrances and exits through this door, trying to summon the courage to tell her plan to the wedding couple. Presently we hear her scream 'Take me! Take me!' offstage, and John Henry enters to report: 'Frankie is in the wedding car and they can't get her out.' Finally Mr Addams drags Frankie onstage saying angrily 'What in the world has come into you?,' and she sits sobbing at the kitchen table with her head in her arms.

Some of the minor characters, like the Portuguese bartender, have, for obvious reasons, been dropped, and the soldier is merely mentioned by Frankie to Berenice. Barney MacKean, instead of committing a 'queer sin' with Frankie, conducts sexual experiments with

8 See, for example, Gerald Weales, *American Drama Since World War II* (New York, Harcourt, Brace and World, Inc., 1962), p. 174 ff.

Helen Fletcher, a neighbouring girl, and reappears in the last scene, after Frankie has confided to Berenice that he puts her in mind of 'a Greek god', to go off in the moving van with Frankie and her new friend, Mary Littlejohn.

One rather wishes that some of the speeches in the play had also been used in the novel. Thus, Frankie's remark to Berenice ('I don't know why you had to get that eye. It has a wrong expression—let alone being blue.') suggests that Berenice's blue eye has another purpose besides the obvious one of imparting to her a certain freak-ishness: it shows *her* desire (which parallels Frankie's) to escape from the identity which requires that her eyes, like her skin, be of a particular colour: she too is doomed to her identity, and longs for the impossible. So viewed, John Henry's remark, 'I like the glass eye better' (also missing in the novel), takes on a special significance as showing his childish preference for the ideal world over the real. On the other hand, some important speeches common to both the novel and the play seem to receive greater emphasis in the latter, because the form is more selective. To this category belongs Frankie's speech in the first act: 'I wish I was somebody else except me.'

Another respect in which the play differs from the novel is in the relative importance of Berenice. In the novel, because it is told from Frankie's point of view and the author consequently enters this character's mind so frequently, Berenice is an accessory character—an important accessory, but nonetheless a satellite. In the play, how-ever, Berenice has almost as many speeches as Frankie, and in this democracy of dialogue she almost succeeds in replacing Frankie as the centre of interest. (Some evidence of this can be seen in the speech, quoted in the preceding paragraph, concerning Berenice's blue eye, which establishes that Frankie is not the only dreamer of the group: this speech does not, as has been said, occur in the novel.) Berenice is omnipresent in the play, the scene of which is limited to the kitchen, while in the novel there are whole sections (like the thirty-two pages at the beginning of Part Two in which Frankie wanders around town telling strangers about the wedding, in which she is entirely absent. In the novel, Berenice's foster-brother, Honey, is working on a chain gang when last we hear of him, but in the play he has hanged himself in his cell, and the violent dénouement of this sub-plot, in which Berenice is involved indirectly, also gives greater importance to her story. Finally, she is more valuable in the symmetry of the play than in the novel: she is the last person to leave the stage, and as she does so she hums the first two lines of the same hymn with which, accompanied by Frankie and John Henry, she ended the second act.

What, in the light of its context, is one to make of this song?—
which runs as follows:

> I sing because I'm happy,
> I sing because I'm free,
> For His eye is on the sparrow,
> And I know He watches me.
>
> Why should I feel discouraged?
> Why should the shadows come?
> Why should my heart be lonely,
> Away from heaven and home?
>
> For Jesus is my portion,
> My constant friend is He,
> For His eye is on the sparrow,
> And I know He watches me.

The words sound appropriate enough, perhaps, in Berenice's mouth,
but there is grim fore-shadowing and irony in the fact that it is John
Henry who begins the song, singing the first stanza alone before he
is joined by Berenice and later by Frankie. And we may be quite
certain that Frankie feels no such sense of security: the whole play
is evidence that she does not. The song is begun by John Henry
immediately after Frankie and Berenice have been discussing the
irrevocability of time, the destructiveness of the atom bomb, the
apparent meaninglessness of life with its 'bolts of chance'.[9] 'There
are so many things about the world I do not understand,' Frankie
observes in the course of this conversation, and its simple assertion
of faith seems scarcely sufficient to dispel such grave doubts as those
which have been worrying Frankie.

As a matter of fact, the inclusion of this song into the play came
about quite fortuitously. (It does not appear in the original acting
version.) Ethel Waters is a singer—she is also, of course, a great
actress—and it was felt that her musical talent would enrich the
quality of the performance. The hymn was of her own choosing—it
was one she had heard at her grandmother's knee, and, as she explained in an interview in *The New York Times*, had always meant a
great deal to her: 'I sing the hymn to myself, and it comes to me that
God will not put more on me than I can bear; that wherever I go He
will take care of me . . . Anyhow, I sang it for Carson, and when I

[9] Carson McCullers, 'The Vision Shared', *Theatre Arts*, April 1950, p. 30.

finished she got in my lap and cried just like Frankie does in the play.'[10]

Regardless of how it may have struck an opening-night audience, who heard Ethel Waters sing it in her rich, magical contralto, *His Eye Is on the Sparrow* is not a 'theme song' in the usual sense at all : the world which it describes is not the world of the play—a world in which 'some of the cards are missing', where atom bombs are manufactured and used, and where all is chance and chaos. There is, alas, abundant reason for Berenice to be 'discouraged', and if little John Henry is 'happy' as he sings in his quavering child's voice, he is not allowed to remain so for very long.

3

The evening of 5th June 1950, was an unforgettable one for Mrs McCullers, who knew for the first time the peculiar satisfaction that a playwright feels when he sees his work come to life on the stage. When this happens to a play—the event for which it is ultimately designed and by whose success it must stand or fall—it ceases to be the property of the author alone. So many other considerations are involved—the direction, the staging, the acting—that the actual production of a play is rather a collaboration than an individual accomplishment. And Mrs McCullers was extremely fortunate in having a sensitive director (Harold Clurman), an imaginative set designer (Lester Polakov), and a brilliantly talented trio of principals : Julie Harris as Frankie, Ethel Waters as Berenice, and Brandon de Wilde as John Henry.

They were all a little nervous, for the Philadelphia tryout had caused some reviewers to predict that the play was too fragile an item to last long on Broadway. But almost from the moment the curtain parted it was obvious that the production was going to be a success. When the cast finally took their bows the audience actually stood and cheered—a very rare occurrence on Broadway. The applause rose to such a roar that Miss Harris burst into tears and had to flee to her dressing room where she was besieged by dozens of people and toasted, together with the rest of the cast, with champagne. There was a big party afterwards, and by the time it was over the morning papers had come out with the news that *The Member of the Wedding* was the new smash hit of the season.

Brooks Atkinson announced :

Mr Clurman has staged a performance by Ethel Waters, Julie

10   30th April 1950, II, p. 2.

Harris, and young Brandon de Wilde that has incomparable insight, grace, and beauty. Anyone who loves art ought to be humbly grateful for such acting and direction. Like Mrs Mc-Cullers' character portraitures, they are masterly pieces of work . . . In view of the rare quality of the writing and acting, the fact that *The Member of the Wedding* has practically no dramatic movement does not seem to be very important. It may not be a play, but it is art. That is the important thing.[11]

In *The New York Daily Telegram,* William Hawkins wrote :

I have never before heard what happened last night at the curtain calls for *Member of the Wedding* when hundreds cried out as if with one voice for Ethel Waters and Julie Harris. The two actresses are splendid beyond compare in this curious play about the tragedy of loneliness.[12]

John Chapman, the influential critic of *The Daily News,* proclaimed :

We are still short of water,[13] but, thank goodness, the theatrical drought is over. A new play, *The Member of the Wedding,* came to the Empire Theatre last night, and at the fall of the third-act curtain a play-parched audience gave voice to its relief with loud, honest cheers . . . As a piece of playmaking it is not ideal . . . Ideal or not, *The Member of the Wedding* is an absorbing study of an adolescent girl.[14]

In *The Daily Mirror* (New York), Robert Coleman observed :

In *The Member of the Wedding* Carson McCullers has created a mood rather than a well-made play, but it is a mood that held an audience spellbound in the Empire Theatre last night. So fascinated by the McCullers characterizations were first-nighters that they threw their yardsticks away and enjoyed themselves immensely.[15]

Of the daily reviewers, only Howard Barnes of *The New York Herald-Tribune* was lukewarm : he praised the acting, but found the play structureless and essentially undramatic.

11   *New York Times,* 6th January 1950, p. 26.
12   Cited in *New York Theatre Critics' Reviews,* XI (1950), p. 399.
13   New York was experiencing a water shortage at the time.
14   Cited in *New York Theatre Critics' Reviews,* XI (1950), p. 398.
15   Cited in *New York Theatre Critics' Reviews,* XI (1950), p. 397.

The New York weeklies continued the almost unanimous praise of the newspapers.[16]

The only emphatic denunciation of *The Member of the Wedding* came from the pen of George Jean Nathan, the reactionary drama critic of *Esquire* who had consistently attacked Tennessee Williams's plays as they made their separate appearances. Mr Nathan made no secret of his personal dislike of Mr Williams, and it is not unlikely that he allowed this subjective attitude to colour his opinion of Mrs McCullers, whose friend Williams was known to be. At any rate he wrote :

> There is no dramatization and little play . . . What the author has done is rather to diminish what degree of drama there was in the novel and to place its two [sic] principal characters on a stage, and, for the greater part of the evening have them engage in a series of inactive dialogues. At the last moment, thinking to lend the dialogue some appearance of a play, she introduces a touch of relative drama, albeit off-stage and merely talked about, but it is too late; the occasion has long since expired of vocal exhaustion.[17]

The charge that the play lacked action was, as we have seen, made even by some of its enthusiastic admirers. Clurman, whose eclecticism included an awareness of the experiments then in progress in European *avant-garde* theatre, decided to clarify this issue publicly in the light of his experience in directing *The Member of the Wedding*. In a memorable article published in *The New Republic,* he declared :

> It is impossible to direct a play that has no action. When a play is well acted, it means that a line of action has been found in it. It means that action was in it, however obscure it may have seemed at first sight. Without action, it would not play. The reason why Chekhov's 'Seagull' did not seem to have action when it was first produced was that the original company had not found it, just as opera singers first thought Wagner unsingable, and a still later generation was to begin by declaring Debussy's 'Mélisande' unoperatic. The directors and actors of the Moscow Art Theatre discovered the play in 'The Seagull'.
> I am convinced that Ethel Waters, Brandon de Wilde and the other actors of 'The Member of the Wedding', following the

16   See Wolcott Gibbs in *The New Yorker,* 14th January 1950, p. 46; Margaret Marshall in *The Nation,* 14th January 1950, p. 44; and Kappo Phelan in *Commonweal,* 27th January 1950, pp. 437-438.

17   *The Theatre Book of the Year* (New York, Alfred A. Knopf, 1950), pp. 164-166.

line of action I sensed in it as a director, have made a play of 'The Member of the Wedding' because it was a play to begin with—albeit of a different kind than any other we had previously done. Ibsen once said of his 'Brand' and 'Peer Gynt': 'If these weren't poetry before, they have become poetry now.' A renewal of faith in the sensitivity and awareness of our New York theatregoing public was perhaps the greatest lesson I learned from 'The Member of the Wedding'.[18]

Mr Clurman's article had a very considerable influence. Mr Atkinson, for example, who had objected to the play's static quality, now modified his original opinion:

If it were not for *The Glass Menagerie, A Streetcar Named Desire,* and *Summer and Smoke,* Mrs McCullers might have had difficulty in finding the proper audience for her play, and audiences might have difficulty in surrendering to it so completely. Tennessee Williams is the pioneer in this particular genre, which has rescued one aspect of the theatre from mathematics and geometry.[19]

Meanwhile, the play continued to play to standee trade. The advance sale of tickets (originally $6,000) climbed in a few weeks to $112,000, and by the second week of March, or ten weeks after the opening, the backers were repaid their entire investment. On March 30th, in an article in *Theatre Arts* entitled 'The Vision Shared', Mrs McCullers defined her intentions in *The Member of the Wedding* and justified its form as follows:

Any form of art can only develop by means of single mutations by individual creators. If only traditional conventions are used an art will die, and the widening of an art form is bound to seem strange at first, and awkward. Any growing thing must go through awkward stages. The creator who is misunderstood because of his breach of convention may say to himself, 'I seem strange to you, but I am alive.'
It seemed to me after my first experiences that the theatre was the most pragmatic of all art media. The first question of ordinary producers is: 'Will it get across on Broadway?' The merit of a play is a secondary consideration and they shy from any play whose formula has not been proved a number of times. *The Member of the Wedding* is unconventional because it is not a *literal* kind of play. It is an *inward* play, and the conflicts are inward conflicts. The antagonist is not personified, but is a

18   30th January 1950, pp. 28-29.
19   17th September 1950, II, p. 1.

human condition of life: the sense of moral isolation. In this respect *The Member of the Wedding* has an affinity with classical plays—which we are not used to in the modern theatre where the protagonist and antagonist are present in palpable conflict on the stage. The play has other abstract values; it is concerned with the weight of time, the hazard of human existence, bolts of chance. The reaction of the characters to these abstract phenomena projects the movement of the play. Some observers who failed to apprehend this *modus operandi* felt the play to be fragmentary because they did not account for this aesthetic concept . . . Some observers have wondered if any drama as unconventional as this should be called a play. I cannot comment on that. I only know that *The Member of the Wedding* is a vision that a number of artists have realized with fidelity and love.[20]

In recent years, critics have gone so far as to maintain that *The Member of the Wedding* is important in the history of American drama not merely in its own right, but *because* it violated the traditional concept of what constitutes action in the theatre. Thus, in 1962, Gerald Weales, in the most detailed analysis of the play yet in print, says that 'a case might well be made for *The Member of the Wedding* as the most obvious structural innovation in the recent American theatre.'[21] Comparing the play with another adaptation, Truman Capote's *The Grass Harp*, he says: '*Member* is a better play than *Harp* not simply because Mrs McCullers has retained the flavor of the original, but because the original has substance as well as flavor . . . There is an archness in the play version of *The Grass Harp* that the novel avoids, but, in comparison to *The Member of the Wedding*, both novel and play seem to be self-conscious constructions, built by a clever and talented draftsman out of materials he has used successfully before and which have had some vogue.' It is regrettable, however, that Mr Weales, whose book is often discerning—though his discussion of Williams and Albee leaves much to be desired—should align himself with those critics (see Chapter IX) who fail to see the 'reason' for John Henry's death:

It is never clear, in the play or in the novel, why violence and death are necessary for Frankie's passage into adolescence; the fall and the beginning of school would have broken open the ring around the kitchen of that summer and, if a more specific event were needed, the wedding could have served. It may be that the double death in the play (in the novel Honey ends on

20 April 1950, p. 80.
2i Op. cit., p. 177.

the chain gang) is a kind of emotional mannerism necessary to the genre of Southern writing to which Mrs McCullers contributes.

However, as if conscious that this last sentence does not do justice to Mrs McCullers's intentions, he goes on to speculate:

It is possible that the novelist and playwright has something more in mind, wants to indicate that the climactic events of so many novels and plays are not formative, are only incidents on the edge of a process that will take place without them.

Here, of course, he is closer to the truth.

4

On 5th April, 1950, the Drama Critics' Circle met to cast their votes for the best Broadway production for the period from 1st April 1949, to 31st March 1950. When the results came in, it was found that an overwhelming majority of the critics had chosen *The Member of the Wedding*. (The competition, such as it was, was divided between William Inge's *Come Back, Little Sheba,* and Gian-Carlo Menotti's opera, *The Consul*.) The play ran for fourteen and a half months, also winning the Donaldson Awards (sponsored by *Billboard*, the theatrical weekly) for the best play of the season as well as for the best first play to be produced during the year. Individual awards, decided by a vote of three thousand representatives of all members of the theatre, went to Julie Harris, Brandon de Wilde, and Harold Clurman; and Ethel Waters received the religious medal of St Genesius, patron saint of actors, from the American National Theatre and Academy. The play closed on 17th March 1951, after a total of 501 performances. Since then *The Member of the Wedding* has been enjoyed by audiences all over the world[22] and has also become a favourite with amateur theatrical groups and summer stock companies in the United States: as recently as 1963, when it was revived on the West Coast with Ethel Waters once more (after thirteen years) in the role of Berenice, it broke all previous records at the Pasadena Playhouse. In 1953 it was made into a successful motion picture; the producer was Stanley Kramer, and the cast of principals remained the same.

[22] *The Member of the Wedding* was produced at the Royal Court Theatre in London in February 1957.

* * *

CHAPTER ELEVEN

RETURN TO BROADWAY

1

After the production of *The Member of the Wedding*, and the publication in America (1951) and England (1952) of her collected edition, Mrs McCullers's literary reputation was secure. Publishers begged for options on her unpublished fiction, and producers clamoured for her to write another play. Already, in her early thirties, she had become a kind of literary legend. As Gore Vidal says:

> She was an American legend from the beginning . . . The publicity was the work of those fashion magazines where a dish of black-eyed peas can be made to seem the roe of some rare fish, photographed by Avedon; yet Carson McCullers' dreaming androgynous face, looking out at us from glossy pages, in its ikon elegance subtly confounded the chic of the lingerie ads all about her.[1]

She was the idol of the youthful literary set in America, and in the next few years she became personally acquainted with many famous European writers such as Edith Sitwell, Elizabeth Bowen, Rosamund Lehmann, and Alberto Moravia. It seemed as though she had everything that any writer could possibly ask for, except good health. Her physical condition made it difficult for her to work at the typewriter, and she was unable to indulge her favourite recreation of playing the piano.

With some of the proceeds from the play, Carson bought a house, 'L'Ancienne Presbytère,' a few miles north of Paris in the Oise Valley at Bachvillers, a village of about 150 inhabitants: she and Reeves were the only Americans in the area. The house, which they acquired for less than five thousand dollars, had central heating, fireplaces, and plumbing. It was surrounded by a big stone fence; there was a large orchard with nine kinds of fruit trees, also a vegetable

---

[1] *The Reporter*, 28th September 1961, p. 50.

and a flower garden. They hired an eccentric Russian housekeeper who claimed to be a direct lineal descendant of Genghis Khan, but she had not been with them very long before her reason broke down completely, whereupon they engaged a local couple. For the next three years Carson and Reeves—and their big boxer dog Kristin and her six pups—made their headquarters here, with frequent visits back and forth to the States.

In the late summer of 1951, at a dinner party given in London by her English publisher, Carson met Dr Katherine Cohen, a physician who appeared to take both a personal and a professional interest in her case. After putting her through a series of physical tests, she declared that there was no organic reason for her strokes, and suggested that her paralysis might be psychosomatic and could be cured by hypnosis. Carson, desperate for help, agreed to treatment and entered St George's Hospital for a week, but neither Dr Cohen nor another hypnotist whom she called in was able to induce hypnosis successfully, and the experiment was a failure. Carson later learned that Dr Cohen, who died a few years after this, was a manic-depressive!

Carson's health was not her only source of concern at this time. Reeves's drinking, which had always tended to be excessive, had, since the resumption of their marriage, begun to assume clinical proportions. Like so many other successful soldiers, he seemed incapable of coping with the challenge which the peace presented: as Janet Flanner has wisely said: 'Perhaps his part in the war had led him astray, destroyed his resistance to ordinary life, to rationality, and the patterns of living without excitement and without authority.'[2] Except for his youthful dream of becoming a writer like his wife (a dream he had long since abandoned), he had never been conscious of a real mission or calling in life. The war had given him a temporary purpose, but that was now a thing of the past. For a time he thought seriously of going to Harvard and getting a degree (there was an accelerated programme for veterans whereby he could have received one in less than three years), but, although Carson agreed to go with him, he did nothing about it.

Now the danger signals were becoming unmistakable. Carson saw them, and was alarmed. In his behaviour towards her, Reeves would alternate between fits of abusive violence, during which he would threaten her life—and his own—and spells of abject remorse during which he would beg her forgiveness: one day he would forge a cheque in her name, and the next he would make her a present of

[2] Unpublished letter (dated 5th December 1953) from Janet Flanner to Carson McCullers.

some expensive item which she neither needed nor desired. She finally persuaded him, during one of their trips to New York, to undergo psychiatric treatment there, but when she returned to Europe on the *Queen Elizabeth* he, without her knowledge, booked passage on the same ship (taking the only available accommodation, the bridal suite) and did not make his presence known to her until they were far out at sea. Carson was both touched and alarmed: the incident was proof at once of his dependence upon her and of his need for professional treatment. Some of her own experience during this trying period undoubtedly went into the short story, 'A Domestic Dilemma' (1951),[3] which is the story of a man with an alcoholic wife whom he both loves and pities.

Carson spent the spring of 1952 at Yaddo, where she finished a group of poems[4] which appeared later that same year in *Botteghe Oscure*, and resumed work on a new novel, *Clock Without Hands*. Also at Yaddo that year were Truman Capote, Marguerite Young, and Marguerite Yourcenar. Miss Young recalls that Carson, who was by far the most famous writer at the colony, was not much in evidence, and that because of her habits she created a rather mysterious impression: during the day she would sleep, wearing a small black mask against the light, and worked in the small hours of the morning. During these weeks Reeves stayed in Nyack with Mrs Smith, who had bought the big house on South Broadway where Carson now makes her home. In the summer they sailed for Europe on the *Constitution*. Miss Young, who was on the same vessel, remembers that Carson showed little interest in her surroundings and read Proust throughout the entire voyage. They disembarked in Italy, which that summer was full of American visitors (including Carson's friends Tennessee Williams, W. H. Auden, and Truman Capote), and went to spend a few days with Princess Marguerite Caetani, the editor of *Botteghe Oscure*, in her eleventh-century castle between Rome and Naples.

Reeves, meanwhile, had greatly worsened: in addition to drinking, he had begun to take drugs; when he was under their influence he behaved like a maniac, and she began to fear for her safety—in particular he seemed fascinated by the idea of a double suicide. There were a few lucid intervals, during which they were still able

---

[3] Mrs McCullers' original title was 'Evening at Home'.

[4] 'The Dual Angel: a Meditation of Origin and Choice', containing five poems: 'Incantation to Lucifer', 'Hymen, O Hymen', 'Love and the Rind of Time', 'The Dual Angel', and 'Father, Upon Thy Image We are Spanned'. The group was published in Rome in *Botteghe Oscure*, IX (1952), and in the United States in *Mademoiselle* (July, 1952).

to enjoy a relative happiness. (Thus, he wrote to Mrs Smith on 5th January 1953: 'We spent a quiet Christmas and New Year. A friend came up from Rome and we had several people out from Paris.'[5]) But they were occurring further and further apart, and the interim was a nightmare, made worse by Carson's own disability and the snail's pace at which *Clock Without Hands* was proceeding. Finally she decided to sell 'L'Ancienne Presbytère' and return to the States alone, which she did in the autumn of 1953. She had been back in Nyack only a few weeks when she learned of Reeves's death, which occurred in the first week of December.

The details, as she later learned them from friends in Paris, were as follows: After the sale of the house, Reeves had been staying with John and Simone Brown in their home outside Paris. He talked constantly of committing suicide, and Mrs Brown, who did not know to what extent he was in earnest, and who was concerned about the effect such an incident might have on her children, begged him not to do so in their house. Going into the city he checked into a hotel and sent Janet Flanner an enormous quantity of flowers. When she chided him on the telephone for his extravagance he answered, 'Don't worry—it's my funeral.' The next morning he was found dead in his room, evidently from an overdose of sleeping pills. A note lay beside him asking Bob Myers, Carson's doctor at the American Hospital, to close his eyes.

Reeves was given a veteran's military funeral and buried in the cemetery at Neuilly. Janet Flanner, who attended the ceremony with Truman Capote and the Browns, described it to Carson in a letter written immediately afterwards.[6] At Carson's request, the organ played Bach, and John Brown read the Twenty-third Psalm. With her left hand Miss Flanner dropped a narcissus into the open coffin and with her right hand a great red rose saying as she did so: 'This is good-bye from Carson. She wanted me to kiss you good-bye.' So ended Carson McCullers's second marriage to the same man—a man whom she had never ceased to love in spite of his many failings. It may be true that, as Biff Brannon said of Leroy and Lucile, these two were not 'suited for each other', and that had he married a less remarkable woman his shortcomings would perhaps have been less obvious. About that it is useless to speculate. One thing is certain: Reeves worshipped Carson, even at those terrifying moments when he threatened her life: in certain natures, and in certain circumstances, love can sometimes express itself only in violence. And

5 Unpublished letter from Reeves McCullers to Mrs Lamar Smith.
6 Unpublished letter (dated 5th December 1953) from Janet Flanner to Carson McCullers.

in some respects he had been a good husband: he had given her sound advice, which she badly needed, about how to invest her profits from the Broadway production of *The Member of the Wedding*, so that today she is able to live comfortably, chiefly on the fruits of these investments. Reeves McCullers was essentially a good man to whom the accidents of circumstance, the 'bolts of chance', had been anything but kind. Those who knew him best towards the end agree that he was a war casualty—one of those uncounted thousands whose wounds are not apparent on the surface.

Carson was to receive two more shocks within the near future. Her favourite aunt, Mrs C. Graham Johnson (Mrs Smith's sister) died suddenly while Carson was visiting her in Columbus, and this upsetting event was followed only a few months later (early in 1955) by the death (from a bleeding ulcer) of her own mother, to whom, as we know, Carson had always been extremely close. Dazed by these happenings, to whose successive impacts she had not had sufficient time to adjust, and handicapped by her own continuing ill health, she nevertheless continued to work away on *Clock Without Hands*, the first chapter of which, entitled 'The Pestle', had created a stir of admiration in literary circles when it appeared in 1953 in *Botteghe Oscure* and *Mademoiselle*. She had also, shortly before her mother's death, begun a second play, and the novel was progressing so slowly and so painfully that she decided to abandon it temporarily for the newer project.

2

The Square Root of Wonderful, like the earlier play, is to a large extent autobiographical. When it appeared in book form, the author explained in her preface:

> In *The Square Root of Wonderful* I recognize many of the compulsions that made me write this play. My husband wanted to be a writer and his failure in that was one of the disappointments that led to his death. When I started *The Square Root of Wonderful* my mother was very ill and after a few months she died. I wanted to recreate my mother—to remember her tranquil beauty and sense of joy in life. So, unconsciously, the life-death theme of *The Square Root of Wonderful* emerged.

The play's protagonist is a young woman, Mollie Lovejoy, who has been twice married to and divorced from the same man, a once-famous writer who, after the failure of his latest play, has attempted suicide and is convalescing in a rest home. Mollie has meanwhile fallen in love with an architect, John, and is on the point of marrying him when Phillip, her ex-husband, returns. The two men are opposites: John is dull but strong; Phillip is weak and has learned to use his weakness to advantage with women, but he is charming and perceptive. He does not love Mollie—it is made clear that he is incapable of loving anyone—but he needs her desperately and insists that she love *him*. In a moment of weakness she yields to him once more but repents almost immediately, and when Phillip realizes he has lost her for good he drowns himself; Mollie is then free to marry John. Other characters are Mollie's thirteen-year-old son, Paris; Mother Lovejoy, a fatuous, domineering woman whose mismanagement of Phillip's childhood is responsible for many of his problems (he loathes her, calling her to her face a 'babbling old horror'); and Sister, her daughter, a homely spinster who compensates for the drabness of her situation by inventing fantasies involving Latin lovers.

From what Mrs McCullers has said in her preface, the reader is obviously expected to identify Phillip with Reeves McCullers, and Mollie Lovejoy with Mrs Smith. But it is not quite so simple as that; the careful reader will note at once that it is Phillip and not his wife who was successful as a writer, even if he is now a 'has-been'. (The identity of Phillip is further complicated, for in the play it is John and not Phillip who has been a war hero.) And the circumstance of Mollie's having married the same man twice reminds us not of Mrs Smith but of Mrs McCullers. What the author has done is to identify herself now with Phillip (in the speeches in which he discusses his writing), now with Mollie (in the dialogue which she exchanges with her ex-husband). This is of course perfectly proper: it is what most authors do when they create characters, so that the result is seldom an authentic portrait of a single individual but a composite or amalgam. But it is useful for us to realize that the author, consciously or unconsciously, has not kept herself out of the play quite as much as her preface might suggest—useful because it explains the lack of aesthetic distance which separates her from her characters. For if this is Mrs McCullers's weakest performance—and I believe it is—the reason for it may well be that she is still too close to her materials. In *The Heart is a Lonely Hunter* and *The Member of the Wedding* she was on safer ground, because she was further from her subject.

Mollie's relationship to Phillip throughout reminds us forcibly of Mrs McCullers's to her own husband (and of Lucile's to Leroy in *The Heart Is a Lonely Hunter*). Thus, when John asks her, 'Why did you remarry Phillip Lovejoy?' she replies, 'I—I was under a spell—a strange spell.' She also tells John how Phillip has mistreated her: 'He struck me, he beat me up so many times. And I stood it.' John again asks, 'Why?' and she answers: 'I—why—we—I—in spite of all Phillip's terrible failings he had a lot of charm. A redeeming charm, somebody once said.' It is also obvious that her love for him is strongly compounded with pity (if we reverse the sexual roles we have exactly the same situation as in 'A Domestic Dilemma'). To John's question if her love for Phillip is 'just pity' she counters: ' "Just" is too small a word for pity. It's like saying 'just food, just God.' John, however, has the last word—and, incidentally, one of the best lines in the play: 'When will you be strong enough to love the strong?'

Though her choice of a life-death theme suggests that Mrs McCullers has consciously chosen a new area of literary interest, the reader will remember that the same theme was present in *Reflections in a Golden Eye*. Captain Penderton's personality, we recall, was 'heavily weighted' toward death, and in fact the resemblance between him and Phillip is too obvious to be overlooked: Penderton's need of the soldier parallels Phillip's need of Mollie, for both men, whose orientation is towards death, are seeking to correct this imbalance by establishing a vicarious contact with life. When Mollie asks Phillip, 'If you don't love me, why did you come back?' he says: 'Like the sick person watches the well. Like the dying watches the living.' He has come back, in short, to feed on her own vitality—a situation which is foreshadowed in the first few lines of the play when Paris describes his nightmare: 'And when I saw the burglar's face—the burglar was my father—in a burglar's cap.' The polarization of characters in this play also reminds us of *Reflections in a Golden Eye*: John (like Major Langdon) is dull and 'normal' while Phillip (like Penderton) is brilliant and neurotic. The contrast extends also to the women characters: while two men compete for Mollie, Sister is obliged to invent her lovers. In this analogy Sister corresponds somewhat to Alison Langdon, and Mollie (with important differences) to Leonora Penderton.

In his inability to love, Phillip personifies the death principle, or, in Freudian terms, the death wish (it is significant that he takes his own life), and Mollie, who is capable of loving more than one man simultaneously, personifies the *élan vital*. Life triumphs over death in the play, and in a sense it is the triumph of the mediocre over the exceptional, for Phillip is certainly the more interesting character. We may be repelled on moral grounds by the conscious tyranny of his appeal to Mollie's pity and maternal sense, but we must admire his honesty and his insight. When he asserts 'Mollie will never leave me', and John asks 'What makes you so sure?' here is his reply: 'Because I am weak, that's why I'm so sure.' Again, when Mrs Lovejoy asks, 'My son, why do you hate me?', he says, 'Because I hate myself.' And again, speaking of literary success: 'After these times of fallowness and failure, the only thing that really heartens me is to read of someone else's gut-tearing failure. I feed on the failures of others because I can no longer succeed. The first thing I read in the newspapers each morning are the obituaries. My talent is gone.' This scene continues as follows:

Sister: Where has it gone?
Phillip: Where did it come from in the first place? Not from the brain . . .
Sister: Then where, Phillip?
Phillip: From some strange little motor in the soul. And now the motor has stopped.

Phillip is the best realized character in the play, and the best lines are his. The healthy vulgarity of Mollie, who speaks in clichés throughout, reminds one a bit of Stella, in *A Streetcar Named Desire*, and indeed the two plays have rather similar conclusions: Phillip and Blanche Dubois have a number of things in common, and the eerie street cry of Williams's flower vendor ('*Flores— flores para los muertos*') applies as appropriately to Phillip's situation as it does to Blanche's. In both plays cultural accomplishment is associated with neurosis, even insanity (Phillip has had a 'nervous breakdown' prior to his stay in the sanitorium), while health is associated with animality.

Subordinate to the primary theme is a variety of minor motifs (too many, possibly, for the play to maintain its unity) which readers familiar with Mrs McCullers's earlier work will recognize at once. Thus, the irrationality of love is again insisted upon: Mollie says; 'Love is very much like witches and ghosts, and childhood—when it speaks to you you have to answer, and you have to go wherever it tells you'; and John remarks, not very originally, 'You can't plan love, it's something that comes round cornerwise when you least expect it.' So also is the loneliness that springs from an incapacity for love ('I feel surrounded by a zone of loneliness,' Phillip complains), and Sister's fantasies remind us of Mick's and Frankie's.

Again, the experience of love as an absolute, enabling the lover to love all things and all persons (which reminds us of both 'A Tree, A Rock, A Cloud' and *The Member of the Wedding*) is present here. When Mollie asks John, 'What is the square root of wonderful?' he answers simply, 'You.' The dialogue continues:

Mollie: Me? Arithmetic, isn't it?
John: That's right.
Mollie: Does it multiply?
John: No. More like divide.
Mollie: Me divide? To me love multiplies. When I fell in love with Phillip, I loved everybody.
John: Everybody?
Mollie: The manager of the Peach Festival, Tootsie Johnson and Billie Little.
John: Who's Billie Little?
Mollie: Just somebody I knew in those far-off days of love. Luminous, you might say, like this table . . . this chair.
John: This table, this chair?
Mollie: And when I fell in love with you, John, I loved everybody.
John: Everybody again?
Mollie: Phillip, the yardman, Sister, Mother Lovejoy . . . Don't you understand . . . if I had not loved so much, John, how could I love you as I do?

But the most important of the minor themes has to do with time. The relation of time to love is obvious: it is the Great Enemy of love as it is of life, of which love is the surest sign and the happiest manifestation. (Ferris, in the short story 'The Sojourner', presses Jeannine's little boy close to him 'as though an emotion as protean as his love could dominate the pulse of time.') Its relation to the problem of identity is equally obvious, since one's identity, as Frankie learns in *The Member of the Wedding*, changes with its passage.

In relation to loneliness, however, time takes on yet another significance. Thus, in *The Square Root of Wonderful*, Mollie remarks, apropos of the grandfather clock, 'It reminds me of peace and family,' and Phillip replies: 'It puts me in mind of time. You were winding it when I came back. Busily, busily winding time. I hate clocks.' Mollie merely says, 'It has a lovely chime.' Phillip does not dislike clocks because they remind him that time is running out; he dislikes them for the opposite reason, because they remind him of how much time he will have to kill before he finds release from his loneliness: for him, as for all unhappy people, clocks do not run too fast but too slow. Time passes quickly for the lover, and in that sense may be thought of as a traitor and an enemy, but it is an even greater enemy to the loveless. Phillip refers to it as 'that endless idiot that goes screaming round the world' (a line which, like several others he speaks toward the end of Act Two, is taken *verbatim* from a poem which Mrs McCullers wrote in 1948[7]), and he conceives of hell as 'noticed clocks on winter afternoons'. When the living room clock chimes at the end of this act, he smashes it with his fists, and the stage directions tell us that he looks 'frightened' as the clock 'chimes on and on' in what is one of the most effective moments of the play.[8]

Except in the case of Phillip (and, to a less extent, Mollie) the characterization is thin and lacking in complexity. John, Paris, Sister, and Mother Lovejoy are all type characters. Mother Lovejoy particularly is the type of female dragon (subtype, Domineering Parent) who has only to enter the stage for us to classify her immediately. She has, however, a few lines whose wit recalls some of the best of Restoration comedy. 'Such a fair will,' she murmurs when Uncle Willie makes her, a cousin twice removed, his chief beneficiary. 'Such a fair will and such a surprise to everybody.' And again: 'I'd always set my cap for Sister to marry a doctor. Not that she's sick, but sometimes I'm ailing.' But she bears too obvious a resemblance to Amanda Wingfield in *The Glass Menagerie*. She boasts of the many gentlemen callers she received before marrying her husband, who, (like Amanda's) later walked out on her, and her attitude toward Sister, a mixture of impatience and disappointment, is identical to Amanda's toward Laura. Like Amanda, she tries unsuccessfully to make a match for her daughter (with John, ironically), and, again like Amanda, she disapproves of her son because he refuses to hold down an ordinary job and wants to write. As for Paris, his speeches reveal a sophistication that is not in character. A thirteen-year-old boy, normal in other respects, does not use the word *zany* in casual conversation, nor would he be likely to say: 'Mother, you eavesdrop and read diaries. I don't respect anybody who reads diaries. Sly people.' Or: 'The door opened like a hinged window. You know how queer dream windows are.'

The Square Root of Wonderful is occasionally also guilty of humour on a rather low level. An example of this occurs in Act One, when, speaking of the Ten Commandments, John asks Mollie if she has ever coveted her neighbour's ox or ass. 'My neighbor's ass?' Mollie repeats (one can almost hear the snickers in the gallery), and

---

7 'When We Are Lost', *Voices, December* 1952, p. 12. The poem first appeared in *New Directions X* (1948), p. 509, where it was run together, by a printer's error, with another poem, 'The Mortgaged Heart'.

8 There is a striking resemblance between this scene and that in Faulkner's *The Sound and the Fury*, in which Quentin, another death-oriented character, smashes his watch shortly before *he* commits suicide.

John says, 'We'll check that one off.' To isolate such speeches is not, of course, to do justice to the play as a whole, for they occur but seldom. Technically, *The Square Root of Wonderful* is a well-made play (it makes surprisingly good reading), and the fact that it did not succeed on Broadway may merely mean that a popular audience is less interested in the personal problems of a literary has-been than in those of a fourteen-year-old girl—who might be the one next door—with growing pains. In this play Mrs McCullers is concerned with too specialized an area of human interest and experience—another way, perhaps, of saying that she is too close to her materials.

Produced by Saint Subber and Figaro Incorporated, directed by George Keathley, and with sets by Jo Mielziner, *The Square Root of Wonderful* opened at the National Theatre in New York on the evening of 30th October 1957. Anne Baxter, the popular screen actress, was cast in the role of Mollie, and Phillip was played by William Smithers.

It received a thorough and almost unanimous drubbing from the critics. A typical reaction was that of John Chapman, who wrote in *The New York Daily News*:

> *The Square Root of Wonderful,* which was handsomely and intelligently presented at the National Theatre last evening, might be described as a trauma in three acts. Watching and hearing it, I had the odd and uneasy feeling that I was a reluctant psychiatrist listening to the confidences of strangers. Since I did not know or particularly care for these strangers, I was uncomfortable.[9]

Louis Kronenberger observed:

> The author of *The Member of the Wedding* this time wrote on a variety of themes, in a variety of tones, at a variety of tempos. A work containing enough material for several plays emerged, for lack of integration, no play at all. The parts were not greater than the whole; they destroyed the whole . . . Jangling with false notes, *Square Root* could not mate humor with horror, or get its varied themes to coalesce; and in the attempt, Miss McCullers' genuine individuality and especial feeling for life became sadly blurred. What emerged was a square root in a round hole.[10]

[9] Cited in *New York Theatre Critics' Reviews,* XVIII (1957), p. 202.
[10] In *The Best Plays of 1957-58,* ed. by Louis Kronenberger (New York, Dodd, Mead, & Company, 1958), pp. 12-14.

In *The New York Herald-Tribune*, Walter Kerr reported:

> In the production at the National Theatre, the big laughs are landed. They are not, in themselves, bad laughs . . . And somewhere in the world there is no doubt a form capable of embracing both the wayward, almost unconscious humor that overtakes people in crises, and the terrifying crises themselves. (Perhaps Chekhov holds the patent.) Miss McCullers does not, in this instance, bring off the mating. One tone defies the other. Each jovial eruption snaps whatever tragic or pathetic thread we may have begun to cling to.[11]

More generous than most, Brooks Atkinson remarked:

> After *The Member of the Wedding*, Carson McCullers' second play seems commonplace. Especially at the end, there are passages of the precise though allusive prose with which Mrs McCullers can weave golden sentiments and wistful dreams out of common material. But most of *The Square Root of Wonderful* remains earthbound. The characters are hardly distinguishable from inhabitants of the conventional comedy of manners.[12]

It is interesting to note that the least charitable of all the reviewers was the same Harold Clurman who had done such a brilliant job of directing *The Member of the Wedding*. Writing in *The Nation*, he called the play a 'total dud' and attacked not only the direction, sets, and acting, but also the way in which the author presented the situation:

> The characters often fall out of focus, and it is one of the mistakes of the play's composition that the author felt constrained to make her story straightforward so that it might appear logical to the prosaic mind. The script might have been better if it had the faults natural to its author's genius.[13]

To the disappointment of everyone involved in its production, *The Square Root of Wonderful* closed after forty-five performances, on 7th December, a bare five weeks after it opened.[14]

---

11 Cited in *New York Theatre Critics' Reviews*, XVIII (1957), p. 202.
12 Cited in *New York Theatre Critics' Reviews*, XVIII (1957), p. 200.
13 *The Nation*, 23rd November 1957, p. 394.
14 *The Square Root of Wonderful* has never been produced in London, but the Group Theatre of Glasgow staged a production at the Palace of Art in Glasgow in March 1963.

* * *

CHAPTER TWELVE

THE SEARCH FOR THE SELF

1

Shortly before Mrs Smith died, Carson bought from her the big house in Nyack, and she has lived here ever since her return from France. It was here, typing laboriously with a single hand at the rate of a page a day and harassed by a series of physical misfortunes almost as numerous as they were painful, that she composed the bulk of *Clock Without Hands* and finally finished it in the spring of 1961: it had been nearly ten years in the making. She now regards Nyack as her permanent home, and has no wish to travel further. 'I have always,' she said recently, 'wanted to wander—fleeing, I suppose, from something—and now I want to settle. I was always homesick for a place I had never seen, and now I have found it. It is here—this house, this town.'

The completion of *Clock Without Hands* in the face of so many difficulties cannot be regarded as anything other than a moral triumph. There was even a time (in the spring of 1958) when she lost the will to write altogether. It was in an effort to recover this, which she had always regarded as the primary reason of her existence, that she paid a visit to a psychiatrist, Dr Mary Mercer. One bitterly cold day, when she was returning from her third session with Dr Mercer, she climbed, with a little more difficulty than usual, the long flight of stairs which led from the doctor's office to the street, entered a cab, and was barely seated in it when she collapsed and had to be taken into a hospital in a condition of acute cardiac failure. This alarming incident resulted in a complete revaluation of Carson's physical condition: a cardiologist made a diagnosis of chronic rheumatic heart disease. It was decided that her strokes, of which she lived in daily terror, were not caused by a congenital anomaly of the cerebral blood vessels (the diagnosis which had been made ten years previously), but rather by emboli from her damaged heart. Dr F. Randolph Baily, of Columbia-Presbyterian Hospital, thereupon set up a new pattern of physical care which has had the effect, among others, of relieving her fear of recurrences. A series of operations to relieve the spasm of her left arm and hand was performed during the next four years. At the end of one year, when the will to write returned and she resumed work on *Clock Without Hands*, psychotherapy was discontinued. Dr Mercer has since become one of her most intimate friends, and it was to her, as a token of gratitude, that Carson dedicated her new novel.

Not surprisingly, Carson had been discouraged by the reception of *The Square Root of Wonderful*.[1] No one seemed to notice its good points: everyone seized upon its weaknesses and made comparisons, sometimes quite pointless ones, with *The Member of the Wedding*. But granting, as I think one must, that this play is the least successful of her works, there is one sense in which it is important: it represents a widening of the author's perspective to include other metaphysical problems than those with which she had previously been occupied. For, with the publication of *The Member of the Wedding*, she had arrived at that critical point in a writer's career where, if he is to avoid repeating himself, it is necessary for him to choose another subject. *The Square Root of Wonderful*, if it was nothing else, was proof of Mrs McCullers's capacity to do this, at the same time that it repeated some of the familiar patterns of her earlier work. *Clock Without Hands* offers further—and more successful—evidence of this widening of interest and perspective.

There are four main characters: J. T. Malone, a forty-one-year-old pharmacist; his friend, Judge Clane, a militant white supremacist, aged eighty-five; the Judge's grandson, Jester, who is nineteen; and a blue-eyed Negro youth named Sherman Pew. When the novel opens, Malone has been told by his physician that he has leukaemia; though he knows he must die he does not know when, and is thus like a man watching a clock without hands. Malone is a sheeplike man who has allowed his life to be managed for him by other people, and, in a flash of self-knowledge born of the realization of his approaching death, he sees that he has never really lived: how then, he wonders, can he die? He is determined to acquire an identity in the few months remaining to him so that his life, before it ends, will have some meaning. Jester, likewise, is in search of an identity: he has not yet decided what he wants to be in life; though he has many passing interests he feels no 'call' for any particular vocation, and the anonymity of his situation is symbolized in the fact that he has never known either of his parents, his father having committed suicide shortly before his mother died in giving him birth. Still a third character, Sherman, is seeking to know himself,

1 See Chapter 11.

and in his case the fact coincides directly with the symbol, as he was a foundling who received his surname from the circumstance of his having been abandoned in a church.

The mystery surrounding Sherman's parentage adds much to the interest of the plot on a realistic level, and it is connected with the mystery surrounding the suicide of Jester's father. Jester finally learns from the Judge that he and his son had not seen eye-to-eye on the race problem (neither do Jester and the Judge, incidentally), and that his (Jester's) father, a lawyer, had fallen in love with one of his clients, a white woman whose Negro lover was on trial for murdering her husband. Jester's father tried to convince the all-white jury that the killing was in self defence, which it was, but the trial, at which the Judge presided (taking no pains to conceal his partiality to the prosecuting attorney instead of to his own son, the defence counsel), proved a mockery of justice: the Negro was hanged, and the woman, who had refused to testify against him, cursed Jester's father on her deathbed—she died in childbirth shortly after the trial—for losing the case. Maddened by his failure, by the injustice of the incident and his father's role in it, by the frustration of his love, and by the death of his client, who never guessed that he took more than a professional interest in the case, Jester's father shot himself. Sherman Pew was this woman's son by her Negro lover.

Jester's inherent liberalism is strengthened by the knowledge that racial injustice has been partly to blame for the tragedy of his father's life, and he resolves to become a lawyer himself and take up the battle where his father left off: his life thus achieves moral direction. Sherman is not so fortunate; he is to find his identity in martyrdom, for when he moves into a white neighbourhood his house is bombed, and, though he has been warned by Jester, he refuses to flee and loses his life. As for Malone, who has taken orders all his life, his opportunity comes when, at a drawing of lots to determine who shall bomb Sherman's house, the job falls to him and he refuses it. Shortly after this he dies with the consolation of having made a moral choice and thus of having lived at last, however briefly.

2

In all of Mrs McCullers's earlier work—even in *The Square Root of Wonderful*—she was concerned with the loneliness that results from a lack of rapport with other individuals; in *Clock Without Hands* she is concerned with the loneliness that results from a lack of rapport with the self. The search for self is the theme of her latest novel, and in its insistence upon the necessity for moral engagement and upon the importance of moral choice it is impossible not to recognize the impact of existential doctrine in the manner of Sartre (that is to say, anti-religious): indeed, the 'existential crisis'—the achievement of identity through engagement and choice—is at the very centre of the narrative. (The book that Malone chooses to read in the hospital is Kierkegaard's *Sickness Unto Death*, and the sentence in it which most impresses him is: 'The greatest danger, that of losing one's own self, may pass off as if it were nothing; every other loss, that of an arm, a leg, five dollars, a wife, etc., is sure to be noticed.')

How the theme of identity is related to that of loneliness has been explained in the preceding chapter, and they are both related to the time phenomenon: loss of identity results in loneliness, and when one is lonely time, as we have noted, passes with maddening slowness. It is for this reason that Malone, while he is waiting for his death—or rather for the moment of free engagement which will give meaning to his life—complains of a 'zone of loneliness' (the same phrase that Phillip uses in *The Square Root of Wonderful*[2]); that the summer seems interminable to Jester, lounging in his grandfather's big house; and that Sherman, in spite of the job the Judge gives him as his 'private amanuensis', is horribly bored and haunted towards the end by a feeling that he must 'do something'. The old Judge is lonely also, not because he lacks identity—he has made all the wrong choices!—but because when his wife, whom he loved sincerely, died, his capacity for love died with her. He does not love his grandson so much as he is hurt by the knowledge (which he tries to conceal from himself) that Jester can no longer love *him*.

The theme of identity is also related to that of ideal love. Like Frankie in *The Member of the Wedding*, both Jester and Sherman yearn to identify themselves with something bigger than themselves and outside themselves, which is merely another way of saying that they are unconsciously seeking a love-object. This is symbolized on the literal level by the fact that Jester cannot love his grandfather, whose ideas he despises—though he does pity him occasionally— and that Sherman, longing for a mother, invents a fantasy that she is Marian Anderson. The same is true of Malone, of whom it is signifi-

2 Numerous echoes of the play occur in the novel: both Judge Clane and Mother Lovejoy have for their favourite quotation Shakespeare's lines from *King Lear*, 'How sharper than a serpent's tooth it is/To have a thankless child'; and Jester, like Sister, is given to sudden spells of vomiting.

cant that he cannot, except in his moment of final weakness[3], love his wife: he is seeking an ideal love, not a physical one (like Frankie, he does not wish to be joined to any particular person but to *that which joins all people*—as Frankie puts it, 'the "we" of me'). It is by thus identifying themselves with something larger than themselves—in this case the idea of social justice—that all of them become conscious of their individual identities. This paradox (that selfhood can only be attained by identification with something outside the self) occurs, as the reader will remember, elsewhere in Mrs McCullers's work, particularly in *The Member of the Wedding*: not until Frankie thinks of herself as a 'we' person can she rid herself of her childish fantasies and know 'who she is' and 'where she is going'. Compare, in this connection, the following passages, the first from *The Member of the Wedding*, the second from *Clock Without Hands*:

> Frankie stood looking into the sky. For when the old question came to her—the who she was and what she would be in the world, and why she was standing there that minute—when the old question came to her, she did not feel hurt and unanswered. At last she knew who she was and understood where she was going . . . And finally, after the scared spring and the crazy summer, she was no more afraid.

and

> Who am I? What am I? Where am I going? Those questions, the ghosts that haunt the adolescent heart, were finally answered for Jester . . . Gone were the dreams of saving Sherman from a mob and losing his own life while Sherman looked on, broken with grief. Gone also were the dreams of saving Marilyn Monroe from an avalanche in Switzerland and riding through a hero's ticker tape parade in New York . . . His dreams were nearly always in foreign countries. Never in Milan, never in Georgia, but always in Switzerland or Bali or someplace. But now his dreams had strangely shifted . . . Night after night he dreamed of his father. And having found his father he was able to find himself. He was his father's son and he was going to be a lawyer. Once the bewilderment of too many choices was cleared away, Jester felt happy and free.

The search for identity parallels the search for ideal love, but in

---

[3] Lubbers, I think, misinterprets this scene. He writes (op. cit., p. 204): 'Malone's love for his wife has returned just as Martin Meadows in a short story "A Domestic Dilemma" finds back to "the immense complexity of love". Thus the burden of impersonal love that Biff takes up and that is rationalized in "A Tree, A Rock, A Cloud" is replaced by mutual love for the first time. Malone's change, however, is not caused by a spiritual transformation but by physical exhaustion: his 'livingness' is leaving him, as the author tells us in so many words.

Clock Without Hands, as elsewhere in Mrs McCullers's work, love on the physical level is doomed to disappointment: Malone's marriage is a failure sexually and his only acquaintance with physical passion has been an affair guiltily carried on in his wife's absence many years ago; Malone's daughter, Ellen, loves Jester, who is scarcely aware of her existence; Jester is secretly in love with Sherman, who constantly mistreats him; and Sherman worships another Negro, Zippo, whose 'house guest' he is and who mistreats *him.* The pattern is even carried back to an earlier generation, for it will be remembered that Jester's father was in love with his client, who cursed him with her dying breath. Here, as in *The Ballad of the Sad Café,* love 'chases its own tail',[4] and the beloved 'fears and hates' the lover: when Jester attempts to kiss Sherman he fares no better than Marvin Macy—the kiss is returned with a blow; and when Malone's wife makes advances to him he, like Miss Amelia, is repelled and rushes from the house. And just as Mrs McCullers in her other novels was careful to select characters between whom any physical union was out of the question (like the man-like Amelia and the homosexual dwarf) she has here been at pains to depict another impossible situation, since Sherman is not only of the same sex as Jester but is also a Negro. For these reasons I find it difficult to agree with Lubbers when he claims that in Mrs McCullers's later work she has 'tended to emphasize the one side of Brannon's vision, putting more stress on "radiance" and "faith" than upon "irony" and "darkness".'[5] It is true that her themes have multiplied and widened, but her vision of life remains profoundly pessimistic. Here is Malone leaving church, where the text of the sermon has been 'The Salvation that Draws the Bead on Death':

> But, although the sermon was long, death remained a mystery, and after the first elation he felt a little cheated when he left the church. How could you draw a bead on death? It was like aiming at the sky. Malone stared up at the blue, unclouded sky until his neck felt strained.

[4] The phrase is Lubbers's, who applies it to *The Ballad of the Sad Café* but not to *Clock Without Hands*: 'The theme of love chasing its own tail forms the logical capstone of an evolution through the three previous works. Its morbidity is made bearable and convincing by narrative detachment, remoteness in time and the witnessing town that stays outside the emotional boundary line. With *Clock Without Hands* a new concept of order is announced. Life becomes a state in which, at least at the end, everything is in its right place.' But everything is *not* in its right place, either at the end or at the beginning: Lubbers is forcing the narrative to fit his thesis rather than allowing his thesis to be shaped by the narrative.

[5] Op. cit., p. 204.

Like the men in Stephen Crane's 'Open Boat' he here acknowledges the depressing probability that nature 'would not maim the universe by disposing of him'. The word *unclouded* is a stroke of genius, implying as it does the indifference of nature (like the windmill in Crane's story) to the fact that Malone is a dying man.[6] And organized religion is made to appear as ineffectual in *Clock Without Hands* as in the existential literature by which it was more directly influenced. When Malone, seeking comfort from his minister, inquires about the after-life, the latter is embarrassed:

> In church, and after twenty years of experience, Dr Watson could make glib speeches about the soul; but in his own home, with only one man asking, his glibness turned to embarrassment and he only said, 'I don't know what you mean, Mr Malone.'

When Malone persists, Dr Watson thinks the conversation is 'getting morbid' and ends it with a shibboleth: 'It's not up to man's judgment to decide what is good and what is bad. God sees the truth, and is our Savior.'

In *Clock Without Hands* there is the same peculiar mixture of love and pity that, as we have seen, defined the relationship of Singer and Antonapoulos, of Mrs Langdon and Anacleto, of Martin and Emily Meadows, and of Amelia and Cousin Lymon. For Mrs Malone's ill-timed advances towards her husband are made in the knowledge that he has not long to live, and Jester feels sorry for Sherman because of his race. Another familiar idea in this novel is that illusions are necessary to enable men to endure their existence. Just as Mick dreams of becoming a concert pianist and Frankie dreams of travelling around the world, and just as Sister chooses her lovers from the Mediterranean area, so here Jester dreams of rescuing Sherman from a lynching and of saving Marilyn Monroe from an avalanche. Sherman, for his part, dreams of being gloriously martyred to the tune of 'John Brown's Body'; of deserting his fiancée, a lily-white French girl whom he has impregnated, at the altar; and of the day when Marian Anderson (to whom he writes letters that are never answered) will acknowledge him openly as her son. 'A lot of my life', he admits, 'I've had to make up stories because the real, actual was either too dull or too hard to take'. Even the old Judge has his dreams, which centre about the restoration of Confederate currency by the federal government. As for

6 The same brand of naturalism occasionally occurs in Emily Dickinson, where it is placed in an oddly religious context. See, for example, the poem 'Apparently with No Surprise', where the sun remains 'unmoved' at the spectacle of the flowers' death and God Himself gives an 'approving nod'.

Malone, bored (like Biff Brannon) with his wife and work, he day-dreams constantly—of snow, of faraway places, and of the one illicit and genuine love of his life. His situation also reminds us somewhat of Frankie Addams's, for he, no less than she (and Captain Penderton and Sister) is destined for the commonplace. Malone, indeed, is Everyman, with Everyman's share of faults but also with his dignity and capacity for the moral life. And of course the shadow of his impending death is the shadow under which all men labour: to this extent we are all watching a 'clock without hands'.

3

Clock Without Hands, then, is both like and unlike Mrs Mc-Cullers's earlier work. There is one important respect in which it harks back to her first novel, and that is in its concern with the racial problem—a theme which is missing in *Reflections in a Golden Eye*, *The Ballad of the Sad Café*, *The Square Root of Wonderful*, and which is present only secondarily in *The Member of the Wedding*. The institutions she attacked in *The Heart Is a Lonely Hunter* were wage slavery and Jim Crowism, but in *Clock Without Hands* her criticism is directed almost exclusively at the latter. The central problem of identity, in the case of each of the main characters, is solved in terms of the peculiar relationship that exists between Negroes and whites in the South. And of all Mrs McCullers's books, this is the one that calls most urgently for specific reform. In *The Heart Is a Lonely Hunter*, the mill workers and the Negroes for whom Jake Blount and Dr Copeland are prepared, respectively, to make such sacrifices, leave a good bit to be desired; they are, almost as much as their oppressors, content with their *status quo*. Dr Copeland himself is a sick man, a fanatic, and his efforts to improve the lot of his people are largely ineffectual—just as are Blount's to further the cause of communism, and for the same reason. But in *Clock Without Hands* the lines are more clearly drawn, and one is made to feel that some tangible benefits may result from Jester's sober determination to right the wrongs against which his father battled unsuccessfully during his short lifetime. The author seems to be saying that it is boys like this, educated and possessing a sense of fairness, upon whom the South must depend eventually for its moral salvation. In this respect at least *Clock Without Hands* is the most positive of Mrs McCullers's works. The casual clubbing to death by a white policeman of the half-witted Grown Boy, the bombing of Sherman Pew's newly-rented house (filled with instalment-bought furniture) while he sits singing at the piano—these are incidents successfully calculated to induce in the reader a sense of

horror and dismay with none of the melodrama that in less skilful
hands would have been certain to ruin the narrative. For this is
dangerous material, inviting the reader to a cliché response that is
rather an appeal to his humanitarian sympathies than to his aesthetic
sense.

Against the forces of reason and justice, personified by Jester and
his father, we have the massive bulk of old Judge Clane, representa-
tive of bigotry and expedience (backed by the 'white trash' element
which gathers in Malone's pharmacy for the lot drawing[7]), who wins
the first battle—against his son—but who will not win the second,
in which his grandson and Malone, feeble as he is, are to be the
victors. His complete breakdown at the end of the novel symbolizes
the collapse of the old order in the South: when the schools are
ordered to integrate he attempts to make a speech over the radio, but
his rage renders him inarticulate, his reason and memory desert
him, and he finds himself, to the horror of his hearers, reciting Lincoln's Gettysburg Address. Mrs Malone, listening, comments to her
husband, 'I don't know what he was talking about. What happened?'
and the dying man answers: 'Nothing, darling. Nothing that was not
a long time in the making.' Malone's reply can be interpreted both as
meaning that the South has finally been made to acknowledge the
implications of Lincoln's message, and that the struggle in the Judge
between conscience and self-interest (a struggle which began with
the suicide of his son and which has tortured him on the unconscious
level ever since) has finally succeeded in destroying his mind.

Judge Clane has made a lifelong habit of dishonesty; he has never
paid his state income tax and reads the *Kinsey Report* behind the
dust jacket of Gibbons's *Decline and Fall of the Roman Empire* at
the same time that he causes it to be banned from the public library.
He is also a master of self-deception, seeing only what he wishes to
see and hearing only what he wishes to hear. After suffering a stroke,
this is his reaction:

> He would not admit it was a true stroke—spoke of 'a light case
> of polio', 'little seizure', etc. When he was up and around, he
> declared he used the walking stick because he liked it and that
> the 'little attack' had probably benefited him as his mind had
> grown keener because of contemplation and 'new studies'.

He will not face the fact that his wife, 'Miss Missy', is dying of
cancer:

---

[7] This group recalls the mill workers who exasperate Jake Blount in *The
Heart Is a Lonely Hunter* and the delegation which calls on Miss Amelia in
The Ballad of the Sad Café.

When it was apparent that his wife was failing, he didn't want to know and tried to deceive both her and himself . . . When it was obvious that his wife was in pain, the Judge would tiptoe softly to the refrigerator, eat without tasting what he ate, thinking only that his wife had been very sick and was just recovering from a serious operation. So he steadied himself to his secret everyday grief, and would not let himself understand.

After her death, his actions remind us of Berenice's:

His wife had sung in the choir and he loved to watch the throats and bosoms of women when they sang. There were some lovely ladies in the First Baptist choir, especially one soprano whom the Judge watched constantly. But there were other church choirs in the town. With a feeling of heresy, the Judge went to the Presbyterian church where there was a blond singer . . . his wife had been blond . . . whose singing throat and breast fascinated him, although otherwise she was not quite to his taste. So, dressed to kill and sitting on one of the front rows, the Judge visited the various churches of the town and watched and judged the choirs, in spite of the fact that he had very little ear for music and was always singing off key and very loudly.

And again:

There had begun a veiled, subconscious search for his dead wife. Miss Missy was a pure woman, and automatically he considered only the pure. A choir singer, only choir singers attracted him. But Miss Missy had also been an excellent poker player; and unmarried, pure choir singers who are also canny poker players are somewhat rare.

But the Judge's portrait is not one-dimensional. He is not merely sad and ridiculous; he is also, on occasion, both wise (though his wisdom is very much of this world) and shrewd. 'It is a sad commentary', he tells Malone, 'but every man has to have somebody to look down on', and shortly thereafter Sherman, who has nobody to look down on, proves him right by killing the family dog, who loves him, in a wild fit of frustration. Concerning local juries, the Judge has advised his son: 'Talk on their own level and for God's sake don't try to lift them above it':

But would Johnny do that? He argued as if those Georgia crackers, millhands, and tenant farmers were trained jurors of the Supreme Court itself. Such talent. But not a grain of common sense.

Had Johnny remembered his father's advice, he might well have won his case.

Taken all in all, old Judge Clane, with his turnip greens and his classical allusions, is, with the exception of Mick Kelly and Frankie Addams, Mrs McCullers's most thoroughly realized character to date. Only superficially is he a caricature, and he manages to be ludicrous, pathetic, and contemptible all at the same time. The glimpses we have of him shuffling about in the kitchen preparing his solitary breakfast, or hiding his grandson's photograph when he is displeased about something, or even relieving himself in the bathroom ('When the odor rose, he was not annoyed by this; on the contrary, since he was pleased by anything that belonged to him, and his feces were no exception') are unforgettable, little masterpieces of realism, and the moment one finds himself admitting this he almost wishes it were not so. For Judge Clane, though he dominates the book, is relevant in only a mechanical way to the central allegory. One is grateful for having met him, but the design of the novel requires that he play a relatively minor part. The protagonist ought to be Malone; it is he, not Judge Clane, who is Everyman, Everyman sentenced to die and watching a clock without hands. *Clock Without Hands* is a novel whose climax occurs when the various characters find their separate identities: its interest lies in their moral progression, and in the Judge's case there is no progression, only deterioration. The author has allowed herself to be carried away in the process of creating a character who, for all his lifelikeness, is minor to her essential purpose. The realistic level of the story is concerned with his activities, and they are so engrossing in themselves that they detract from the primary theme. *Clock Without Hands,* in fact, raises an interesting critical question: the extent to which realism may be desirable in the novel of ideas. For, particularly in allegory, the realistic level, while coherent, must always be secondary to the symbolic. In Kafka, for example, the realistic level is negligible: the reader understands from the first that it is not to be taken as seriously as the symbolic, and if his characters are less convincing as human beings than Mrs McCullers's they are for that reason more effective as symbols.

4

There are other flaws. Sherman Pew is the least successful in the long gallery of Mrs McCullers's grotesques, and here we have a similar difficulty, for he is at once too *outré* to be credible on realistic terms and not sufficiently so to be a genuine grotesque like, say, Cousin Lymon. (Chapter IV, which relates his initial encounter with

Jester, is unquestionably the weakest in the book.) Some of the minor characters are crudely, even carelessly drawn, like the police-man who, after his lethal clubbing of Grown Boy, unexpectedly con-fides to Jester:

> When you break up a crowd with a billy stick you don't know how hard you are hitting. I don't like violence any more than you do. Maybe I shouldn't even have joined the force.

If these remarks are sincere they do not convince because they have not been properly prepared for; if, on the other hand, they are in-sincere, the insincerity should have been made more obvious.

As against these defects, *Clock Without Hands* exhibits a greater sophistication than any of Mrs McCullers's other works. The psycho-logical subtlety of which she is capable is nowhere more in evidence or more admirable, expressing itself in a variety of insights, frequently of an ironical or paradoxical nature. When Jester says to Sherman, 'It must give you a funny feeling not to know who your mother was', this is how he responds:

> 'No, it don't . . . Once you get used to it it don't bother you at all.' He said this because he had never gotten accustomed to it.

And again, when Jester asks, 'Why is it so hard to be friends with you?':

> 'Because I don't want friends,' Sherman lied, because next to a mother, he wanted a friend the most.

Speaking of the sense of humour which was almost the only thing that Judge Clane and his son had in common, Mrs McCullers wrote:

> Often the father and son who responded to the ridiculous in the same manner were caught by such laughter. This side of their relationship had prompted the Judge to a further assumption, to a fallacy often common in fathers. 'Johnny and I are more like two brothers than father and son. The same love of fishing and hunting, same sterling sense of values—I have never known my son to tell a lie—same interests, same fun.' So the Judge would harp on such fraternal similarities to his audiences in Malone's pharmacy, in the courthouse, in the back room of the New York Café and in the barbershop. His listeners, seeing little relation between the shy young Johnny Clane and his town-character father, made no comment. When the Judge himself realized the widening difference between his son and himself, he harped

on the father-son theme more than ever, as though words could turn the wish into reality.

In *Clock Without Hands*, as in *The Ballad of the Sad Café*, the author occasionally ignores Flaubertian rules of technique to make a generalization about human nature; when she does this the result, as in the case of the earlier story, is nearly always striking. Not the least impressive of what Tennessee Williams has called Mrs Mc-Cullers's 'stunning array of gifts'[8] is the one which enables her to utter universal truths with such simplicity and directness that it seems inconceivable to the reader that he has not encountered them previously, stated in these very words, yet he will search his memory for them in vain. To this category belongs the opening sentence, 'Death is always the same, but each man dies in his own way', and, perhaps even more emphatically : 'When hurt has been caused by a loved one, only the loved one can comfort.' In a scene where Malone and the Judge are seized simultaneously with a hysterical fit of laughter, she observes: 'The laughter of disaster does not stop easily, and so they laughed for a long time, each for his own disaster.' And of Jester she tells us that he 'knew dimly that fury is unleashed more freely against those you are most close to . . . so close that there is the trust that anger and ugliness will be forgiven'. It is of course possible to argue, as did Ford Madox Ford with immense per-suasiveness, that such observations have no place in fiction, but if this be so many of the most universally admired works in Western literature (some of which, incidentally, Ford praised in his *March of Literature*) would not meet with our approval : ought we not rather to alter our criteria and agree instead that pronouncements of this kind are as interesting—or as dull—as the minds from which they proceed?

5

Clock Without Hands was reviewed simultaneously (September 17th, 1961) in *The New York Times* and *The New York Herald-Tribune*, and both papers ran full-page advertisements containing blurbs by Graham Greene ('I've read the new Carson McCullers with the usual pleasure. Other novels are visible and audible, but hers seem to have a taste and a smell as well—a sharp unmistakable quality.'); Tennessee Williams ('She has once again, and more deeply than ever before, examined the heart of man, with an understanding beyond knowledge, a compassion beyond sentiment.'); and Kathryn

---

8   In his introduction to the reprint of *Reflections in a Golden Eye* which New Directions issued in 1950.

Hulme ('I can never find critical words for such a rare novel as Carson McCullers' *Clock Without Hands*. I am most grateful to have had an advance look at this masterpiece.' The same advertisements quoted David Garnett to the effect that Mrs McCullers was 'the best living American writer' and Dame Edith Sitwell: 'Carson McCullers has a great poet's eye and mind and senses, together with a great prose writer's sense of construction and character. She is a transcendental writer. There can be no slightest doubt about that.'

Notwithstanding this publicity, *Clock Without Hands* has proved to be the most controversial of Mrs McCullers's books. On the same Sunday that Irving Howe smashed it to pieces in *The New York Times*, Rumer Godden, in *The New York Herald-Tribune*, gave it the most prominent place in the house. Mr Howe wrote:

> Mrs McCullers clearly had in mind a symbolic scheme: the white judge and Negro boy seem to represent varieties of the social fantasy choking the South, while Malone embodies the ineradicable truth about human existence. Yet the book is so poorly constructed—one is troubled throughout by a disharmony between the sober realism of the Malone section and the grotesque capers of the section dealing with the Judge and Sherman Pew—that the symbolic scheme fails to carry strength or conviction . . . What is most disturbing about *Clock Without Hands* is the lethargic flatness of the prose. The style of her new novel . . . is that of a novelist mechanically going through the motions, and commiting to paper not an integrated vision of life but an unadorned and scrappy scenario for a not-yet-written novel. Nothing, to be sure, is more difficult for the critic to establish than the absence of inner conviction and imaginative energy in a novel; yet once all serious intentions have been honored and all technical problems noted, only this conviction, only this energy really matters. And in *Clock Without Hands*, I regret to say, it is not to be found.[9]

And Miss Godden:

> For me not a word could be added or taken away from this marvel of a novel by Carson McCullers . . . Above all her gift is apart, aloof, inevitably lonely: it owes nothing to any other writer and is paradoxical, a sure sign of richness: it is powerful yet humble, dignified yet utterly unpretentious.

She added shrewdly:

9 Book Review Section, p. 5.

Of course truth is not always palatable. There are parts in this book that may even now shock in their matter-of-fact treatment of certain subjects. Truth, too, can give an uncomfortable bleakness, and one can well understand that, of Mrs McCullers' novels, only *The Member of the Wedding,* a masterpiece, has become universally popular. This new book may well be too strange and strong, too frank, for many people.[10]

Granville Hicks, in *Saturday Review,* while maintaining 'Nothing she has done is quite as good as her first book,' observed:

In an important sense this is a novel about the race problem . . . But Mrs McCullers is not trying to underline the obvious fact that there is a problem, nor has she a solution she wishes to thrust upon us, her purpose is to share the problem at the deepest possible level, as it penetrates the secret recesses of human souls.[11]

Reading the various reviews, one sometimes rubs one's eyes. Thus, concerning the novel's point of view, Gore Vidal wrote: 'Technically it is breathtaking to watch Mrs McCullers set a scene and then dart from character to character, opening up in a phrase, in a line, a life.'[12] But here is Robert O. Bowen: 'The action skips about so much from one point of view to another that the impression is fleeting and superficial as in watching a television show replete with commercials.'[13] According to *The Times Literary Supplement,* Sherman Pew is 'the most brilliantly realized of the three characters',[14] but John Gross, of *The New Statesman,* found him 'cold and cruel, a sad disappointment after the Negroes in the earlier stories',[15] and Louis D. Rubin, in *The Sewanee Review,* pronounced him a 'failure'.[16] Of the style, Mr Vidal said: 'Mrs McCullers writes in exact prose closer to the Flaubert of *Un Coeur Simple* than to *Absalom! Absalom!* There is never a false note. Her genius for prose remains one of the few satisfactory achievements of our second-rate culture.' But Mr Howe, as we have seen, objected to the 'lethargic flatness' of the writing, and Whitney Balliett, of *The New Yorker,* wrote: 'Mrs

10   *Books,* p. 5.
11   23rd September 1961, p. 15.
12   Op. cit., loc. cit.
13   *The Catholic World,* December 1961, p. 186.
14   20th October 1961, p. 749.
15   27th October 1961, p. 614.
16   Summer 1962, p. 509.

McCullers's prose, rumpled and gossipy, gives the peculiar impression of having been slept in.'[17] There must, indeed, be few contemporary novels which have elicited such extremes of criticism, the reviewers either echoing the ecstatic admiration of Miss Godden or agreeing with Robert O. Bowen that it was 'a comic book for the intellectual delinquent':

> Clock Without Hands is Southern Gothic of an almost purely Partisan Review-New Yorker-Guggenheim Foundation bias . . . The McCullers recipe for Southern Gothic follows the rules for form and content set down by Truman Capote and Flannery O'Connor as a dash of sympathy for homosexuals, a bit of the macabre, some basting with lavatory-wall vulgarisms and a garnish of pseudo-liberal canards on race and religion.

But though their reactions tended to polarize, only a few critics felt that Clock Without Hands was Mrs McCullers's best novel. Mr Vidal thought that she was not, for the first time, completely at ease with her materials, that her proper domain was not the public world but the private one of her own transcendental vision. And Louis D. Rubin reached a somewhat similar conclusion:

> However much one may sympathize with Miss McCullers' attitude toward the segregation issue, as a work of fiction Clock Without Hands is a confusing book. For the political and social issues which apparently provide the motivations and the plights of her characters do not in fact do so. Her people aren't really the sort who care about such things . . . It is as if Miss McCullers determined to write a novel 'about' the segregation issue, and fashioned her people entirely with this issue in mind. The result is not a novel but a tract. The failure is exemplified in the failure of Sherman Pew as a character; sometimes he is a symbol, sometimes a human being, but never both at the same time.

The judgment of Jean Martin, in The Nation, was exceptional:

> From the standpoint of its author, Clock Without Hands is a step forward, a success, for it eschews the pointed and labored allegory of her earlier works and the frequently trumped-up Southern characters have now been blended happily into a believable story level. Carson McCullers has always been a writer's writer; darling of the 'Southern Group', lavishly praised by Tennessee Williams, Truman Capote, et al, visited by Françoise Sagan on her recent tour of the American beaches. McCullers is

[17] 23rd September 1961, p. 179.

reported to be considered by Europeans as our best American novelist. From the viewpoint of her fellow-writers, Mrs Mc-Cullers' outstanding quality is her courage. Ever since she published *The Heart Is a Lonely Hunter,* at twenty-two, she has had to write with the albatross of reputation hanging around her neck and the thumping signboard of 'genius' staring her in the teeth. That she has managed to grow in the face of this has taken guts. *Clock Without Hands* is warm, funny, and readable; its point may not quite click, but the writing is quietly superb.[18]

To Mrs McCullers, one of the most heartening aspects of the book's publication was the way it was received in England, where, almost simultaneously with the American edition, it was issued by Cresset. Almost without exception the British critics reviewed *Clock Without Hands* soberly and respectfully. *The Times Literary Supplement,* for example, commented:

> Novels of the South have at the moment a sharply topical relevance. The problems of race which they naturally explore confront us all in one shape or another; and the sense of a larger, expectant audience is a temptation to melodrama and exaggeration. It is vastly to Mrs McCullers' credit that she avoids such pitfalls, while subtly presenting the moral issues and analyzing the psychology of the distressing situation. She has been able by dint of honesty as much as by technical skill to write a good and moving book which comes up to all the demands raised by her reputation.[19]

6

Though it received a mixed press in the U.S.A., *Clock Without Hands* immediately found a place on *The New York Times's* Best Seller list: a month after publication it was the seventh best-selling novel in the nation, and it remained for five months on this list. Doubtless it is still too early for a critic to evaluate *Clock Without Hands* with the proper degree of perspective. My own feeling is: granted that the book is uneven stylistically, that it suffers from a division of narrative purpose, and that its themes do not combine so smoothly as one might wish, Mrs McCullers's latest novel is, after *The Member of the Wedding,* the best of her full-length works. (I am excluding, of course, since it is a novella, *The Ballad of the Sad Café.*) It is less ambiguous in its implications than the first novel, its psychology is subtler and more complex, its compassion is more

18   18th November 1961, p. 411.
19   20th October 1961, p. 749.

authentic and all-embracing, its form is firmer, and its style is generally more impressive. It lacks the high polish and the formal perfection of *Reflections in a Golden Eye,* but it is a much maturer work, and infinitely more difficult of achievement. What mars it, finally, is not so much that its author, as Mr Vidal believes, lacks that knowledge of the world of public events which would enable her to describe it convincingly (one must not underestimate the imagination that enabled a sheltered girl of twenty-two to create so successfully the atmosphere of an army camp), nor is it that the characters who interest her are not, as Mr Rubin contends, the sort who take public events seriously : I think there is some truth in what both these critics say (Mr Rubin is exactly right about Sherman Pew), but to my mind Mrs McCullers's greatest defect is a defect of *form,* of the vehicle or medium by means of which she chooses to communicate her meaning. When, as in *The Ballad of the Sad Café,* the medium is uniformly abstract, the result is high art. When, as in *The Member of the Wedding,* the medium is an almost perfect compromise or adjustment between the abstract and the concrete, the symbolic and the realistic, the result is, again, high art. On the other hand, when the medium is uncertain, when realism struggles with allegory, and the concrete alternates and is made to compete with the abstract, the result is a hybrid. *The Heart Is a Lonely Hunter* is such a hybrid; so also, I think, is *Clock Without Hands.* And both are among the most interesting American novels of the last quarter century.

* * *

CHAPTER THIRTEEN

AT THE MOMENT

1

One might have hoped that a correct diagnosis and a programme of reconstructive surgery might have put an end to Carson's physical problems, but this was not to be the case. Cancer of the right breast developed in the spring of 1962; it was removed in June, in a double operation lasting eight hours during which final surgery was also performed upon her left hand. By August of the following year she was well enough to work with Edward Albee on his dramatization of *The Ballad of the Sad Café*.[1] However, only a month later, there was cause for further worry: a suspicion of cancer of the cervix, which, fortunately, was dispelled by a biopsy in September 1963. But in May 1964 disaster occurred once more: Carson fell to the bathroom floor and shattered her left hip. Again surgery was performed, and a metal cap inserted over the femur. Misfortune even

[1] Readers interested in Mr Albee's experience in adapting this play from the novel should consult *The Transatlantic Review*, Summer, 1963, in which he is interviewed by Digby Diehl. The interview ran in part as follows:

Mr Diehl: What about the McCullers novel? Why did you choose to do a task that you yourself have said has not been done well in the past?

Mr Albee: Exactly that reason. No, two reasons really, but one of them is that I am interested in finding out what happens when people do adaptations of novels for the stage. Usually there's a tendency to cheapen—to lessen the work that's adapted . . . I am interested in finding out if it is possible to do an adaptation of somebody else's work—to move it from the pages of the novel to the life of the stage—without cheapening or lessening the work. And then again, ten years ago—Is it ten?, yes, probably eleven years now—when I first read *The Ballad of the Sad Café*, I said to myself, If I ever start writing plays I'd like to make this into a play . . . My responsibility, of course, in putting Carson McCullers' novel on the stage is to make it seem as if Carson McCullers had written it for the stage. So I must indeed become Carson McCullers. The novella *The Ballad of the Sad Café* has two lines of dialogue. That's all in the entire 110-page book. It's my intention (and I hope I succeed in it) to turn all of that narration into dialogue which sounds as if it were written by Carson McCullers . . .

Mr. Diehl: You think you're attempting to speak in her voice.

Mr Albee: I am using my judgment and whatever craft I have (and naturally I must be speaking my own voice). I am using whatever craft I have to make the piece completely Carson McCullers.

followed her out of the hospital, for her convalescence was complicated by severe and repeated onslaughts of pneumonia in the big
house at Nyack, and not until August was she strong enough to com-
mence physiotherapy designed to enable her to walk again. On 2nd
September 1964, a date she will never forget—for she had begun to
fear she would be permanently bedridden—she was able to walk
from her bedroom to the living room. She had to return in a wheel-
chair, but her achievement was a cause of rejoicing both to her and
her friends.

Mrs McCullers's life in recent years, however, has not been altogether Job-like. As recently as February 1959, she was able to dance
with Arthur Miller at a luncheon party which she gave in Nyack for
her friend Isak Dinesen (in private life the Baroness Karen Blixen
Finecke). She had met the Baroness at a dinner of the American
Academy of Arts and Letters. On that occasion, when she learned
that the distinguished Danish authoress whom she so admired, and
whose work had such an affinity with her own, was to be among the
guests, she had asked the president of the Academy if she might be
seated near her. To her astonishment he replied that the Baroness,
who was familiar with her books, had already requested that Carson
be seated next to her: the place cards were already on the table!
'When I met her,' Mrs McCullers has written, 'she was very, very
frail and old but as she talked her face was lit like a candle in an old
church.'[2] The Baroness had also expressed a wish to meet Marilyn
Monroe, and as Arthur Miller, with whom Carson was acquainted,
was seated at the next table, she decided to invite him and his
beautiful wife to a luncheon party at which the Baroness would be
the guest of honour. Mrs McCullers, in the tribute which she paid
Isak Dinesen in *The Saturday Review* following her death in September, 1962, thus describes the party:

> Tanya [the Baroness] ate only oysters and drank only cham-
> pagne. At the luncheon we had many oysters and for the big
> eaters several large soufflés. Arthur asked what doctor put her
> on that diet of nothing but oysters and champagne. She looked
> at him and said rather sharply, 'Doctor? The doctors are horri-
> fied by my diet but I love champagne and I love oysters and
> they agree with me.' Then she added, 'It is sad, though, when
> oysters are not in season, for then I have to turn back to aspara-
> gus in those dreary months.' Arthur mentioned something about
> proteins and Tanya said, 'I don't know anything about that but
> I am old and I eat what I want and what agrees with me' . . .
> After lunch everybody danced and sang. A friend of Ida's [Mrs

2 *The Saturday Review*, 16th March 1963, p. 29.

McCullers' cook] had brought in a motion picture camera, and there were pictures of Tanya dancing with Marilyn, me dancing with Arthur, and a great round of general dancing.[3]

Again, when another writer whom she greatly admired, William Faulkner, was visiting the Military Academy at West Point (where Carson's cousin, Major Simeon Smith, is an English instructor), she was able to attend the dinner given in his honour: when Faulkner, during cocktails, saw her standing in the distance and learned who she was, he deserted the circle of 'top brass' which surrounded him and crossed the room to join Carson and her cousin, an incident which caused some of the officers' wives to raise their brows.

She was even able, in the autumn of 1962, to accept an offer from England to participate, with all her expenses paid, in the Cheltenham Festival of Literature. (She was one of three Americans represented there.) Wearing a cast on her left arm, and attended by a private nurse, she flew to London, where she was interviewed on television by Elizabeth Jane Howard. The trip, which lasted two weeks, exhausted her physically, but she enjoyed herself thoroughly and was particularly pleased to see again her old friends Peter Pears, Edith Sitwell, and Cecil Beaton, as well as two of her most enthusiastic British critics: David Garnett and V. S. Pritchett. Mr Beaton, with whom she had tea in his elegant apartment at Pelham Place,[4] had recently returned from Copenhagen, where he visited Isak Dinesen shortly before her death.

The house on South Broadway is a three-storey Victorian structure with a cupola, which gives, in spite of its size, an impression of lightness and airiness. It is set back slightly from the street, and there is a large back yard which formerly contained both a flower and vegetable garden (Carson's mother liked to grow her own vegetables), but only the flowers have been kept up. The interior has something of the quality of a small Southern mansion: the ceilings are tall, making for coolness in the summer, and there were once chandeliers in all the larger rooms. (Now there is only one, a dazzling crystal affair from France, in the dining room.) To the right of the entrance hall is the living room where, until her recent fall, Carson spent most of her time in an armchair. It contains a simple but elegant fireplace, and is filled with souvenirs and mementoes of her career: there are three paintings by her friend, Henry Varnum Poor, and a plaster

3   Ibid.
4   For Mrs McCullers's description of this visit, see *The Saturday Review* for 16th March 1963.

plaque of Carson's head by the same artist; a tall secretaire, its book-case containing editions of her works in many languages; and a huge Chinese bowl, ancient and fragile, of the most delicate shade of blue imaginable, which she discovered in a New Orleans antique shop.

In the adjacent dining room, books—many of them with personal inscriptions by their authors—line two walls from top to bottom, and on a third wall hangs a portrait of Carson—a sensitive line drawing by Vertès. Underneath the big chandelier is a long table of Italian marble. This room opens on to an outdoor porch which is lined with flower boxes and commands a fine view of the Hudson River. Across the hall from the living room is Carson's bedroom, where, propped against pillows and wearing a colourful Persian dressing-gown, she receives her friends. This room contains, besides books (books are in evidence throughout the house), her gramo-phone; the manuscripts on which she still continues painfully to work; a bed-stand of blood-red marble, breathtakingly beautiful; family photographs; and two of her favourite pictures: a small Whistler and a Dufy watercolour, the latter a gift from Tennessee Williams. There is also a small folding table which, when she invites a few intimate friends for a meal, can be opened and set for four, while Carson 'joins' them sitting up in bed.

For Carson is never lonely. She receives visitors not only from New York, but from all over the country, and from Europe as well.[5] Many of these are strangers to her—readers who have undertaken the pilgrimage to Nyack in order to express in person their appreci-ation of her work. And of course some of the most distinguished personalities in the modern literary and theatrical world have en-joyed the hospitality at her house: they are not likely to forget the warmth with which their hostess, ailing as she is, invariably receives them—nor, should they be asked to stay for dinner, Ida's fried chicken or cheese soufflé. And throughout her various illnesses Car-son has been sustained by the devotion and professional care of a circle of friends which includes, in addition to Dr Mercer, whom she regards as her 'guardian angel', Floria V. Lasky, the lawyer whom she has constituted her power of attorney; Robert Lantz, her literary agent; Ida Reeder, the coloured housekeeper who has served her family faithfully for many years; Ethel Kirkland, her private nurse; and Jack Dobbin, a neighbour who has written her cheques every Sunday for the past nineteen years. The only assistant of whom she

[5]   One of the latter, the Belgian critic René Micha, has described his visit to the house in an article recently published in France, 'Carson McCullers ou la Cabane de l'Enfance,' (*Critique*, Août-Septembre, 1962).

is presently in need is a secretary—someone capable of taking dicta-
tion and who, preferably, would be willing to live on the premises:
one might think the problem a simple one, but Carson has not found
it so.

Habitually reticent about her work in progress, she has nevertheless confided that her next project will be a book which, partly autobiographical in character, will expound her convictions on the craft
of writing, with particular emphasis on the sources of literary inspiration. She is also contemplating another novel, but about this she
is reluctant to talk at present.

2

Carson McCullers is quite possibly the most controversial living
American writer. The controversy began in 1940, with the publication of *The Heart Is a Lonely Hunter,* and it is still going strong.
Reviewing it, one notices that, with certain exceptions (some of them
quite distinguished exceptions, as in the case of Edmund Wilson),
the censure has come from professional book reviewers while the
praise has come either from other novelists (and a few poets and
playwrights) or from a group of critics whom, for want of a better
term, I shall call academic—that is, men whose profession is teaching and whose avocation is scholarly criticism. There is therefore
some evidence for believing that Mrs McCullers is both a 'writer's
writer' and one whose work requires, or at least lends itself to, a
considerable amount of explication—more, at any rate, than the
popular reviewer, either for reasons of space or because he lacks
the proper literary background, is prepared to supply. I think this
is emphatically the case, though I am by no means certain that it
explains the controversy. The truth, I suspect, is that Mrs Mc-
Cullers's is a very special sensibility with which many readers, even
highly cultivated readers, are, for some reason, simply unable to
establish a rapport. Mrs McCullers is not unique among novelists in
this respect (the case of Ford Madox Ford, a very different kind of
writer, is somewhat similar), and in a sense the phenomenon is proof
of her individuality and her originality as an artist.

It is possible, however, to suggest a few more specific reasons why
this author's work is not, at present, more widely appreciated. The
first of these is psychological, and has to do with the effect of her
'message'—what she has to say—upon the reader. In her best work,
Mrs McCullers has always been concerned with exploring what
Hawthorne called the 'labyrinth of the human heart', and what she
has found therein has not always proved cause for rejoicing. What
she conceives to be the truth about human nature is a melancholy

truth: each man is surrounded by a 'zone of loneliness', serving a life sentence of solitary confinement. The only way in which he can communicate with his fellow prisoners is through love: this affords him a certain measure of relief, but the relief is incomplete and temporary since love is seldom a completely mutual experience and is also subject to time. This view of life and love received its most pessimistic statement, of course, in *The Ballad of the Sad Café*, which added the startling notion that the beloved 'fears and hates' the lover. A flaw thus exists in the very nature of love, and frustration is the lot of man.

These are not popular ideas. They do not flatter the reader. They are uncomfortable to live with. We are reluctant to acknowledge that they correspond to reality—and our very reluctance may be evidence of a sneaking suspicion that they do. This may well account for some of the aversion which many readers feel for her work: we do not wish to have the truth told to us quite so plainly, and unpopularity is the not infrequent price of honesty. (How Mr Tennessee Williams, a writer with a somewhat similar message, has avoided paying it remains something of a mystery.) We like to believe—it may even be necessary for many of us to believe—that the deck of cards with which we attempt to play the game of life is, unlike the deck in Frankie Addams's kitchen, perfect and complete; and to suggest that some of the cards may be missing is disconcerting to say the least.

Another reason Mrs McCullers has suffered unfavourable criticism is her choice of characters and materials. It must be admitted that her characters are not always the kind one is likely to encounter in ordinary experience, and that the situations in which she places them are frequently uncommon, even implausible. But, as I have shown in this book, there is a reason for this, and a good one. The theme of Mrs McCullers's best work is spiritual isolation, and it should be obvious that any kind of deviation, physical or psychological, increases this sense of isolation. It is not because Mrs McCullers is indulging a taste for the freakish that she causes Singer, in *The Heart Is a Lonely Hunter*, to be a deaf-mute; it is because, being such, he constitutes an ideal symbol of man's inability to communicate with his neighbour. Similarly with Captain Penderton in *Reflections in a Golden Eye* and the dwarf in *The Ballad of the Sad Café*: their mutilations are not irrelevant but symbolize the factors that make for the loneliness of Everyman. As Paul Engle noted more than a decade ago,[6] Mrs McCullers uses freaks *as symbols of the*

6 *The Chicago Tribune*, 10th June 1951, p. 5.

normal. To call her Gothic is therefore to misuse the term, for Gothic horror is horror for its own sake, and while Faulkner has occasionally been guilty of this, notably in *Sanctuary,* Mrs McCullers has not.

As for her situations, if they sometimes have an artificial, stylized quality it is because they have been contrived deliberately to dramatize a thesis, not to imitate situations in real life. Thus, Mrs McCullers's notion that 'the most outlandish people can be the stimulus for love . . . the value and quality of any love is determined by the lover himself' is illustrated by Singer's love for the half-witted Antonapoulos in *The Heart Is a Lonely Hunter* and by Amelia's love for the dwarf in *The Ballad of the Sad Café*. Since frustration is a common theme, and since of all emotional frustrations frustrated love is probably the most painful, Mrs McCullers logically prefers situations that lead inevitably to disappointment: love, the attempt at ideal communication, is usually unreturned, unrecognized, mistaken for its opposite, or made difficult if not impossible by social and sometimes even biological considerations.

It is doubtful that any American writer since Hawthorne and Melville has handled the difficult form of allegory quite so well as Carson McCullers. A didactic writer in an age when didacticism, in the United States at any rate, is suspect (unless the message involved be one that flatters the reader at the same time that it does not make very considerable demands upon his intelligence), she may yet live to see the fulfilment of Mr Gore Vidal's prediction that 'of all our Southern writers Carson McCullers is the one most likely to endure.'[7] A constantly expanding corpus of critical writings is testimony to the increasing interest in her work in the United States, while in England and in continental Europe her reputation is decidedly on the increase. As a bibliographer, Stanley Stewart, has observed: 'It is important to note that Mrs McCullers is highly respected on the Continent; certainly foreign publications and critical estimates of her work would seem to be the logical next step in research on this author.'[8] Her writing is almost never peripheral, as that of Faulkner often is: it goes straight to the heart of its subject, and it rarely fumbles. And while it is true that her talent lacks the impressive range of Faulkner's, within its limits she has succeeded in creating certain effects that are inimitable. Had she written nothing except *The Ballad of the Sad Café* her position among the half dozen or so who comprise the highest echelon of living American authors would still be unassailable.

7   Op. cit., loc. cit.
8   *Bulletin of Bibliography*, January-April 1959, p. 182.

Author's Outline of THE MUTE

(later published as *The Heart is a Lonely Hunter*)

GENERAL REMARKS

The broad principal theme of this book is indicated in the first dozen pages. This is the theme of man's revolt against his own inner isolation and his urge to express himself as fully as is possible. Surrounding this general idea there are several counter themes and some of these may be stated briefly as follows : (1) There is a deep need in man to express himself by creating some unifying principle or God. A personal God created by a man is a reflection of himself and in substance this God is most often inferior to his creator. (2) In a disorganized society these individual Gods or principles are likely to be chimerical and fantastic. (3) Each man must express himself in his own way—but this is often denied to him by a wasteful, shortsighted society. (4) Human beings are innately cooperative, but an unnatural social tradition makes them behave in ways that are not in accord with their deepest nature. (5) Some men are heroes by nature in that they will give all that is in them without regard to the effort or to the personal returns.

Of course these themes are never stated nakedly in the book. Their overtones are felt through the characters and situations. Much will depend upon the insight of the reader and the care with which the book is read. In some parts the underlying ideas will be concealed far down below the surface of a scene and at other times these ideas will be shown with a certain emphasis. In the last few pages the various motifs which have been recurring from time to time throughout the book are drawn sharply together and the work ends with a sense of cohesive finality.

The general outline of this work can be expressed very simply. It is the story of five isolated, lonely people in their search for expression and spiritual integration with something greater than themselves. One of these five persons is a deaf mute, John Singer—and it is around him that the whole book pivots. Because of their loneliness these other four people see in the mute a certain mystic superiority and he becomes in a sense their ideal. Because of Singer's infirmity his outward character is vague and unlimited. His friends are able to impute to him all the qualities which they would wish for him to have. Each one of these four people creates his understanding of the mute from his own desires. Singer can read lips and understand what is said to him. In his eternal silence there is something compelling. Each one of these persons makes the mute the repository for his most personal feelings and ideas.

This situation between the four people and the mute has an almost exact parallel in the relation between Singer and his deaf-mute friend, Antonapoulos. Singer is the only person who could attribute to Antonapoulos dignity and a certain wisdom. Singer's love for Antonapoulos threads through the whole book from the first page until the very end. No part of Singer is left untouched by this love and when they are separated his life is meaningless and he is only marking time until he can be with his friend again. Yet the four people who count themselves as Singer's friends know nothing about Antonapoulos at all until the book is nearly ended. The irony of this situation grows slowly and steadily more apparent as the story progresses.

When Antonapoulos dies finally of Bright's disease Singer, overwhelmed by loneliness and despondency, turns on the gas and kills himself. Only then do these other four characters begin to understand the real Singer at all.

About this central idea there is much of the quality and tone of a legend. All the parts dealing directly with Singer are written in the simple style of a parable.

Before the reasons why this situation came about can be fully understood it is necessary to know each of the principal characters in some detail. But the characters cannot be described adequately without the events which happen to them being involved. Nearly all of the happenings in the book spring directly from the characters. During the space of this book each person is shown in his strongest and most typical actions.

Of course it must be understood that none of these personal characteristics are told in the didactic manner in which they are set down here. They are implied in one successive scene after another—and it is only at the end, when the sum of these implications is considered, that the real characters are understood in all of their deeper aspects.

CHARACTERS AND EVENTS

John Singer

Of all the main characters in the book Singer is the simplest. Because of his deaf-mutism he is isolated from the ordinary human emotions of other people to a psychopathic degree. He is very observant and intuitive. On the surface he is a model of kindness and cooperativeness—but nothing which goes on around him disturbs his inner self. All of his deeper emotions are involved in the only friend to whom he can express himself, Antonapoulos. In the second chapter Biff Brannon thinks of Singer's eyes as being 'cold and gentle as a cat's.' It is this same remoteness that gives him an air of wisdom and superiority.

Singer is the first character in the book only in the sense that he is the symbol of isolation and thwarted expression and because the story pivots about him. In reality each one of his satellites is of far more importance than himself. The book will take all of its body and strength in the development of the four people who revolve about the mute.

The parts concerning Singer are never treated in a subjective manner. The style is oblique. This is partly because the mute, although he is educated, does not think in words but in visual impressions. That, of course, is a natural outcome of his deafness. Except when he is understood through the eyes of other people the style is for the main part simple and declarative. No attempt will be made to enter intimately into his subconscious. He is a flat character in the sense that from the second chapter on through the rest of the book his essential self does not change.

At his death there is a strange little note from the cousin of Antonapoulos found in his pocket:

Dear Mr Singer,
> No address on corner of letters. They all sent back to me. Spiros Antonapoulos died and was buried with his kidneys last month. Sorry to tell same but no use writing letters to the dead.
>> Yours truly,
>> Charles Parker.

When the man is considered in his deepest nature (because of his inner character and peculiar situation) his suicide at the death of Antonapoulos is a necessity.

Mick Kelly

Mick is perhaps the most outstanding character in the book. Because of her age and her temperament her relation with the mute is more accentuated than any other person's. At the beginning of the second part of the work she steps out boldly—and from then on, up until the last section, she commands more space and interest than anyone else. Her story is that of the violent struggle of a gifted child to get what she needs from an unyielding environment. When Mick first appears she is at the age of thirteen, and when the book ends she is fourteen months older. Many things of great importance happen to her during this time. At the beginning she is a crude child on the threshold of a period of quick awakening and development. Her energy and the possibilities before her are without limits. She begins to go forward boldly in the face of all obstacles before her and during the next few months there is great development. In the end, after the finances of her family have completely given way, she has to get a job working ten hours a day in a ten-cent store. Her tragedy does not come in any way from herself—she is robbed of her freedom and energy by an unprincipled and wasteful society.

To Mick music is the symbol of beauty and freedom. She has had no musical background at all and her chances for educating herself are very small. Her family does not have a radio and in the summer she roams around the streets of the town pulling her two baby brothers in a wagon and listening to any music she can hear from other people's houses. She begins reading at the public library and from books she learns some of the things she needs to know. In the fall when she enters the Vocational High School she arranges to have rudimentary lessons on the piano with a girl in her class. In exchange for the lessons she does all the girl's home work in algebra and arithmetic and gives her also fifteen cents a week from her lunch money. During the afternoon Mick can sometimes practice on the piano in the gymnasium—but the place is always noisy and over-crowded and she never knows when she will be interrupted suddenly by a blow on the head from a basket ball.

Her love for music is instinctive, and her taste is naturally never pure at this stage. At first there is Mozart. After that she learns about Beethoven. From then on she goes hungrily from one composer to another whenever she gets a chance to hear them on other people's radios—Bach, Brahms, Wagner, Sibelius, etc. Her information is often very garbled but always the feeling is there. Mick's love for music is intensely creative. She is always making up little tunes for herself—and she plans to compose great symphonies and operas.

Her plans are always definite in a certain way. She will conduct all of her music herself and her initials will always be written in big red letters on the curtains of the stage. She will conduct her music either in a red satin evening dress or else she will wear a real man's evening suit. Mick is thoroughly egoistic—and the crudely childish side of her nature comes in side by side with the mature.

Mick must always have some person to love and admire. Her childhood was a series of passionate, reasonless admirations for a motley cavalcade of persons, one after another. And now she centers this undirected love on Singer. He gives her a book about Beethoven on her birthday and his room is always quiet and comfortable. In her imagination she makes the mute just the sort of teacher and friend that she needs. He is the only person who seems to show any interest in her at all. She confides in the mute—and when an important crisis occurs at the end of the book it is to him that she wants to turn for help.

This crisis, although on the surface the most striking thing that happens to Mick, is really subordinate to her feeling for Singer and to her struggle against the social forces working against her. In the fall when she enters Vocational High she prefers to take 'mechanical shop' with the boys rather than attend the stenographic classes. In this class she meets a fifteen-year-old boy, Harry West, and gradually they become good comrades. They are attracted to each other by a similar intensity of character and by their mutual interest in mechanics. Harry, like Mick, is made restless by an abundance of undirected energy. In the spring they try to construct a glider together in the Kellys' backyard and, although because of inadequate materials they can never get the contraption to fly, they work at it very hard together. All of this time their friendship is blunt and childish.

In the late spring Mick and Harry begin going out together on Saturday for little trips in the country. Harry has a bicycle and they go out about ten miles from town to a certain creek in the woods. Feelings that neither of them fully understands begin to come about between them. The outcome is very abrupt. They start to the country one Saturday afternoon in great excitement and full of childish animal energy—and before they return they have, without any premeditation at all, experienced each other sexually. It is absolutely necessary that this facet of the book be treated with extreme reticence. What has happened is made plain through a short, halting dialogue between Mick and Harry in which a great deal is implied but very little is actually said.

Although it is plain that this premature experience will affect both of them deeply, there is the feeling that the eventual results will be more serious for Harry than for Mick. Their reactions are rather more mature than would be expected. However, they both decide that they will never want to marry or have the same experience again. They are both stunned by a sense of evil. They decide that they will never see each other again—and that night Harry takes a can of soup from his kitchen shelf, breaks his nickel bank, and hitch-hikes from the town to Atlanta where he hopes to find some sort of job.

The restraint with which this scene between Mick and Harry must be told cannot be stressed too strongly.

For a while Mick is greatly oppressed by this that has happened to her. She turns to her music more vehemently than ever. She has always looked on sex with a cold, infantile remoteness—and now the experience she has had seems to be uniquely personal and strange. She tries ruthlessly to forget about it, but the secret weighs on her mind. She feels that if she can just tell some person about it she would be easier. But she is not close enough to her sisters and her mother to confide in them, and she has no especial friends of her own age. She wants to tell Mr Singer and she tries to imagine how to go about this. She is still taking consolation in the possibility that she might be able to confide in Mr Singer about this when the mute kills himself.

After the death of Singer, Mick feels very alone and defenseless. She works even harder than ever with her music. But the pressing economic condition of her family which has been growing steadily worse all through the past months is now just about as bad as it can be. The two elder children in the family are barely able to support themselves and can be of no help to their parents. It is essential that Mick get work of some kind. She fights this bitterly, for she wants to go back at least one more year to High School and to have some sort of chance with her music. But nothing can be done and at the beginning of the summer she gets a job working from eight-thirty to six-thirty as a clerk in a ten-cent store. The work is very wearing, but when the manager wants any of the girls to stay overtime he always picks Mick—for she can stand longer and endure more fatigue than any other person in the store.

The essential traits of Mick Kelly are great creative energy and courage. She is defeated by society on all the main issues before she can even begin, but still there is something in her and in those like her that cannot and will not ever be destroyed.

Jake Blount

Jake's struggle with social conditions is direct and conscious. The spirit of revolution is very strong in him. His deepest motive is to do all that he can to change the predatory, unnatural social conditions existing today. It is his tragedy that his energies can find no channel in which to flow. He is fettered by abstractions and conflicting ideas—and in practical application he can do no more than throw himself against windmills. He feels that the present social tradition is soon to collapse completely, but his dreams of the civilization of the future are alternately full of hope and of distrust.

His attitude towards his fellow man vacillates continually between hate and the most unselfish love. His attitude towards the principles of communism are much the same as his attitude toward man. Deep inside him he is an earnest communist, but he feels that in concrete application all communistic societies up until the present have degenerated into bureaucracies. He is unwilling to compromise and his is the attitude of all or nothing. His inner and outward motives are so contradictory at times that it is hardly an exaggeration to speak of the man as being deranged. The burden which he has taken on himself is too much for him.

Jake is the product of his peculiar environment. During the time of this book he is twenty-nine years old. He was born in a textile town in South Carolina, a town very similar to the one in which the action of this book takes place. His childhood was passed among conditions of absolute poverty and degradation. At the age of nine years (this was the time of the last World War) he was working fourteen hours a day in a cotton mill. He had to snatch for himself whatever education he could get. At twelve he left home on his own initiative and his self teachings and wanderings began. At one time or another he has lived and worked in almost every section of this country.

Jake's inner instability reflects markedly on his outer personality. In physique he suggests a stunted giant. He is nervous and irritable. All of his life he has had difficulty in keeping his lips from betraying his emotions—in order to overcome this he has grown a flourishing mustache which only accentuates this weakness and gives him a comic, jerky look. Because of his nervous whims it is hard for him to get along with his neighbors and people hold aloof from him. This causes him either to drop into self-conscious buffoonery or else to take on an exaggerated misplaced dignity.

If Jake cannot act he has to talk. The mute is an excellent repository for conversation. Singer attracts Jake because of his seeming stability and calm. He is a stranger in the town and the circumstance of his loneliness makes him seek out the mute. Talking to Singer and spending the evening with him becomes a sedative habit with him. At the end, when the mute is dead, he feels as though he has lost a certain inner ballast. He has the vague feeling that he has been tricked, too, and that all of the conclusions and visions that he has told the mute are forever lost.

Jake depends heavily on alcohol—and he can drink in tremendous quantities with no seeming ill effect. Occasionally he will try to break himself of this habit, but he is as unable to discipline himself in this as he is in more important matters.

Jake's stay in the town ends in a fiasco. As usual, he has been trying during these months to do what he can to right social injustice. At the end of the book the growing resentment between the Negroes and the white factory workers who patronize the show is nourished by several trifling quarrels between individuals. Day by day one thing leads to another and then late one Saturday night there is a wild brawl. (This scene occurs during the week after Singer's death.) All the white workers fight bitterly against the Negroes. Jake tries to keep order for a while and then he, too, loses control of himself and goes berserk. The fight grows into an affair in which there is no organization at all and each man is simply fighting for himself. This brawl is finally broken up by the police and several persons are arrested. Jake escapes but the fight seems to him to be a symbol of his own life. Singer is dead and he leaves the town just as he came to it—a stranger.

Dr Benedict Mady Copeland

Dr Copeland presents the bitter spectacle of the educated Negro in the South. Dr Copeland, like Jake Blount, is warped by his long years of effort to do his part to change certain existing conditions. At the opening of the book he is fifty-one years old, but already he is an old man.

He has practiced among the Negroes of the town for twenty-five years. He has always felt, though, that his work as a doctor was only secondary to his efforts at teaching his people. His ideas are laboriously thought out and inflexible. For a long while he was interested mainly in birth control, as he felt that indiscriminate sexual relations and haphazard and prolific propagation were re- sponsible in a large part for the weakness of the Negro. He is greatly opposed to miscegenation—but this opposition comes mainly from personal pride and resentment. The great flaw in all of his theories is that he will not admit the racial culture of the Negro. Theoretically he is against the grafting of the Negroid way of living to the Caucasian. His ideal would be a race of Negro ascetics.

Parallel with Dr Copeland's ambition for his race is his love for his family. But because of his inflexibility his relations with his four children are a complete failure. His own temperament is partly responsible for this, too. All of his life Dr Copeland has gone against the grain of his own racial nature. His passionate asceticism and the strain of his work have their effect on him. At home, when he felt the children escaping from his influence, he was subject to wild and sudden outbreaks of rage. This lack of control was finally the cause of his separation from his wife and children.

While still a young man Dr Copeland suffered at one time from pulmonary tuberculosis, a disease to which the Negro is particularly susceptible. His illness was arrested—but now when he is fifty-one years old his left lung is involved again. If there were an adequate sanitorium he would enter it for treatment—but of course there is no decent hospital for Negroes in the state. He ignores the disease and keeps up his practice—although now his work is not as extensive as it was in the past.

To Dr Copeland the mute seems to be the embodiment of the control and asceticism of a certain type of white man. All of his life Dr Copeland has suffered because of slights and humiliations from the white race. Singer's politeness and consideration make Dr Copeland pitiably grateful. He is always careful to keep up his 'dignity' with the mute—but Singer's friendship is of great importance to him.

The mute's face has a slightly Semitic cast and Dr Copeland thinks that he is a Jew. The Jewish people, because they are a racially persecuted minority, have always interested Dr Copeland. Two of his heroes are Jews—Benedict Spinoza and Karl Marx.

Dr Copeland realizes very fully and bitterly that his life work has been a failure. Although he is respected to the point of awe by most of the Negroes of the town his teachings have been too foreign to the nature of the race to have any palpable effect.

In the beginning of the book Dr Copeland's economic situation is very uncertain. His house and most of his medical equipment are mortgaged. For fifteen years he had received a small but steady income from his work as a member of the staff of the city hospital—but his personal ideas about social situations have led to his discharge. As a pretext for dismissal he was accused, and rightly, of performing abortions in certain cases where a child was an economic impossibility. Since the loss of this post, Dr Copeland has had no dependable income. His patients are for the most part totally unable to pay fees for treatment. His illness is a hindrance and he steadily loses ground. At the end the house is taken away from him and after a lifetime of service he is left a pauper. His wife's relations take him out to spend the short remaining part of his life on their farm in the country.

Biff Brannon

Of the four people who revolve around the mute Biff is the most disinterested. It is typical of him that he is always the observer. About Biff there is much that is austere and classical. In contrast with the driving enthusiasms of Mick and Jake and Dr Copeland, Biff is nearly always coldly reflective. The second chapter of the book opens with him and in the closing pages his meditations bring the work to a thoughtful and objective finish.

Biff's humorous aspects are to be brought out in all the parts dealing with him. Technically he is a thoroughly rounded character in that he will be seen completely from all sides. At the time the book opens he is forty-four years old and has spent the best part of his life standing behind the cash register in the restaurant and making his own particular observations. He has a passion for detail. It is typical of him that he has a small room in the back of his place devoted to a complete and neatly catalogued file of the daily evening newspaper dating back without a break for eighteen years. His problem is to get the main outlines of a situation from all the cluttering details in his mind, and he goes about this with his own painstaking patience.

Biff is strongly influenced by his own specific sexual experiences. At forty-four years he is prematurely impotent—and the cause of this lies in psychic as well as physical reasons. He has been married to Alice for twenty-three years. From the beginning their marriage was a mistake, and it has endured mainly because of economic necessity and habit.

Perhaps as a compensation for his own dilemma Biff comes to his own curious conclusion that marital relations are not the primary functions of the sexual impulse. He believes that human beings are fundamentally ambi-sexual—and for confirmation he turns to the periods of childhood and senility.

Two persons have a great emotional hold on Biff. These are Mick Kelly and a certain old man named Mr Alfred Simms. Mick has been coming in the restaurant all through her childhood to get candy with her brother and to play the slot machine. She is always friendly with Biff, but of course she has no idea of his feelings for her. As a matter of fact, Biff is not exactly clear himself on that point, either. Mr Simms is a pitiable, fragile old fellow whose senses are muddled.

During middle life he had been a wealthy man but now he is penniless and alone. The old man keeps up a great pretense of being a busy person of affairs. Every day he comes out on the street in clean ragged clothes and holding an old woman's pocket-book. He goes from one bank to another in an effort to 'settle his accounts'. Mr Simms used to like to come into Biff's restaurant and sit for a little while. He always sat at a table quietly and never disturbed anyone. With his queer clothes and the big pocket-book clutched against his chest he looked like an old woman. At that time Biff did not have any particular interest in Mr Simms. He would kindly pour him out a beer now and then, but he did not think much about him.

One night (this was a few weeks before the opening of the book) the restaurant was crowded and the table where Mr Simms was sitting was needed. Alice insisted that Biff put the old man out. Biff was used to ejecting all sorts of people from the place and he went up to the old man without thinking much about it and asked him if he thought the table was a park bench. Mr Simms did not understand at first and smiled up happily at Biff. Then Biff was disconcerted and he repeated the words in a much rougher way than he had intended. Tears came to the old man's eyes. He tried to keep up his dignity before the people around him, fumbled uselessly in his pocket-book and went out crushed.

This little episode is described here in some detail because of its effect on Biff. The happening is made clear in a chapter in the second part of the book. All through the story Biff's thoughts are continually going back to the old man. His treatment of Mr Simms comes to be for him the embodiment of all the evil he has ever done. At the same time the old man is the symbol of the declining period of life which Biff is now approaching.

Mick brings up in Biff nostalgic feelings of youth and heroism. She is at the age where she possesses both the qualities of a girl and of a boy. Also, Biff has always wanted to have a little daughter and of course she reminds him of this, too. At the end of the book, when Mick begins to mature, Biff's feelings for her slowly diminish.

Toward his wife Biff is entirely cold. When Alice dies in the second part of the book Biff feels not the slightest pity or regret for her at all. His only remorse is that he did not ever fully understand Alice as a person. It piques him that he could have lived so long with a woman and still understand her so confusedly. After her death Biff takes off the crepe paper streamers from under the electric fans and sews mourning tokens on his sleeves. These gestures are not so much for Alice as they are a reflection of his own feeling for his approaching decline and death. After his wife dies certain female elements become more pronounced in Biff. He begins to rinse his hair in lemon juice and to take exaggerated care of his skin. Alice had always been a much better business manager than Biff and after her death the restaurant begins to stagnate.

In spite of certain quirks in Biff's nature he is perhaps the most balanced person in the book. He has that faculty for seeing the things which happen around him with cold objectivity—without instinctively connecting them with himself. He sees and hears and remembers everything. He is curious to a comic degree. And nearly always, despite the vast amount of details in his mind, he can work his way patiently to the very skeleton of a situation and see affairs in their entirety.

Biff is far too wary to be drawn into any mystic admiration of Singer. He likes the mute and is of course very curious about him. Singer occupies a good deal of his thoughts and he values his reserve and common sense. He is the only one of the four main characters who sees the situation as it really is. In the last few pages he threads through the details of the story and arrives at the most salient points. In his reflections at the end Biff himself thinks of the word 'parable' in connection with what has happened—and of course this is the only time that this designation is used. His reflections bring the book to a close with a final, objective roundness.

Subordinate Characters

There are several minor characters who play very important parts in the story. None of these persons are treated in a subjective manner—and from the point of view of the novel the things that happen to them are of more importance in the effects on the main characters than because of the change that they bring about among these characters.

Spiros Antonapoulos

Antonapoulos has been described with complete detail in the first chapter. His mental, sexual and spiritual development is that of a child of about seven years old.

Portia Copeland Jones, Highboy Jones, and Willie Copeland

A great deal of interest is centered around these three characters. Portia is the most dominant member of this trio. In actual space she occupies almost as much of the book as any one of the main characters, except Mick—but she is always placed in a subordinate position. Portia is the embodiment of the maternal instincts. Highboy, her husband, and Willie, her brother, are inseparable from herself. These three characters are just the opposite of Dr Copeland and the other central characters in that they make no effort to go against circumstance.

The tragedy that comes to this group plays an important part on all the phases of the book. At the beginning of the second section Willie is arrested on a charge of burglary. He was walking down a side alley after midnight and two young white boys told him they were looking for someone, gave him a dollar, and instructed him to whistle when the person they were looking for came down the alley. Only when Willie saw two policemen coming towards him did he realize what had happened. In the meantime the boys had broken in a drug store. Later in the fall Willie is sentenced along with them for a year of hard labor. All of this is revealed through Portia as she tells this great trouble to the Kelly children. 'Willie he so busy looking at that dollar bill he don't have no time to think. And then they asks him how come he run when he seen them police. They might just as soon ask how come a person jerk their hand off a hot stove when they lays it there by mistake.'

This is the first of their trouble. Now that the household arrangements are disturbed, Highboy begins keeping company with another girl. This too is told by Portia to the Kelly children and Dr Copeland: 'I could realize this better if she were a light-colored, good looking girl. But she at least ten shades blacker than I is. She the ugliest girl I ever seen. She walk like she haves a egg between her legs and don't want to break it. She not even clean.'

The most brutal tragedy in the book comes to these three people. Willie and four other Negroes were guilty of some little misbehavior on the chain-gang where they were working. It was February and the camp was stationed a couple of hundred miles north of the town. As punishment they were put together in a solitary room. Their shoes were taken off and their feet suspended. They were left like this for three full days. It was cold and as their blood did not circulate the boys' feet froze and they developed gangrene. One boy died of pneumonia and the other four had to have one or both of their feet amputated. They were all manual laborers and of course this completely took away their means for future livelihood. This part is of course revealed by Portia, too. It is told in only a few blunt broken paragraphs and left at that.

This happening has a great effect on the main characters. Dr Copeland is shattered by the news and is in delirium for several weeks. Mick feels all the impact of the horror. Biff had formerly employed

Willie in his restaurant and he broods over all the aspects of the affair.

Jake wants to bring it all to light and make of it a national example. But this is impossible for several reasons. Willie is terribly afraid—for it has been impressed upon him at the camp to keep quiet about what has been done to him. The state has been careful to separate the boys immediately after the happening and they have lost track of each other. Also, Willie and the other boys are really children in a certain way—they do not understand what their co-operation would mean. Suffering had strained their nerves so much that during the three days and nights in the room they had quarrelled angrily among themselves and when it was over they had no wish to see each other again. From the long view their childish bitterness towards each other and lack of cooperation is the worst part of the whole tragedy.

Highboy comes back to Portia after Willie returns and, handicapped by Willie's infirmity, the three of them start their way of living all over again.

The thread of this story runs through the whole book. Most of it is told through Portia's own vivid, rhythmic language at intervals as it happens.

Harry West

Harry has already been briefly described in the section given to Mick. During the first part of the year, when he and Mick started their friendship, he was infatuated with a certain little flirting girl at High School. His eyes had always given him much trouble and he wore thick-lensed glasses. The girl thought the glasses made him look sissy and he tried to stumble around without them for several months. This aggravated his eye trouble. His friendship with Mick is very different from his infatuation with the other little girl at High School.

Harry has the exaggeratedly developed sense of right and wrong that sometimes is a characteristic of adolescence. He is also of a brooding nature. There is the implication that his abrupt experience with Mick will leave its mark on him for a long time.

Lily Mae Jenkins

Lily Mae is an abandoned, waifish Negro homosexual who haunts the Sunny Dixie Show where Jake works. He is always dancing. His mind and feelings are childish and he is totally unfit to earn his living. Because of his skill in music and dancing he is a friend of Willie's. He is always half starved and he hangs around Portia's kitchen constantly in the hopes of getting a meal. When Highboy and Willie are gone Portia takes some comfort in Lily Mae.

Lily Mae is presented in the book in exactly the same naive way that his friends understand him. Portia describes Lily Mae to Dr Copeland in this manner: 'Lily Mae is right pitiful now. I don't know if you ever noticed any boys like this but he cares for mens instead of girls. When he were younger he used to be real cute. He were all the time dressing up in girls' clothes and laughing. Everybody thought he were real cute then. But now he getting old and he seem different. He all the time hungry and he real pitiful. He loves to come set and talk with me in the kitchen. He dances for me and I gives him a little dinner.'

The Kelly children—Bill, Hazel, Etta, Bubber and Ralph

No great interest is focussed on any of these children individually. They are all seen through the eyes of Mick. All three of the older children are confused, in varying degrees, by the problem of trying to find their places in a society that is not prepared to absorb them. Each one of these youngsters is seen sharply—but not with complex fullness.

It is Mick's permanent duty to nurse Bubber and the baby during all the time when she is not actually at school. This chore is something of a burden for an adventurous roamer like Mick—but she has a warm and deep affection for these youngest children. At one time she makes these rambling remarks concerning her sisters and brothers as a whole: 'A person's got to fight for every single little thing they ever get. And I've noticed a lot of times that the farther down a kid comes in a family the better the kid really is. Youngest kids are always the toughest. I'm pretty hard because I have a lot of them on top of me. Bubber—he looks sick but he's got guts underneath that. If all this is true Ralph sure ought to be a real strong one when he's big enough to get around. Even though he's just thirteen months old I can read something hard and tough in that Ralph's face already.'

Interrelations of Characters:

It can easily be seen that in spirit Dr Copeland, Mick Kelly and Jake Blount are very similar. Each one of these three people has struggled to progress to his own mental proportions in spite of fettering circumstances. They are like plants that have had to grow under a rock from the beginning. The great effort of each of them has been to give and there has been no thought of personal returns.

The likeness between Dr Copeland and Jake Blount is so marked that they might be called spiritual brothers. The greatest real difference between them is one of race and of years. Dr Copeland's earlier life was spent in more favorable circumstances and from the start his duty was clear to him. The injustices inflicted on the Negro race are much more plainly marked than the ancient vastly scattered mismanagements of capitalism as a whole. Dr Copeland was able to set to work immediately in a certain narrow sphere, while the conditions which Jake hates are too fluid for him to get his shoulder to them. Dr Copeland has the simplicity and dignity of a person who has lived all of his life in one place and given the best of himself to one work. Jake has the jerky nervousness of a man whose inner and outer life has been no more stable than a whirlwind.

The conscientiousness of both these men is heightened by artificial stimulation—Dr Copeland is running a diurnal temperature and Jake is drinking steadily every day. In certain persons the effects of these stimulants can be very much the same.

Dr Copeland and Jake come into direct contact with each other only once during the book. Casual encounters are not considered here. They meet and misunderstand each other in the second chapter when Jake tries to make the doctor come into Biff's restaurant and drink with him. After that they see each other once on the stairs at the Kelly boarding house and then on two occasions they meet briefly in Singer's room. But the only time they directly confront each other takes place in Dr Copeland's own house under dramatic circumstances.

This is the night in which Willie has come home from the prison hospital. Dr Copeland is in bed with an inflammation of the pleura, delirious, and thought to be dying. The crippled Willie is on the cot in the kitchen and a swarm of friends and neighbours are trying to crowd in through the back door to see and hear of Willie's situation. Jake has heard of the whole affair from Portia and when Singer goes to sit with Dr Copeland during the night Jake asks to accompany him.

Jake comes to the house with the intention of questioning Willie as closely as possible. But before the evening is over he is drawn to Dr Copeland and it is he, instead of Singer, who sits through the night with the sick man. In the kitchen Willie is meeting his friends for the first time in almost a year. At first in the back of the house there is a sullen atmosphere of grief and hopelessness. Willie's story is repeated over and over in sullen monotones. Then this atmosphere begins to change. Willie sits up on the cot and begins to play his harp. Lily Mae starts dancing. As the evening progresses the atmosphere changes to a wild artificial release of merriment.

This is the background for Jake's meeting with Dr Copeland. The two men are together in the bedroom and the sounds from the kitchen come in during the night through the closed door. Jake is drunk and Dr Copeland is almost out of his head with fever. Yet their dialogue comes from the marrow of their inner selves. They both lapse into the rhythmic, illiterate vernacularisms of their early childhood. The inner purpose of each man is seen fully by the other. In the course of a few hours these two men, after a lifetime of isolation, come as close to each other as it is possible for two human beings to be. Very early in the morning Singer drops by the house before going to work and he finds them both asleep together, Jake sprawled loosely on the foot of the bed and Dr Copeland sleeping with healthy naturalness.

The interrelations between the other characters will not have to be described in such detail. Mick, Jake and Biff see each other frequently. Each one of these people occupies a certain key position in the town; Mick is nearly always on the streets. At the restaurant Biff comes in frequent contact with all the main characters except Dr Copeland. Jake is constantly watching a whole cross section of the town at the show where he works—later when he drives a taxi he becomes acquainted with nearly all of the characters, major and minor, in the book. Mick's relations toward each of these people are childish and matter of fact. Biff, except for his affinity for Mick, is coldly appraising. Certain small scenes and developments take place between all of these people in a variety of combinations.

On the whole the interrelations between the people of this book can be described as being like the spokes of a wheel—with Singer representing the center point. This situation, with all of its attendant irony, expresses the most important theme of the book.

General Structure and Outline:
TIME:
The first chapter serves as a prelude to the book and the reckoning of time starts with Chapter Two. The story covers a period of fourteen months—from May until the July of the following year.

The whole work is divided into three parts. The body of the book is contained in the middle section. In the actual number of pages this is the longest of the three parts and nearly all of the months in the time scheme take place in this division.

PART I

The first writing of Part I is already completed and so there is no need to take up this section in detail. The time extends from the middle of May to the middle of July. Each of the main characters is introduced in detail. The salient points of each person are clearly implied and the general direction each character will take is indicated. The tale of Singer and Antonapoulos is told. The meetings of each one of the main characters with Singer are presented—and the general web of the book is begun.

PART II

There is a quickening of movement at the beginning of this middle section. There will be more than a dozen chapters in this part, but the handling of these chapters is much more flexible than in Part I. Many of the chapters are very short and they are more dependent upon each other than the first six chapters. Almost half of the actual space is devoted to Mick, her growth and progress, and the increasing intensity of her admiration for Singer. Her story, and the separate parts developed from her point of view, weave in and out of the chapters about the other characters.

This part opens with Mick on one of her nocturnal wanderings. During the summer she has been hearing concerts under unusual circumstances. She has found out that in certain wealthier districts in the town a few families get fairly good programs on their radios. There is one house in particular that tunes in every Friday evening for a certain symphony concert. Of course the windows are all open at this time of the year and the music can be heard very plainly from the outside. Mick saunters into the yard at night just before the program is to begin and sits down in the dark behind the shrubbery under the living room window. Sometimes after the concert she will stand looking in at the family in the house for some time before going on. Because she gets so much from their radio she is half in love with all of the people in the house.

It would take many dozens of pages to go into a synopsis of this second part in complete detail. A complete and explanatory account would take actually longer than the whole part as it will be when it is completed—for a good book implies a great deal more than the words actually say. For convenience it is best to set down a few skeleton notations with the purpose of getting the sequence of events into a pattern. These rough notes mean very little in themselves and can only be understood after a thorough reading of the part of these remarks which goes under the heading of Characters and Events.

This rough outline is still in a tentative stage and is only meant to be indicative of the general formation of this central part.

Late Summer

Mick's night wandering and the concert. Resumé of the growth that is taking place in Mick this summer. On the morning after the concert Portia tells Mick and the other Kelly children of Willie's arrest. Mick's morning wanderings.

Jake Blount's experience at the Sunny Dixie Show.

Autumn

Mick's first day at Vocational High.

Dr Copeland on his medical rounds. Another visit from Portia in which she tells her father that Highboy has left her.

Mick becomes acquainted with Harry West.

Biff's wife, Alice, dies—his meditations.

Mick and her music again. Mick's sister, Etta, takes French leave of her family and tries to run away to Hollywood, but returns in a few days. Mick goes with the little girl who teaches her music to a 'real' piano lesson. She experiences a great embarrassment when she boldly tells the teacher she is a musician and sits down to try to play on a 'real' piano. (This takes place at the house where Mick was listening to the concert at the opening of this section—and Mick already knows this teacher and her family quite well after watching them through the window during the summer.)

Winter

Christmas. Dr Copeland gives his two annual Christmas parties— one in the morning for children and another in the late afternoon for adults. These parties have been given by him every year for two decades and he serves refreshments to his patients and then makes a short talk. The relation between Dr Copeland and the human material with which he works is brought out clearly.

Singer visits Antonapoulos.

Jake Blount's experience in the town as a ten-cent taxi driver.

Mick and Singer. Mick begins plans for the glider with Harry West.

The tragedy of Willie and the other four boys is told by Portia in the Kelly kitchen to Mick, Jake Blount and Singer.

Spring

Further meditations of Biff Brannon—and scene between Mick and Biff at the restaurant.

Mick and her music again—Mick and Harry work on the glider. Willie returns. The meeting of Dr Copeland and Jake.

The experience between Harry and Mick comes to its abrupt fulfillment and finish. Harry's departure. Mick's oppressive secret. The Kellys' financial condition. Mick's energetic plans and her music.

Singer's death.

This outline does not indicate the main web of the story—that of the relations of each main character with the mute. These relations are so gradual and so much a part of the persons themselves that it is impossible to put them down in such blunt notations. However, from these notes a general idea of the time scheme and of sequence can be gathered.

PART III

Singer's death overshadows all of the final section of the book. In actual length this part requires about the same number of pages as does the first part. In technical treatment the similarity between these sections is pronounced. This part takes place during the months of June and July. There are four chapters and each of the main characters is given his last presentation. A rough outline of this conclusive part may be suggested as follows:

Dr Copeland. The finish of his work and teachings—his departure to the country. Portia, Willie and Highboy start again.

Jake Blount. Jake writes curious social manifestoes and distributes them through the town. The brawl at the Sunny Dixie Show; Jake prepares to leave the town.

Mick Kelly. Mick begins her new work at the ten-cent store.

Biff Brannon. Final scene between Biff, Mick and Jake at the restaurant. Meditations of Biff concluded.

PLACE—THE TOWN

This story, in its essence, could have occurred at any place and in any time. But as the book is written, however, there are many aspects of the content which are peculiar to the America of this decade—and more specifically to the southern part of the United States. The town is never mentioned in the book by its name. The town is located in the very western part of Georgia, bordering the Chattahoochee River and just across the boundary line from Alabama. The population of the town is around 40,000—and about one third of the people in the town are Negroes. This is a typical factory community and nearly all of the business set-up centers around the textile mills and small retail stores.

Industrial organization has made no headway at all among the workers in the town. Conditions of great poverty prevail. The average cotton mill worker is very unlike the miner or a worker in the automobile industry—south of Gastonia, s.c., the average cotton mill worker has been conditioned to a very apathetic, listless state. For the most part he makes no effort to determine the causes of poverty and unemployment. His immediate resentment is directed toward the only social group beneath him—the Negro. When the mills are slack this town is veritably a place of lost and hungry people.

TECHNIQUE AND SUMMARY:

This book is planned according to a definite and balanced design. The form is contrapuntal throughout. Like a voice in a fugue each one of the main characters is an entirety in himself—but his personality takes on a new richness when contrasted and woven in with the other characters in the book.

It is in the actual style in which the book will be written that the work's affinity to contrapuntal music is seen most clearly. There are five distinct styles of writing—one for each of the main characters who is treated subjectively and an objective, legendary style for the mute. The object in each of these methods of writing is to come as close as possible to the inner psychic rhythms of the character from whose point of view it is written. This likeness between style and character is fairly plain in the first part—but this closeness progresses gradually in each instance until at the end the style expresses the inner man just as deeply as is possible without lapsing into the unintelligible unconscious.

This book will be complete in all of its phases. No loose ends will be left dangling and at the close there will be a feeling of balanced completion. The fundamental idea of the book is ironic—but the reader is not left with a sense of futility. The book reflects the past and also indicates the future. A few of the people in this book come very near to being heroes and they are not the only human beings of their kind. Because of the essence of these people there is the feeling that, no matter how many times their efforts are wasted and their personal ideals are shown to be false, they will someday be united and they will come into their own.

INDEX

Adams, Robert M., 58
Addams, Charles, 76
Albee, Edward, 143, 145, 156, 188
American Academy of Arts and Letters, 97, 189
Ames, Elizabeth, 86, 99, 117
Anderson, Sherwood, 28, 54, 135, 139
Arnold, Matthew, 121
Atkinson, Brooks, 152, 155, 169
Auden, W. H., 82, 84, 85, 86, 92, 134n, 160

Bachvillers (France), 158, 161
Baily, F. Randolph (Dr), 170
Balakian, Nona, 17n
Baldanza, Frank, 46, 76, 77n, 79, 89, 93, 94, 95, 96, 107, 111, 112, 113, 125
BALLAD OF THE SAD CAFE, THE, 9, 17, 17n, 18, 25, 50, 51, 62, 71, 79, 86, 95, 114, 126-143, 175, 177, 178n, 182, 186, 187, 188, 193, 194
  Characters:
  Amelia Evans, 17n, 25, 50, 51, 127-140 *passim*, 175, 176, 178n, 194
  "Cousin" Lymon, 25, 50, 62, 86, 126-137 *passim*, 175, 176, 180, 193
  Marvin Macy, 25, 127-137 *passim*, 175
Balliett, Whitney, 184
Barnes, Howard, 153
Bates, Sylvia Chatfield, 32, 34, 39
Baxter, Anne, 168
Beaton, Cecil, 190
Beckett, Samuel, 145
Beecher, H. W., 84
Berman, Eugene, 83
Bernstein, Leonard, 83
Blitzstein, Marc, 83
Bowen, Elizabeth, 118, 158
Bowen, Robert, 184, 185
Bowles, Jane, 83
Bowles, Paul, 21, 83, 86

Boyle, Kay, 99, 147
Breuer, Bessie, 99
Brickell, Herschel, 88
Britten, Benjamin, 82
Brodin, Pierre, 22n
Brook Farm, 82
Brooklyn, N.Y., 82, 84, 86
Brooks, Cleanth, 90, 137
Brown, John, 147, 161
Brown, Simone, 161
Bunyan, John, 121
Burnett, Whit, 33-34

Caetani, Marguerite (Princess), 160
Capote, Truman, 10, 17n, 95, 146, 156, 160, 161, 185
Chapman, John, 153, 168
Chekhov, Anton, 57, 72, 133, 154, 169
Cheltenham Festival of Literature, 190
Clancy, W. P., 139-140
CLOCK WITHOUT HANDS, 9, 17, 18, 24, 25, 36n, 38, 108, 110, 112, 160, 161, 162, 170-187
  Characters:
  J. T. Malone, 17, 25, 171-183
  Jester Clane, 24, 25, 36n, 171-182 *passim*
  Judge Clane, 112, 171-183 *passim*
  "Miss Missy", 178-179
  Sherman Pew, 24, 25, 171-187 *passim*
  Zippo, 24, 175
Clurman, Harold, 152, 154-155, 169
Cohen, Katherine (Dr), 159
Coleman, Robert, 153
Coleridge, S.T., 90-92, 119, 120
Columbia University, 29, 30, 31, 32, 33
Columbus, Ga., 9, 18, 22, 28, 29, 32, 33, 34, 35, 36, 42, 86, 87, 97, 148, 162
Crane, Hart, 84, 86

216